APPOINTMENTS WITH BONHOEFFER

T&T Clark New Studies in Bonhoeffer's Theology and Ethics

Series Editors
Jennifer McBride
Michael Mawson
Philip G. Ziegler

APPOINTMENTS WITH BONHOEFFER

Personal Faith and Public Responsibility in a Fragmenting World

Keith Clements

LONDON • NEW YORK • OXFORD • NEW DELHI • SYDNEY

T&T CLARK
Bloomsbury Publishing Plc
50 Bedford Square, London, WC1B 3DP, UK
1385 Broadway, New York, NY 10018, USA
29 Earlsfort Terrace, Dublin 2, Ireland

BLOOMSBURY, T&T CLARK and the T&T Clark logo are trademarks
of Bloomsbury Publishing Plc

First published in Great Britain 2022
Paperback edition published 2024

Copyright © Keith Clements, 2022

Keith Clements has asserted his right under the Copyright, Designs and
Patents Act, 1988, to be identified as Author of this work.

For legal purposes the Acknowledgements on p. xii constitute an
extension of this copyright page.

All rights reserved. No part of this publication may be reproduced or transmitted in
any form or by any means, electronic or mechanical, including photocopying,
recording, or any information storage or retrieval system, without prior permission in
writing from the publishers.

Bloomsbury Publishing Plc does not have any control over, or responsibility for,
any third-party websites referred to or in this book. All internet addresses given in this
book were correct at the time of going to press. The author and publisher regret any
inconvenience caused if addresses have changed or sites have ceased to exist,
but can accept no responsibility for any such changes.

A catalogue record for this book is available from the British Library.

Library of Congress Cataloging-in-Publication Data
Names: Clements, K. W. (Keith W.), author.
Title: Appointments with Bonhoeffer : personal faith and public
responsibility in a fragmenting world / Keith Clements.
Description: London ; New York : T&T Clark, 2022. |
Series: T&T Clark new studies in Bonhoeffer's theology and ethics |
Includes bibliographical references and index. |
Identifiers: LCCN 2021060973 (print) | LCCN 2021060974 (ebook) |
ISBN 9780567707055 (hardback) | ISBN 9780567707109 (paperback) |
ISBN 9780567707062 (pdf) | ISBN 9780567707093 (epub)
Subjects: LCSH: Bonhoeffer, Dietrich, 1906–1945. | Christian ethics. | Public theology.
Classification: LCC BX4827.B57 C535 2022 (print) | LCC BX4827.B57 (ebook) |
DDC 241–dc23/eng/20220404
LC record available at https://lccn.loc.gov/2021060973
LC ebook record available at https://lccn.loc.gov/2021060974

ISBN: HB: 978-0-5677-0705-5
PB: 978-0-5677-0710-9
ePDF: 978-0-5677-0706-2
eBook: 978-0-5677-0709-3

Series: T&T Clark New Studies in Bonhoeffer's Theology and Ethics

Typeset by Newgen KnowledgeWorks Pvt. Ltd., Chennai, India

To find out more about our authors and books visit www.bloomsbury.com
and sign up for our newsletters.

CONTENTS

Preface	vii
Foreword	x
Acknowledgements	xii
List of Abbreviations and Acronyms	xiii

Part I
RECEIVING BONHOEFFER

Chapter 1
WHO IS DIETRICH BONHOEFFER FOR US TODAY? — 3

Chapter 2
AFTER MARTYRDOM: BONHOEFFER'S POSTHUMOUS JOURNEY THROUGH COLD WAR EAST EUROPE — 11

Chapter 3
PUBLIC ETHICS AND THE RECEPTION OF BONHOEFFER IN BRITAIN — 23

Part II
WORLDLY FAITH AND A TRANSCENDENT GOD

Chapter 4
CENTURIES APART YET NEIGHBOURS IN SPIRIT: THE WORLDLY HOLINESS OF THOMAS TRAHERNE AND DIETRICH BONHOEFFER — 35

Chapter 5
'IF YOU ENGLISH HAD READ HIM YOU WOULD NOT HAVE NEEDED TO READ KARL BARTH': BONHOEFFER ON THE CATHOLIC MODERNIST FRIEDRICH VON HÜGEL — 51

Chapter 6
BETWEEN A CONFESSING CHURCH AND CONTEXTUAL ETHICS: BONHOEFFER, THE CRISIS OF 1934 AND THE CONTINUING ECUMENICAL QUEST FOR A PUBLIC THEOLOGY — 71

Chapter 7
'WHAT DOES IT MEAN TO TELL THE TRUTH?' THE CHURCH AND THE ALLEGATION OF 2015 AGAINST BISHOP GEORGE BELL IN THE LIGHT OF BONHOEFFER'S 1943 PRISON ESSAY — 81

Part III
PEACE, COMMUNITY AND RECONCILIATION: THE COSTLY WAY

Chapter 8
FROM EAST AND WEST, FROM NORTH AND SOUTH: THE GOSPEL
SUBVERTING TRIBALISM   93

Chapter 9
LIFE TOGETHER, LIFE FOR OTHERS: DIETRICH BONHOEFFER'S
WISDOM FOR MINISTRY IN A POST-CHRISTIAN WORLD   97

Chapter 10
BELONGING WHOLLY TO THE WORLD: THE STILL UNREALIZED
ECUMENICAL CALLING   113

Chapter 11
'THE BURNING FIRE OF LOVE, THE NUCLEUS OF RECONCILIATION':
RELEARNING WHAT LOVE MEANS   127

Part IV
TAKING RESPONSIBILITY

Chapter 12
ULTIMATE AND PENULTIMATE: SOME BONHOEFFERIAN INSIGHTS
FOR FAITH AND DEMOCRACY IN A TIME OF EXTREMISMS   143

Chapter 13
THE 'WHO AM I?' QUESTION WRIT LARGE: BRITAIN, EUROPE AND
THE CHURCHES   155

Chapter 14
'ARE WE STILL OF ANY USE?' WORDS FOR FAILING PUBLIC SERVANTS
AND FRIGHTENED CITIZENS   173

Chapter 15
A NEW ETHIC – OR THE END OF ETHICS? LOVE AGAINST THE PLAGUE   181

Bibliography   195
Index   199

PREFACE

Dietrich Bonhoeffer, a few months before his arrest in 1943, wrote a notable essay, 'After Ten Years', reflecting on a decade of life under Hitler and resistance to the regime. This present book comprises lectures, addresses and articles on Bonhoeffer and related subjects over the decade 2011 to 2021 – but any parallel with that earlier fateful decade and Bonhoeffer's reflections on it is absolutely not intended. It is rather that Bonhoeffer continues to excite interest and debate more than seventy-five years after his death in the execution yard at Flossenbürg, and this book is offered in the hope of recording that interest and promoting it still further.

One of Bonhoeffer's earliest and most important interpreters to the English-speaking world, the Scottish theologian Ronald Gregor Smith (1913–68) began one of his lectures at Glasgow University by saying that he spoke about Bonhoeffer 'not because I want to but because I must'. Many of us who have studied Bonhoeffer share that sense of compulsion, and I cannot deny it in myself. But what follows in these pages owes less to my own initiative than to invitations and requests for me to speak or write on Bonhoeffer and his significance for life in church and in society today. They therefore reflect on issues of faith, theology, ecumenism and responsibility in the public realm, which have been challenging our generation at local, national and global levels, in the light of how Bonhoeffer wrestled with the challenges of his own time and context. Because the topics are indicated in the list of contents, I need not detail them further here, except to say that they all have to do with how Bonhoeffer addressed the fragmenting world of his time, and how he can be a resource as we face ours.

A warning is in order. The word 'appointments' in the title is deliberately chosen, in preference to 'encounters' or even 'dialogues' (words I myself have used once before in writing on Bonhoeffer). Appointment refers to a meeting arranged with someone whom we wish to consult on matters important to us, and which require more than a quick chat on the phone, or a casual conversation. It means taking time to listen and to think about what has emerged in the meeting, to develop ideas rather than jot down sound bites. It would be a misuse of Bonhoeffer to treat him as an instant oracle on whichever problem or crisis happens to be on top of our contemporary agenda. Bonhoeffer does indeed have much to say to us. But he does so not by taking us quickly to 'Answerland', a term my wife coined to describe the attitude of some of her university students: a seeming belief in a mythical place where ready-made solutions to problems could be obtained, instead of *thinking* for themselves. Bonhoeffer invites us to a fundamental, biblically based rethink of what it means to be human beings created by God, to have God's image restored in us by Christ and in that restoration to live wholly in this world. It means taking on board

Bonhoeffer's unwavering emphasis upon human life as social and relational, a life with others; and on God as relational, the God who in grace freely binds himself to us and our history, and to all creation. It consequently means scrutinizing popular assumptions about those catchwords of our time, 'freedom' and 'identity', and their promotion of the fragmentation of the world: freedom seen as the right to regard oneself alone as the arbiter of one's choices; identity, whether of the individual person or a communal entity, as a self-chosen, self-enclosed, self-protecting, self-asserting, self-justifying possession. It means taking as central the term that will repeatedly appear in these pages, what Bonhoeffer in his mother tongue calls *Stellvertretung*, and is in somewhat ungainly fashion translated as 'vicarious representative action'. It denotes a person standing with and in the place of another. It is the counterstroke to all that sunders and fragments. It is supremely embodied in Christ but also emerges, even if only in partial and provisional forms, as central in our day-to-day social existence. In the area of public responsibility, the last ten years have seen an ever-extending agenda of issues, from Britain's breach with the European Union and the rise of populist politics, from climate change to the Black Lives Matter movement, and most recently the Covid-19 pandemic. Rather than attempting the impossible task of addressing fully all such issues under one cover it is more important to identify the theological framework with which to engage the public arena, and how Bonhoeffer can be a resource for that framework.

It might well be asked if anything really new can still be said about Bonhoeffer. In one sense, the answer is no. For several years now we have had available the full corpus of his known writings available to us, in English and other languages as well as his native German. But the reading and rereading of these texts in the face of our contemporary experiences still make them sound uncannily fresh and new, almost as if we were reading them for the first time. Moreover, I dare to hope that even seasoned readers of Bonhoeffer might find some elements of novelty in what follows in these pages – and even some surprise, as when I invite to the discussion two figures not hitherto (as far as I am aware) associated with him: the seventeenth-century poet and priest Thomas Traherne and, especially, the Catholic Modernist Friedrich von Hügel.

Bonhoeffer, of course, has the stature of a martyr, one who pursued the truth not just academically but with his life and unto his death. But it is a mistake to regard his theology as secondary to his heroism. Each was integral to the other. Australian students have told me what a life-changing experience it has been to take an intensive course on Bonhoeffer which I have taught several times in Melbourne during these ten years and more. I am sure they found Bonhoeffer a challenging and inspiring person. But no less, they discovered in him a mentor who opened their *minds* to new ways of looking at faith, the church, the contemporary world and their responsibility in it.

The chapters are not arranged in chronological order of their original writing or delivery but are grouped more or less thematically. Nor have I sought to revise their content which may, even after only a short passage of time, now seem a little dated (or indeed, with the benefit of hindsight in need, of some correction) since I believe that more interest lies in what was said in addressing a particular occasion than in trying to speak in timeless generalities (something that Bonhoeffer himself abhorred).

I am grateful to those who originally heard or read the contents as lectures, papers and (in two cases) sermons, and who in their responses became part of the conversation which resulted in the book as a whole. I must thank James Bradnock, who during the process of preparing the text for publication scrutinized it for the errors that a seasoned teacher of English unfailingly notices. Great debt is owed to Professor Phil Ziegler of the University of Aberdeen who first encouraged me to publish this collection, and who with the other editors of the T&T Clark Bonhoeffer Series made very apposite and helpful suggestions for improving the text at certain points. Finally, words of gratitude are inadequate for the grace that has enabled me to outlive the two years which were medically predicted for me in 2015. For all the means of that grace, especially the superb ministrations of staff in the National Health Service, and the loving support of thought and prayer from family and friends at home and around the world, *Deo gracias!* As Bonhoeffer himself said in one of his letters from prison to his friend Eberhard Bethge, 'What is certain is that in all this we stand within a community that carries us.'

Portishead
February 2022

FOREWORD

Written in conscious though unspoken debt to the witness of Dietrich Bonhoeffer, this open letter was sent to Patriarch Kirill, head of the Russian Orthodox Church, following the military attack on Ukraine launched on 24 February 2022.

8 March 2022

Your Holiness,

I greet you in the name of our Lord and Saviour Jesus Christ.

During these recent days I have been recalling very clearly the visit which in May 1999 Your Holiness and I together with other church and ecumenical figures made to Belgrade. We met with President Milosevic to present and discuss with him a proposal, drawn up by the Vienna Group of which both of us were members, for ending the conflict over Kosovo. Belgrade at that time was under aerial bombardment by NATO forces. In Belgrade and elsewhere we saw at first hand the effects of such attacks and our visit involved not a little danger to ourselves. But we went willingly, with the aim of contributing towards a cessation of hostilities and the creation of an opportunity for peace. This remains with me as a very positive memory of ecumenical fellowship in pursuit of peace, for which I am deeply grateful.

Today, in Ukraine, we are witnessing attacks on a country and its people, on a far greater scale than anything seen in Europe since 1945. This time, it has to be said in plain truth and in sorrow, the military operations are being carried out not by NATO but by Russian forces under the orders of President Putin. The devastation being wreaked upon Ukraine, its people and its infrastructure, the displacement and flight of civilians now being numbered by the millions are being witnessed by the whole world. It is a situation which cannot be justified by any Christian spirit or conscience and for the sake of the people of Ukraine and of Russia must be ended without delay.

In the same spirit which led us to visit Belgrade in 1999, I appeal to you for a word which acknowledges and addresses this situation in terms befitting a great Church of Jesus Christ. Thus far, we in the world outside have heard words about the desire for peace but not about the things that make for peace: first of all an acknowledgement of the wrong that is being committed against the people of Ukraine, without which no genuine movement towards peace can begin. It is known that there are voices in your Church and in other Christian communities in Russia, which are already expressing these aspirations towards repentance and the hope which repentance brings. I and others hope and pray that you will hear, defend and uphold them.

Many of us are well aware of the real historical factors which are involved in the relationship of Russia and Ukraine. We also realize that all countries, including those in the West, will need to reflect on their policies in Europe over recent decades, and be ready to learn from past mistakes. Moreover we are aware of the constraints which Your Holiness experiences, as leader of a Church with such close ties to the Russian state. But 'the word of God is not chained' (2 Timothy 2:9) and history shows us that there are moments when the Church is challenged to confess, perhaps at great cost but greatly strengthening its witness to the love of God for all people, where its truest and highest allegiance lies. Christians are called to place above all claims of earthly powers their loyalty to Jesus Christ to whom alone 'all authority in heaven and on earth has been given' (Matthew 28:18).

With all those who eagerly await such a word from you, and with continuing prayers for the guidance and inspiration of God's Holy Spirit upon Your Holiness, I remain,

In Christ,
Keith Clements
Former general secretary of the Conference of European Churches 1997–2005

ACKNOWLEDGEMENTS

Extracts from the works of Dietrich Bonhoeffer are printed with permission as follows:

(i) Dietrich Bonhoeffer, *Creation and Temptation*, SCM Press, 1966 © SCM Press. Used by permission of Hymns Ancient & Modern Ltd.
(ii) Dietrich Bonhoeffer, *The Cost of Discipleship*, SCM Translation, 1948, 1959 © SCM Press. Used by permission of Hymns Ancient & Modern Ltd.
(iii) Dietrich Bonhoeffer, *Ethics*, SCM Press, 1955 © SCM Press. Used by permission of Hymns Ancient & Modern Ltd.
(iv) Dietrich Bonhoeffer, *Letters and Papers from Prison, The Enlarged Edition*, SCM Press, 1971 © SCM Press. Used by permission of Hymns Ancient & Modern Ltd.
(v) *Dietrich Bonhoeffer Works*, Volumes 9, 10, 11, 12, 13, 14, 15, 16, published by Fortress Press.

Extracts from the works of Thomas Traherne are printed with permission as follows:

Thomas Traherne, *Works*, Volume 1, edited by Jan Ross, published by D.S. Brewer 2005.

Acknowledgements are also made for permission to use previously published material on which chapters are based, as follows:

The editor, *Crucible. The Journal of Christian Social Ethics* (Chapter 1)
The editor, *Keston Newsletter* (Chapter 2)
Fortress Press (Chapter 3)
The editor, *The Bonhoeffer Legacy* (Chapter 9)
The editor, *Ecumenical* Review, World Council of Churches (Chapter 11)
Religion and Social Policy Network (RASP), Australia (Chapter 12)

Every effort has been made to contact the original publishers of extracts from works included in this volume. In cases where this has not proved possible, the author and publisher of this work will be pleased to hear from the publishers concerned with a view to formalizing the permission.

ABBREVIATIONS AND ACRONYMS

CDU	Christian Democratic Union (in GDR)
CEC	Conference of European Churches
CIMADE	Comité inter-mouvement auprès des évacués
CPC	Christian Peace Conference
DBWE	Dietrich Bonhoeffer Works English Series
EU	European Union
GDR	German Democratic Republic
Gestapo	Geheime Staatspolizei (Secret State Police, in Nazi Germany)
KOR	Committee for the Defence of Workers (Poland)
OSE	Organisation de Secours aux Enfants
SCM	Student Christian Movement
SS	Schutzstaffel (Nazi 'Protection Guards')
Stasi	Staatsicherheitsdienst (State Security Service, in GDR)
UK	United Kingdom of Great Britain and Northern Ireland
UNESCO	United Nations Educational, Scientific and Cultural Organization
WCC	World Council of Churches

Part I

RECEIVING BONHOEFFER

Chapter 1

WHO IS DIETRICH BONHOEFFER FOR US TODAY?

'Who is Christ actually for us today?'[1] More than seventy-five years after his death Dietrich Bonhoeffer's question, penned in a Nazi prison cell, still troubles Christianity and catalyses lively theological debate. This in itself is a remarkable phenomenon. From the 1960s onwards the imminent demise of what some have dubbed 'the Bonhoeffer industry' has been regularly predicted – only to be followed by revivals of interest and fresh outpourings of publications about his life and work. Indeed, 'Dietrich Bonhoeffer seems to grow in popularity the further his death recedes into the past'.[2] The Thirteenth International Bonhoeffer Congress which met in January 2020 in Stellenbosch, South Africa, drew 160 participants from six continents: senior academics, younger research students, laypeople and clergy from nearly all church traditions (or none), to address the overall theme, 'How is the coming generation to go on living? Bonhoeffer and the response to our present crisis and hope.'

As well as plenary lectures, there were more than seventy seminars offered on Bonhoeffer's theology in his own context, and above all on the pertinence of his thought for a wide range of contemporary issues: African religion, Black theology, climate change, medical ethics, guilt and forgiveness in public life, poverty in Central Africa, intergenerational responsibility, interfaith cooperation and much more.

Such a menu of topics might suggest simply an exercise in tagging with the illustrious name of Bonhoeffer whichever issue is a current preoccupation, in order to enhance its importance or to justify the stance being taken on it. That is certainly a danger. But it can equally well be argued that the reason Bonhoeffer is still such a potent figure is not that he himself spoke directly to all the issues we are concerned with now (obviously he did not) but that he offers a profound and original way of looking at the basis of what it is to be human as creatures in God's world, a world claimed and redeemed by Christ; and that this is foundational and

---

Written for and published in *Crucible, The Journal of Christian Social Ethics*, July 2020, to mark the seventy-fifth anniversary of Bonhoeffer's death.

1. DBWE 8, 362.

2. Stephen Haynes, 'Readings and Receptions', in M. Mawson and Philip G. Ziegler (eds). *The Oxford Handbook of Dietrich Bonhoeffer* (Oxford: Oxford University Press, 2019), 482.

creative for the whole range of concerns we have for society and Christian for witness within it. We are dealing with fundamental theology.

Bonhoeffer: A changing image

The received image of Bonhoeffer has certainly varied in the course of time. The progressive unfolding and publication of the full range of his writings, the successive studies of him in his historical context, together with the varying perspectives and interests of his readers, have seen to that. In the years immediately after his death it was Bonhoeffer the martyr who first became known in the English-speaking world: the one who had endured two years' imprisonment and then in the last month of war was executed at Flossenbürg; the one who had refused to bow the knee to the tyrant; the exemplary pastor of the Confessing Church who had lived out and sealed by his own death what in 1937 he had written in his book *Nachfolge* (Discipleship): 'When Jesus calls a man, he bids him come and die.' Significantly, when the first English edition appeared in 1949 the title was enlarged to *The Cost of Discipleship*. In the early 1950s others of his works began to appear in English, notably his *Letters and Papers from Prison* (1953), and *Ethics* (1955). The figure of a serious, exploratory theologian began to emerge, which in the early 1960s morphed into that of the radical, even revolutionary, thinker who in his secret prison writings had declared the need for a 'Christianity without religion' in a 'world come of age'. In Britain it was John A. T. Robinson's *Honest to God* (1963), which highlighted this version of Bonhoeffer, as did certain of the so-called 'death of God' theologies, particularly in the United States. By the 1970s, however, a more complex and contoured picture was arriving with the publication of Bonhoeffer's earlier works on ecclesiology, biblical theology and Christology, and above all in 1970 with the comprehensive and detailed biography by Bonhoeffer's close friend Eberhard Bethge.[3] It was this latter which decisively revised the simplistic martyr-narrative and brought more fully into light Bonhoeffer the willing participant in the conspiracy to overthrow Hitler, with all the moral ambiguity which complicity in an act of violence entailed for the former advocate of pacifism. Political and liberation theologies found an interlocutor in Bonhoeffer, and much debate still focuses on Bonhoeffer the ethicist and his implications for theology in the public realm.

We might well, then, ask, 'Who is *Dietrich Bonhoeffer* actually for us today?' That question was enlivened by the publication in 2010 of the bestselling biography – running into millions worldwide and far outselling any other book on Bonhoeffer – by the American writer Eric Metaxas.[4] Fluently written, it is however

---

3. Eberhard Bethge, *Dietrich Bonhoeffer*, 2nd edn (Minneapolis, MN: Fortress Press, 1999).

4. Eric Metaxas, *Bonhoeffer: Pastor, Martyr, Prophet, Spy* (Nashville, TN: Thomas Nelson, 2010).

flawed by an overly selective use of Bonhoeffer's writings (e.g. he dismisses totally the prison letters) and above all a desire to secure Bonhoeffer as a standard-bearer for the neo-conservative American right (Metaxas is an ardent advocate of Donald Trump). If this is a grotesque misuse of Bonhoeffer, it also underlines the need for care by anyone, from any position on the political or theological spectrum, who presumes to interpret Bonhoeffer for today. Integrity requires more than piecemeal citations from Bonhoeffer's immense output. Interpretation must be tested by what can be identified as the core and main thrust of his thinking, and the realities of the context with which he was engaged.

The case for still taking Bonhoeffer seriously, however, has to counter two assumptions. The first is that Bonhoeffer's context of Nazi tyranny was so extreme as to reduce or nullify his relevance for us today – in Britain at any rate, unless one grossly exaggerates our predicaments to apocalyptic dimensions. To this it must be said that Bonhoeffer forged the distinctive tools of his theology well *before* the advent of Hitler to power in 1933. In his doctoral and postdoctoral dissertations *Sanctorum Communio* (1927) and *Act and Being* (1930), respectively, we already see how he fuses a Christ-centred view of revelation (owing much to Karl Barth) with an intensely relational and social understanding of both the church and humanity at large. The church is 'Christ existing as church-community'; 'the concepts of person, community and God are inseparably and essentially interrelated'.[5] We are thus truly human only in relationship to others. As early as this, too, we read of the 'worldliness' of God. God's transcendent freedom is not a freedom *from* but *for* historical human beings; God's choice is 'to be placed at the disposal of human beings'.[6] In 1932 he expounds the petition 'Thy kingdom come' in a way that anticipates what he was to write over a decade later in prison: 'Whoever evades Earth in order to find God finds only himself ... He who loves God, loves God as the Lord of all the earth as it is; he loves the earth, loves it as God's earth.'[7] Bonhoeffer's theological tools were to be sharpened during the Third Reich, but they were already to hand in the tottering democracy and disintegrating society of the Weimar Republic. Moreover, his later theology in parts of his wartime *Ethics*, and certainly in his prison writings, was anticipating the situation of a post-Hitler, post-war world in which the question facing the church would not be whether it would be persecuted but whether it would be noticed at all.

The second assumption is closely related. It is that Bonhoeffer's theology developed in a linear fashion, punctuated by sharp turns and a final breakthrough from a 'churchly' to a 'worldly' emphasis, culminating in the 'religionless' theology of the prison writings.

Arguments then develop on where the most decisive break was made. Between *Discipleship* and *Ethics*? Between *Ethics* and the prison writings? Or somewhere within the prison writings, most likely at the end of April 1944 when he asks the

---

5. DBWE 1, 34.
6. DBWE 2, 90–1.
7. 'Thy Kingdom Come', DBWE 12, 288.

'Who is Christ?' question, marking the start of the 'radical' letters? There are, however, notable continuities in Bonhoeffer's thinking. The main ingredients remain markedly consistent: a heavily Christocentric, biblically based view of revelation; a determinedly social, anti-individualist understanding of human nature; faith seen as always rooted in this world and worldly responsibility; a suspicion of religion as the human attempt to place God where God can be made to serve partisan human purposes; or as an escape from this world, instead of faith as the acceptance of being with the suffering Christ, the one whom God chooses to be on earth. These ingredients are always found together, though not always with the same emphasis, just as the themes of an orchestral symphony may continually appear and reappear, one for a time in a more leading role than others, but none of them ever completely absent from the score.

So for example in *Discipleship* the main focus is on the narrow way, the exclusive relationship of faith to Jesus Christ in opposition to the claims of the false lords of this world, bedecked with swastikas or other symbols of power. But at the end of that book, the narrow defile of discipleship suddenly opens out into a panorama of the whole world seen anew, because the one who is to be followed so exclusively is the Christ who has made himself one with all humanity in its need: 'In Christ's incarnation all humanity regains the dignity of bearing the image of God.'[8] This theme is followed up in the *Ethics* where it is now the world, of which Christ is the centre, that holds the attention; but the fact that Christ is the centre is never lost sight of.

As for the prison writings, Bonhoeffer himself certainly recognizes that he is taking a new turn in looking for a Christianity which is not a form of 'religion', in a world that no longer needs God as traditionally conceived (the God beyond us, the stopgap God who is brought in from another world and only when human powers give out). Yet here, where his personal situation is becoming so dire, so much of his earlier thought is fused anew into an affirmation of how the transcendent God is indeed to be apprehended in present experience: 'Experience that here there is a reversal of all human existence, in the very fact that Jesus only "is there for others".'[9] The implication for the church is sharp: 'God is the beyond in the midst of our lives. The church stands not at the point where human powers fail, at the boundaries, but in the centre of the village.'[10] God is not an escape from suffering but takes his place at the heart of the world's affliction. With Christ 'one takes seriously no longer one's own sufferings but rather the suffering of God in the world';[11] 'The church is church only when it is there for others.'[12]

---

8. DBWE 4. 285.
9. DBWE 8, 501.
10. Ibid., 367.
11. Ibid., 486.
12. Ibid., 363.

Vicarious representative action

We can be yet more specific about the continuity in Bonhoeffer. There is one term and concept which, more than any other, runs like a thread throughout his theology, and which is crucially significant for linking the life of the church and the life of society. We meet it first in *Sanctorum Communio*. It is the German term *Stellvertretung*, which in earlier translations of Bonhoeffer was rendered as 'deputyship' but in the new English versions becomes 'vicarious representative action', that is, action which bears the needs of another and stands in for that person before God and before others. As Rowan Williams paraphrases, 'We are to stand in the place where the other lives, so that we are vulnerable to what the other is vulnerable to; we are to risk what the other risks'.[13]

For Bonhoeffer, *Stellvertretung* is most fully embodied by Jesus Christ himself who took the place of sinners on the cross, and who always exists as the love shown in that relationship. Equally it defines how members of the body of Christ are called and enabled to relate to one another, to be (as Luther said) Christs to one another, a forgiven and forgiving people. Bonhoeffer takes the traditional evangelical gospel and transmutes it into entirely relational terms. He moved on from *Sanctorum Communio*, but *Stellvertretung* remained a key concept for him, marking the trajectory of his life and thought, in a stream that acquired widening and deepening significance as it flowed on. In *Ethics*, for example, it is seen as the foundation of all responsible human life, secular as well as religious, in which mutuality and solidarity are evident:

> Jesus – the life, our life – the Son of God who became human, lived as our vicarious representative. Through him, therefore, all human life is in its essence vicarious representation … Since he is life, all of life through him is destined to be vicarious representative action.[14]

To quote Williams again, as mandated by God the patterns of interdependent human life 'exist in order to provide human existence with a structure that will eventually appear as the structure of Christ's own life, Christ's-being-for-the-other'.[15] But if all human life in its everyday relationships of family, work, friendship and civic responsibility is marked even there by traces of vicarious representative action there are also occasions when it becomes a more drastic calling. It was this which had enabled Bonhoeffer to write in May 1933, as the state-sanctioned violence against the Jews began, to declare that 'the church has an unconditional obligation toward the victims of any societal order, even if they do not belong to the Christian community'.[16] ' "Speak out for those who cannot speak" – who in the

---

13. Rowan Williams, *Christ the Heart of Creation* (London: Bloomsbury, 2018), 207.
14. DBWE 6, 258–9.
15. Williams, *Christ the Heart of Creation*, 204.
16. 'The Church and the Jewish Question', DBWE 12, 365.

church today still remembers that this is the very least the Bible asks of us in such times as these?', he wrote to a friend in 1934.[17] In the context of the self-limiting religious and social tribalism of Germany at that time, this was truly prophetic. It was equally in the spirit of *Stellvertretung* that on the eve of war in 1939 Bonhoeffer chose to return to Germany from the safety of a lecture tour in the United States to share all the perils of his people, come what may. It was, ultimately, as an act of vicarious representative action that he saw his participation, and that of his family and closest friends, in the political conspiracy: an act which in taking the sword entailed becoming guilty, but doing so on behalf of the whole nation that had betrayed its calling, and an act for which he accepted the consequences.

Being human: Life in relationship

It is as much an anthropological as a theological perspective that Bonhoeffer brings: a view of what it is to be human, revealed by Christ. Human beings, in the light of the biblical narrative of their creation, fall and redemption, do not just *have* their being but *receive* it from God and, because humans are created in and for relationships, receive it from *one another*.

This is personalist, relational and communal understanding of being human at its most profound – so much so as to appear threatening to the sense of self (it has been asked by some commentators whether it could only be expected from someone who was as strong a (male!) personality, secure in his own selfhood, as was Bonhoeffer himself[18]). Above all, Bonhoeffer sees freedom not as a possession which the individual has in isolation but as a relationship with others: 'freedom is a relation between two persons. Being free means "being-free-for-the- other", because I am bound to the other. Only by being in relation with the other am I free.'[19] This runs counter to the self-justifying, self-aggrandizing view of freedom as space to do whatever one wishes, space guaranteed against encounter with others, which is the prevalent assumption of life today.

Bonhoeffer does not deny the reality of the self, or the individual person or the distinctive nation. But he does assert that whatever particular self is in view, its true purpose can only be seen in its relation to others and its calling within the wider whole. Relatively little known but very significant is a lecture he gave to technological college students in Berlin in 1932, the year before the Nazi takeover, on 'The Right to Self-Assertion'. He was clearly aware of how terms like 'freedom' and 'self-sacrifice' were vulnerable to exploitation by the burgeoning Nazi movement with its nationalist and racist ideology:

17. DBWE 13, 217.
18. See Rachel Muers, 'Anthropology', in Mawson and Ziegler, *Oxford Handbook*, 196–207.
19. DBWE 3, 222.

We are not only individuals, but we are also placed within life-communities … Our marriage, our church, Germany are called before the forum of responsibility … Every community, even the great community of the people, lives not only for itself but for the others, lives in responsibility for the brother, for the people to whom one is bound in brotherhood. There is absolutely no isolated life for the people. It is bound through its birth onward to the community and through its life to the peoples [sic] in brotherhood.[20]

Even on the international level, therefore, vicarious representative action is in view. This is a challenge to all the assumptions about freedom and the claims of selfhood, whether the self of the individual, the group or the nation – or even humankind as a whole vis-à-vis the rest of creation – which drives so much of the Western world today. This was all too evident in the debates over Britain and the European Union, preceding and following the referendum vote of 2016. What was most painfully obvious was that the British churches and their leaders, for the most part timidly silent, corporately had no clear perspective to offer on the issues; no critique to make of the unexamined language about 'our freedoms', 'sovereignty' and 'taking back control'; no answer to the populist demonizing of Europe; no positive vision of what a continuing partnership with our fellow-Europeans in the wider world could in fact be; nor even any appreciation to record of how long and deep has been the British churches' involvement with the European project since the Second World War, based on a long-lasting commitment to justice, peace and reconciliation. Who even thought to ask what British departure might mean, not just for ourselves but for Europe as a whole?

Stellvertretung was way beyond the horizon.

Conclusion

Who is Bonhoeffer for us today? It is always tempting to hail Bonhoeffer the courageous prophet who resisted tyranny at its most evil, the martyr faithful unto death, at the expense of attending to the theological basis of his witness. Thereby we are apt to evade the real critique he offers of our present context, and content ourselves with hero-worshipping him from afar. At one level there is some hope that our world today is conscious of being in a 'drift towards interdependence' and of the need for people and communities to become 'part of a larger *us*'.[21] But more immediately, whoever and wherever we are, we are immersed in an individualized and polarizing world, where achievement and self-portrayal (see the social media for example) are so important and in which 'Many people are convinced that integration into a community takes place through the demonstration of efficiency

---

20. 'The Right to Self-Assertion', DBWE 12, 254.
21. Alex Evans, *The Myth Gap* (London: Random House/Transworld, 2017) (citing Robert Wright), 44–5.

and the considerable aspects of one's own life'.[22] In such a context, Bonhoeffer is the one who witnesses to Jesus Christ, mediator of the gift of a very different way to community as the goal of human life, the costly life of the incarnate God with us.

It was as witness to vicarious representative action that in September 1944, weeks after the failure of the plot against Hitler, and fully aware of his own now near-certain fate, he wrote his almost final poem, 'The Death of Moses'. Drawing inspiration from Israel's first and greatest prophet, who saw from afar the Promised Land and knew that he himself would not enter it, he concludes,

> To punish sin, to forgive, you are moved;
> O God, this people have I truly loved.
> That I bore its shame and sacrifices
> and saw its salvation – that suffices.[23]

That was Bonhoeffer's expression of what vicarious representative action meant for him in his own life, where witness was called for in the ultimate extremity. But he was no less concerned for the witness of vicarious representative action in all the penultimate relationships of faithful and loving responsibility, in every walk of life, and at every level in society – which we must fulfil in our time too.

---

22. Christoph Barnbrock, abstract of paper 'Breakthrough to Fellowship', presented at the Thirteenth International Bonhoeffer Congress, Stellenbosch, South Africa, 19–23 January 2020.
23. DBWE 8, 541.

Chapter 2

AFTER MARTYRDOM: BONHOEFFER'S POSTHUMOUS JOURNEY THROUGH COLD WAR EAST EUROPE

Dietrich Bonhoeffer, executed in April 1945, died just before the end of the Second World War in Europe, and some two years before the Cold War descended to divide East and West. Like others who have died yet still speak he has inspired many people, worldwide, who have had to endure oppressive regimes and who have campaigned for justice and human rights, from South Africa to Latin America to East Asia. What is surprising, however, is that relatively little has been said about Bonhoeffer's posthumous role nearer to home, in Cold War Europe. In part that is because his story is bound up with the complexities of the churches' role under communism in Europe, and much of that story is still being told and is still under debate; and the Bonhoeffer part of that story has its own complexities. All I try to do here is sketch his posthumous role in three countries of the Soviet Bloc: the German Democratic Republic (GDR), Czechoslovakia and Poland. 'Role' is of course an ambiguous word in such contexts. It can refer to the use made of his writings and his story – but perhaps their misuse too. Reactions to the posthumous Bonhoeffer can be illuminative of the outlook both of the communist authorities and of churches and Christians in those countries.

The pre-Cold War Bonhoeffer

Bonhoeffer of course in his lifetime was preoccupied with his immediate context of Nazi totalitarianism. But he was aware of the dangers posed by Soviet tyranny. For instance, in the spring of 1939 he was in London seeking, among other matters, to secure a place for the Confessing Church in the ecumenical fellowship represented by the new World Council of Churches (WCC) 'in formation'. While there he wrote a long letter to his great friend George Bell, bishop of Chichester. In this he stresses the need for ecumenical solidarity with churches under oppression: 'I think we failed in earlier years to give our full assistance in advice and fellowship

---

Revised version of lecture given at the Annual General Meeting of the Keston Institute, 3 November 2018, and published in *Keston Newsletter*, No. 20, 2019.

to the Russian Christians'[1] – a clear reference to the persecutions particularly during the massive Stalinist purges of 1936-7. In September 1941 Bonhoeffer made one of his wartime visits to Geneva on behalf of the Confessing Church and the political resistance in Germany, for conversations with W. A. Visser't Hooft, secretary of the WCC. In Geneva, Bonhoeffer and Visser't Hooft prepared two memoranda in response to a book by William Paton, then an assistant general secretary for the WCC in London, on the shape of a post-war, post-Hitler Europe.[2] The second memorandum concludes with a paragraph on 'The Russian Problem'. This acknowledges the great uncertainties about 'the forces at work in Russia and its future role in the world'. The German invasion of the Soviet Union had been launched three months earlier, bringing Russia into the warm embrace of the allies. But as Christians, say the authors,

> we dare not let ourselves be carried away by momentary reactions. Even though we may consider the British-Russian alliance a justifiable and unavoidable political decision, we must not minimise the danger which Russia still represents for all what we hold dear. Unless the war calls forth very fundamental changes in the structure of the Russian state, Bolshevism may well become a tremendous menace to all countries which have been betting on the wrong horse and which will find their Fascist system discredited by a German defeat.[3]

The German Democratic Republic

Bonhoeffer is obviously nearest to home here. Though known only to relatively few even in Germany at the time of his death, his writings and story soon created an impression in both the Western and Eastern Zones, as they were first called, which later solidified as the Federal Republic and the GDR, respectively. At least as important, a number of Bonhoeffer's Confessing Church colleagues and former students had survived the war and were very important in stimulating discussion of his ideas. These included his close friend Eberhard Bethge, the recipient of most of Bonhoeffer's prison letters. A first edition of the *Ethics* edited by Bethge appeared in 1949, and then the prison letters in 1951 under the German title *Widerstand und Ergebung* – 'Resistance and Submission'. This would obviously ring bells with those now living under Soviet domination (as well as being a more provocative title than the one by which we Anglophones know the book, *Letters and Papers from Prison*).

In the GDR, hard-line Marxist-Leninism was promulgated as official government doctrine and policy, perhaps more rigorously than in any other

---

1. DBWE 15, 156.
2. DBWE 16, 528-39.
3. Ibid., 539.

Eastern bloc country. That did not bode well for the churches. On the other hand, the state had to tread somewhat carefully here. The GDR wanted to be seen as an authentically *German* socialist state, and that could not be done if Martin Luther and the Reformation heritage were wholly excised from the country's history, nor if the churches were to be totally suppressed. There was also the awkward fact to consider that while the GDR sought to justify so much of its aims by recalling the horrors of Nazism which it had replaced, significant opposition to that fascism had come from within the churches and people imbued with Christian values. The Marxist jibe about religion being 'the opium of the people' wouldn't quite wash. Containment, if not actual control, rather than abolition of the churches was to mark the GDR's church policy from the 1960s onwards, first under head of state Walter Ulbricht and then from 1971 his successor Erich Honecker. In addition to the ruling Socialist Unity Party (SED) there were several smaller parties sanctioned by the state, including the Christian Democratic Union (CDU), designed to allow some people from the church sector to have a semblance of participation in the organs of government. Not many either inside or outside the churches had much regard for it. When visiting the GDR in 1978 I was in a group that met with some pastors in Weimar and we asked about the CDU. One pastor shook his head and said, 'I never want to see the church in uniform again.' His father had been a Confessing Church pastor and had experienced at first hand the havoc wrought by the so-called German Christian Movement, effectively a Protestant wing of the Nazi party. That memory remained pertinent in the GDR.

What did the GDR authorities make of Bonhoeffer? In one way, quite a lot. By the 1960s his reputation was too great to be ignored. In fact, of all the people variously associated with the conspiracy which culminated in the 20 July 1944 plot, Bonhoeffer was about the only one to receive official praise by the GDR authorities. Most of the others being high-ranking military figures, academics or Junker types were dismissed as bourgeois reactionaries and did not fit the desired socialist narrative of a people's movement. Bonhoeffer at least did not have *von* in front of his family name. But why was Bonhoeffer, who was in fact as upper-class bourgeois as they come, an acceptable exception? It was because in his *Ethics*, written during the war and published soon after, he had written extensively on relations between church and state, and on the state itself. We find statements such as: 'Government is the power set in place by God to exercise world rule with divine authority. Government is the vicarious representative action of God on earth.'[4] A very top-down view, redolent of much traditional Lutheran reading of Romans 13. While the authorities were hardly interested in the theological element of such statements, what Bonhoeffer seemed to be saying sat very well with the requirements of the totalitarian state. Moreover in the GDR there were theologians who were happy to go along with this and much more. One extreme example was Hanfried Müller, professor in Berlin, who in 1961

4. DBWE 6, 504.

brought out a book *Von der Kirche zur Welt* ('From the Church to the World') expounding Bonhoeffer's ideas in his prison writings, on religionless Christianity in a world come of age, as leading to 'a new picture of history', 'a rational and optimistic atheism which is founded upon the freedom of faith'.[5] This of course was tailor-made to fit the official GDR ideology. Few theologians in the GDR actually bought this, but some did give the state the benefit of the doubt, including some Bonhoeffer scholars. (I remember well during the 1980 Congress of the International Bonhoeffer Society in Oxford, sitting at lunch with one such, who set out the cutlery and cruets on the table to construct a map of Eastern Europe and Central Asia, in order to explain the Soviet fears of encirclement and so to justify the invasion of Afghanistan.)

So was Bonhoeffer an unwitting apologist for Soviet communism in the GDR? As so often happens, citations taken out of context are the propagandists' dream. Yes, Bonhoeffer in his *Ethics* had written about the authority of the state – but not as an end in itself, rather as a mandate from God and therefore accountable to God. Moreover, he wrote of government as one of several mandates of equal validity: family, work, culture – and church. Bonhoeffer's intention of portraying the *limitations* of the state and its relation to areas of life over which it did *not* have authority had been written out of the picture for the sake of the totalitarian ideology.[6] Professor Wolf Krötke, who has studied and written extensively on this subject, says entertainingly that by drawing upon any of Bonhoeffer's writings the GDR authorities were in fact laying a cuckoo's egg in their own nest.[7] For Bonhoeffer had also written in a vein quite counter to that misleadingly selected citation about the state. At Christmas 1942, three months before his imprisonment, he had written for his friends and family in the resistance an essay, 'After Ten Years', reflecting on Hitler's decade of power and the experiences of life in resistance. One section is titled 'Civil Courage'. Here he acknowledges the bravery and self-sacrifice that the typical German has habitually shown in obedience to the commission of service to country. That was moving to see. Bonhoeffer continues,

> However, in doing so, [the German] misjudged the world; he did not reckon with the fact that the readiness to subordinate and commit his life to the commission could be misused in the service of evil. When such misuse occurred, exercise of the career itself became questionable, and all the basic moral concepts of the Germans were shaken. What became apparent was that Germans lacked still

---

5. Cf. Hanfried Müller, 'Concerning the Reception and Interpretation of Dietrich Bonhoeffer', in R. Gregor Smith (ed.), *World Come of Age: A Symposium on Dietrich Bonhoeffer* (London: Collins, 1967), 208.

6. DBWE 6, 388–408.

7. See W. Krötke, 'Dietrich Bonhoeffers Verständnis des Staates', in K. Busch Nielsen, Kirsten Busch Nielsen, Ralf K. Wüstenberg and Jens Zimmermann (eds) *Dem Rad in die Speichen fallen/A Spoke in the Wheel* (Gütersloh: Gütersloh Verlagshaus, 2103), 303–24.

one decisive and fundamental idea: that of the need for the free, responsible action even against career and commission. In its place came the irresponsible lack of scruples, on the one hand, and self-tormenting scruples that never led to action, on the other. But civil courage can grow only from the free responsibility of the free man. Only today are Germans beginning to discover what free responsibility means. It is founded in a God who calls for the free venture of faith to responsible action, and who promises forgiveness and consolation to the one who on account of such action becomes a sinner.[8]

This and other thoughts found in Bonhoeffer's *Ethics* were seized upon with zest by those who in the GDR were looking for a different kind of citizenship than that prescribed by or just allowed by the state, and who wanted to be actively involved in creating a more truly democratic society. Over the years many such groups found space and shelter in the churches. The influence of Bonhoeffer can also clearly be seen in those church leaders who sought to resist the marginalizing of the churches to the private religious dimension of life, and heeded Bonhoeffer's call in his prison letters for the church, like God 'the Beyond in the midst', to stand at the centre of life and especially where people are suffering. One such was Heino Falcke, in the 1970s principal of the Gnadau Theological College, and then provost of Erfurt. At a Synod meeting in 1972, and in address to the Baptists, he publicly challenged the state view that socialism was in effect primitive Christianity put into practice and that specifically religious activity was for private life and leisure hours:

To this we must say 'No' ... We cannot accept withdrawal from the secular world ... Were we to settle for that we would be falsifying the Gospel of freedom into a spare-time Gospel ... We would be conceding that man's political maturity depends on his liberation from Christ rather than on his being liberated by Christ.[9]

This stance thus refused either to withdraw totally from the socialist context or to give socialism a carte blanche blessing. Rather, it sought a better kind of socialism than the state was capable of, and therewith appealed for dialogue with the state, and an opening up of public discussion on how people were actually faring in the present socialist society. There was little immediate response from the state to Falcko's plea, but over the years there came a grudging respect for the churches' social role, with frank exchanges on matters such as youth and education, the military education imposed on schools, care of the elderly and opportunities for the church to extend its ministry on the airwaves. It is noteworthy that at this time and into the 1980s the presiding bishop of the Protestant church in the GDR was

---

8. DBWE 8, 41.

9. Cited in Trevor Beeson, *Discretion and Valour: Religious Conditions in Russia and Eastern Europe* (London: Collins, 1974), 185.

Albrecht Schönherr, who had been one of Bonhoeffer's most loyal students. He now proved himself a shrewd diplomat. Associated with him were phrases like 'a church within socialism' and 'critical solidarity' with the socialist state. These were phrases that Schönherr did not invent but felt he could live with. He safeguarded space for the church – 'a church without privileges' – while at the same time insisting that the church must not simply stay in that space away from the wider world but to be, as Bonhoeffer put it, 'the church for others'. Some wished he had spoken out more strongly about conditions in the country – he himself wished he had been more outspoken about conditions in prisons. But when the time came for change at the end of the 1980s, it was evident that here was a church – notwithstanding the pressures upon it including infiltration by the Stasi, the secret police – that had not only retained its integrity as the church of Christ but was now ready to help Germans in both East and West make the most momentous and above all peaceful transition to a unified democracy. In it all, the posthumous influence of Bonhoeffer was very evident.

Czechoslovakia

Today the very name Czechoslovakia is enough to evoke pictures of one of the harshest regimes of the communist era, which right through to the early 1960s enforced the most unyielding Stalinist line. So much so that when in 1956 the Soviet leader Nikita Khrushchev denounced the late Stalin's oppressive policies and initiated an attempt at de-Stalinization, this was resisted by the Czechoslovak Communist party and not until 1963 was any relaxation permitted. Then came the hopes of the Prague Spring under the government of Alexander Dubček and the project of 'socialism with a human face', which was crushed following the invasion by Soviet and Warsaw Pact forces in 1968. A neo-Stalinist regime was installed by the Soviets, determined to repress every sign of independence. The churches were now destined to feel once more the full force of repression, and battled against odds as heavy as could be found anywhere in Eastern Europe outside Albania and the Soviet Union itself.

The largest Czechoslovak church was the Roman Catholic Church, followed by the two main Protestant churches, the Hussite Church and the Evangelical Church of the Czech Brethren (mostly of former Lutheran and Reformed communities), plus the Slovak Lutherans, the Baptists and the Methodists. The Hussite Church is significant as bearing the name of Jan Hus, the fifteenth-century proto-reformer, martyr and the figurehead of much Czech nationalism. There was thus a significant Protestant constituency aligned with the historic Czech national identity, and there is no mistaking the appeal that the martyr-figure of Bonhoeffer made to those who saw themselves as the heirs of the martyr Jan Hus.

There were in fact two levels at which Bonhoeffer's appeal was felt. First, there were those high-level Protestant theologians who believed that Christian witness in the socialist society required Christian dialogue with Marxism. Here a key and controversial figure was the Reformed theologian of Prague, and leading figure in the World Alliance of Reformed Churches, Josef Hromádka (1889–1970). In the late

1950s he with others founded the Christian Peace Conference (CPC) which first met in Prague in 1958, as an ecumenical forum bringing together eastern and western and nonaligned Christians from around the globe.

Appeal was made to Bonhoeffer's own dramatic call in 1934[10] to Fanø for the church at world level to witness for peace. Always there was suspicion in the West that while the CPC claimed political neutrality, it could only have been founded in the East with Soviet backing. Nevertheless for a time it did provide an ecumenical meeting point in addition to the WCC, and people from both East and West found it a significant point of dialogue. It was shaken by the events of 1968, when it appeared that if indeed it existed under Soviet behest the Soviets themselves believed it by now to be a tool of the West! Hromádka died two years later, somewhat broken and feeling betrayed by the socialist forces he had felt called to interpret to the wider world.

If the CPC alone had represented Bonhoeffer's influence in Czechoslovakia, that influence might have effectively disappeared after 1968. But there was a quite other level at which Bonhoeffer journeyed there. The Bohemian tradition dating from Jan Hus and the other pioneers of the Bohemian reformation from which the later Czech Protestants emerged stressed the importance of the local congregations and personal discipleship to Christ. During the 1950s and 1960s, when so much institutional structure and power had been lost to the churches at the national level, these local communities came into their own. Jan Milič Lochmann (1922–2004), another Prague theologian and much inspired by Bonhoeffer, wrote joyously of the vitality of these congregations which, he said, gave strength to his work as a theologian: 'Deprived of their institutional "power", they got a new "glory" of a free, spontaneous, meaningful community. Their institutional element became important; it was a base – in many respects the only base – for Christian organization and service.'[11] It was only to be expected that Bonhoeffer, the author of *Discipleship* and *Life Together*, would be gladly received there. But there was more to it than even that. Ján Liguš, professor in the Hussite Theological Faculty in Prague, recalls that it was Bonhoeffer's prison letters that helped him and others meet the challenge of the Marxist ideology which bore down on every aspect of everyday life of that time.[12] Religion was officially declared to be the opium of the people, and atheism to be the only way forward to achieve a true and just society. Yet Bonhoeffer in his prison writings had made his own attack on 'religion', religion as a way of thought which offered people a life out of this world, as distinct from the gospel which calls us into the world to witness God's renewal of it. Bonhoeffer asked, 'How do we go about being "religionless-worldly Christians ... those who are called out, without understanding ourselves religiously privileged, but instead seeing ourselves

---

10. See below, 71–5, 95, 114–17, 133–4.

11. Cited in Beeson, *Discretion and Valour*, 211.

12. Ján Liguš, 'Rezeption des Bonhoefferschen religioslosen Christentums in der Tschechoslowakei nach dem Jahr 1948', in F. Schmitz and C. Tietz (eds), *Dietrich Bonhoeffers Christentum* (Gütersloh: Gütersloh Verlagshaus, 2011), 381–5.

as belonging wholly to the world?"'[13] Such as Lochmann and Liguš felt this to be a breakthrough in meeting the Marxist challenge. The Marxist attack on religion was off-target as regards the gospel, and so could be set aside by Christians. Their job was, as part of their discipleship to Christ, to work for just relations between people even in a godless atheistic world. (It is interesting that Lochmann was arguing this in 1955 – seven years before Bonhoeffer's prison writings had really hit the headlines in Britain with Bishop John Robinson's *Honest to God*. What became an interesting sort of intellectual discussion in the West was behind the Iron Curtain already a decisive matter for everyday faith in Marxist-Leninist society.)

'It is not the religious act which makes the Christian, rather the participation in the suffering of God in the worldly life', wrote Bonhoeffer.[14] So Ján Liguš, following on from Lochmann, draws on Bonhoeffer to say that we meet the transcendent God not outside but inside every human life-situation, God in the form of the incarnate, crucified risen and glorified Christ. He writes,

> As a good conclusion we can say that Bonhoeffer's *theologia crucis* combines the new life of the Christian and the participation in God's suffering in the world. This combination lights up, like a lighthouse in the darkness, God's hidden ways with the Christian churches in the communist-atheistic society behind the Iron Curtain. This faith in the suffering almighty God in Christ was equally for Christians the greatest comfort in their daily cares and sicknesses and the encouragement willingly to accept suffering and discrimination, and thereby to share in God's suffering in Christ.[15]

Liguš speaks of a 'latent operation' of Bonhoeffer's influence:

> a hidden, secret influence that did not show any public, revolutionary slogans and protests on the outskirts but worked deeply, long and hidden in the hearts of believers, Christians who came into contact with Bonhoeffer publications, which helped them in the long run to understand the socio-political situation and the life orientation of faith in communist-atheistic society in post-war Czechoslovakia.[16]

There was maintained, we could say, a continual tension between *Widerstand* and *Ergebung*.

Poland in transition to democracy

Poland, that most Catholic of countries, which in the 1980s led the way to the emancipation of Eastern Europe from Soviet rule, might seem an odd place to

13. DBWE 8, 364.
14. Ibid., 480.
15. Liguš, 'Rezeption', 383 (my translation).
16. Ibid.

manifest a reception of the Protestant Bonhoeffer, notwithstanding the existence of very active Protestant minority churches there. Yet nowhere in Eastern Europe was the posthumous Bonhoeffer more warmly welcomed than in those circles which from the 1970s onwards were looking to re-shape the post-1945 Polish mind. The story of the liberation and democratization of Poland was of course one in which figures like Lech Walesa and the Solidarity movement, and most notably the Catholic archbishop, Karol Wojtyla, later Pope John Paul II, were central. But that was not the whole story.

First, there is a special and not wholly incidental reason why Bonhoeffer found a welcome in Poland, for in one sense it was a welcome home. Bonhoeffer was born in 1904 in what was then Breslau in Silesia, and today is Wroclaw, part of Poland since the border changes of 1945. In the centre of Wroclaw is the historic and beautiful Elisabeth Church, which by turns over the centuries has been Catholic and Protestant and today is Catholic again. Outside the church, embedded in the pavement, is a striking bronze memorial to this son of Wroclaw, Dietrich Bonhoeffer. There are other Bonhoeffer links. Much of Bonhoeffer's activity from 1935 onwards was in what is now Poland, most notably the underground seminary he directed for the Confessing Church, at Finkenwalde, close to Stettin.

Bonhoeffer comes into the story of Poland's search for a post-communist future in the context of the long-running Polish debate about the authentic national identity and the ambiguity of its long-term development: was it to be a liberal, inclusivist and outward-looking understanding of the nation, or a narrowing, exclusivist chauvinism armed with religion ('to be Polish is to be Catholic') and with ugly anti-Semitic features? Under Soviet communism, what room was there for the former, inclusivist type to develop, or what was there to prevent a reversion to the latter, chauvinist type once the communist yoke was removed? In communist Poland, crucial to the eventual development of a political movement which could be an alternative to the Soviet-imposed system was the need for dialogue between Christians (overwhelmingly of course, but not completely, Roman Catholic) and the reformist, left-of-centre intellectuals. Finding common ground was not easy, as there were suspicions on both sides. Catholics expected secular or humanist thinkers to be ipso facto anti-church or anti-clerical, while the secular intellectuals in turn were apt to assume that theologians attended only to narrowly religious concerns and to safeguarding the interests of the church. If these entrenched positions had been maintained there would have been little chance of a common humane language developing, to enable Poland to develop a civil society, pluralist but with a widely shared respect for human rights, and encouraging citizens to active social responsibility.

Joel Burnell, who teaches in the Evangelical Theological Seminary in Wroclaw, has impressively documented how important Bonhoeffer's writings, especially his *Ethics* (with their emphasis on the freedom of the responsible person in society) and his prison writings (on how to be Christian in a godless world), were for both the secular and theological Polish thinkers of the 1970s and 1980s.[17] The

---

17. Joel Burnell, *Poetry, Providence, and Patriotism: Polish Messianism in Dialogue with Dietrich Bonhoeffer* (Eugene, OR: Pickwick, 2009).

role of the scholar Anna Morawska, associated with the Catholic journal *Więź*, was especially important in the transmission of Bonhoeffer from 1968 onwards. But many secular intellectuals were also impressed. A notable example is Adam Michnik: historian, political activist and member of the 'commandos' (students involved in the 1968 demonstrations); co-founder of the Committee for the Defence of Workers (KOR); advisor to Solidarity; member of Parliament 1989–91; and from 1989 editor of *Gazeta Wyborczc*, Poland's largest daily newspaper. 'Reading Bonhoeffer,' he confessed, 'was essential for me because he explained how to be an anti-totalitarian Christian.' Under an officially atheist regime, Bonhoeffer's provocative ideas, written during the last year of his life in prison, on 'religionless Christianity' and 'living as if God is not given', made both secularists and religious people question their easy assumptions about 'belief' and 'unbelief' – and to call every dogmatism to account in the name of what is truly human. Michnik argued that the Catholic Church and the left shared an antitotalitarian view of the unity of human rights and human duties, as deeply rooted in both Christian and secular traditions, and urged that they should talk to one another. He said he had discovered from Bonhoeffer and his *Ethics* that truth, freedom, dignity and tolerance, social justice and human solidarity stem from Christ and his teaching. One cannot reject this tradition with impunity. 'Belief in the divinity of Christ is a matter of grace, and in this sense is given only to a few. But belief in the hallowed nature of Christ's commandments is the duty of all, because it is the light that protects human freedom and dignity against violence and debasement, against nihilism and the hell of solitude.'[18]

Another leading intellectual activist from the 1970s onwards was Jacerk Kuron, a one-time Marxist but growingly disenchanted with the socialist project. Expelled from the communist party in 1964, he became a leader of the opposition movement and with Adam Michnik, a co-founder of the KOR. In 1989 he wrote of the effect of Bonhoeffer's prison letters and his provocative statement that we must 'live as if there were no God'. 'This statement became another great discovery for me. Up until now ... I suspected that Christian morality was based on the principle of the fear of punishment and the desire for reward. For I did not know how to imagine love for God, and only now did I learn that it might grow out of love for humanity.'[19]

Bonhoeffer was thus a vital influence in the search for a common language and set of values – call it a Christian humanism or a humanist Christianity – that would be a unifying and not a divisive contribution to the making of post-communist Poland. The transition, it has to be said, is not over yet.

Choosing to live across the wall

On my first visit to the GDR in November 1978 I made a train journey from Erfurt to Wittenberg, birthplace of the Lutheran Reformation. I fell into conversation

18. Ibid., 136–7.
19. Ibid., 134.

with a lady sitting opposite me who, when I told her what I was and why I was here, turned out to be a member of the famous Moravian Protestant community at Herrnhut. As the train proceeded through the frost-laden fields, we talked sotto voce a lot about being Christian in the GDR, and she gave me the name and address of the provost of Wittenberg so that having paid homage at the shrine of Luther I could look him up (which in due course I did). Sitting on the other side of the aisle, staring out of the window, was a huge Red Army officer, resplendent in uniform and guarding his bulky briefcase, evidently on his way to some important meeting of the military. It was, I thought, a kind of parable of the Christian situation: under the nose of earthly power, a conversation was going on with people who seemingly had no power. In East Berlin the previous Sunday, with others from the UK, I had attended morning worship in the Marienkirche, a historic church dwarfed by the mighty television tower built as a symbol of the technological prowess of the socialist state. The preacher was Pastor Jürgen Henkys, and his text was from the book of Daniel: Daniel, the apparently powerless exile who yet has the power born out of God's wisdom, which gives him the clue to what is really going on in history. History does not belong to the rulers who want power at all costs but to the Lord of grace, and this gives his people hope in what is true. It was a message preached just a few hundred yards from the palatial Soviet Embassy. Jürgen Henkys, like a number of pastors in the East, had been brought up in the West but had deliberately chosen to live and minister in the East. Another of the new, post-war generation deeply indebted to Bonhoeffer, he was no doubt inspired by Bonhoeffer's decision to return from the safety of America to Germany just before the war, to be in solidarity with his church and people there despite all the complications and risks. It was true, too, of a Baptist pastor I knew in the East, Klaus Fuhrmann, a westerner but who was caught in the East when the Berlin Wall went up in 1961. He told me that after some turmoil he eventually came to think of the wall, in a strange way, as a blessing of God to him, because it removed all doubts as to where his ministry now had to be. Bonhoeffer, as in Czechoslovakia and Poland and elsewhere in the East, was here a powerful source of strength and guidance for those who wished neither to be unrealistic revolutionaries nor escapees from the situation but to be with Christ in and for that situation, and so live in hope and give hope to others. As Bonhoeffer himself said in that 1942 Christmas essay, 'The ultimately responsible question is not how I extricate myself heroically from a situation but [how the] coming generation is to go on living.'[20]

20. DBWE 8, 42.

Chapter 3

PUBLIC ETHICS AND THE RECEPTION OF BONHOEFFER IN BRITAIN

It would be pleasing to be able to describe in a quite straightforward way how the reception of Dietrich Bonhoeffer in Britain made an impact on public ethics there. That is not possible, however, because it did not happen quite like that. It would be truer to say that it was a prior and significant concern with public issues that in fact led to the ready reception of Bonhoeffer in Britain. From the start, that reception was most marked among certain ecumenical figures who were already wrestling with critical social and international challenges. Two in particular were outstanding. The first was the ecumenical pioneer and social thinker J. H. Oldham (1874–1969), who had known Bonhoeffer personally from the early 1930s, and was study organizer for the 1937 Oxford Conference on Church, Community and State. He had at the outset of the Second World War started the *Christian News-Letter*, a weekly bulletin of information and comment on a whole range of social and international issues. This continued after the war, and it was in the issue of 14 November 1945 (Number 247) that the first published tribute to Bonhoeffer appeared, over the name of Reinhold Niebuhr.[1] During the war, in 1942, Oldham had also founded the Christian Frontier Council, a forum designed to bring together laypeople, whether committed members of the church or not, who had common responsibilities in secular life and who shared a concern for social order. His stated advocacy of such a group resonates strikingly with Bonhoeffer's perception in his prison writings a year later, of the divorce between the church and the world in which people actually have to live, and the need for a new language of faith for the contemporary world – even a new meaning for 'God'.

> The word God, for example, which is the foundation of everything, has for many people ceased to have an intelligible meaning and lost the power to evoke any emotional response. The only way in which the words used in the pulpit can

---

Revised version of a paper presented at the conference 'Bonhoeffer for the Coming Generations' at Union Theological Seminary, New York, November 2011, and published in C. J. Green and G. C. Carter (eds), *Interpreting Bonhoeffer: Historical Perspectives, Emerging Issues* (Minneapolis, MN: Fortress Press, 2013), 25–33.

1. Compare Reinhold Niebuhr, 'The Death of a Martyr', *Christianity and Crisis* 5.1 (25 June 1945), 6–7.

regain their depth and richness of meaning is that they should be re-enforced by actions in the practical sphere informed by the truths which Christianity asserts.[2]

Further, it was Oldham who coined the phrase 'the responsible society' as the motif for two whole decades of ecumenical social thinking under the aegis of the World Council of Churches from 1947 till about 1968. Not surprisingly, Oldham was drawn to Bonhoeffer's prison writings when they were published, in fact before they were translated into English, and he drew upon them in his 1953 book on the meaning of Christianity today, *Life Is Commitment*.[3]

Second, there was George Bell (1883–1958), bishop of Chichester, the great friend of Bonhoeffer during his lifetime and, almost immediately following the news of his death, an advocate of his significance as a martyr. It was Bell who preached the sermon at the memorial service for Dietrich and Klaus Bonhoeffer held in London on 27 July 1945, and broadcast to the world by the BBC. It was he who wrote the foreword to the first English edition of *The Cost of Discipleship*; who constantly spoke in public about what Bonhoeffer meant for the post-war world and church, especially in witnessing to the existence of 'another Germany' (a senior Anglican cleric has told me how as a boy in the 1940s he first heard of Bonhoeffer when Bell came to his boarding school to conduct a confirmation service, and after dinner spoke to the entire school about Bonhoeffer). But Bell was a public theologian in his own right, and indeed concerned with many more issues even than those which prompted him to protest during the war, such as the area bombing of German cities. His wartime book *Christianity and World Order*[4] (1940) makes that clear, surveying as it does the whole sweep of issues revealed by the present crisis: modern secularism, peace and war, the universal church and the separated churches; and, even at that early stage in the conflict, the need for reconstruction and a new international order after the war. The post-war years saw Bell's ecumenical activity and stature rise still more with his service as chairman of the Central Committee of the new World Council of Churches, inaugurated in 1948. His book *The Kingship of Christ*[5] was a panoramic sketch of the whole ecumenical scene since the launch of the WCC, including Interchurch Aid and Refugee Service, action for justice and peace, and the role of laypeople. Its concluding chapter 'Christ the Hope of the World', detailing the Christian obligation to work for peace and justice, racial equality and freedom from fear and want, sounds a note now familiar to many of us:

> The Christian hope is a hope of our earthly calling. The difference between the Christian hope of resurrection and a mythological hope is that the Christian

---

2. Cited in Keith Clements, *Faith on the Frontier: A Life of J. H. Oldham* (Edinburgh: T&T Clark; Geneva: WCC, 1999), 413.
3. London: SCM Press, 1953.
4. London: Penguin Books, 1940.
5. London: Penguin Books, 1954.

hope sends a man back to his life on earth in a wholly new way which is even more sharply defined than it is in the Old Testament. The Christian, unlike the devotees of the salvation myths dos not need a last refuge in the eternal from earthly tasks and difficulties. But like Christ himself ('My God, my God, why hast thou forsaken me?') he must drink the earthly cup to the lees, and only in his doing that is the crucified and risen Lord with him, and he crucified and risen with Christ.[6]

Those who know Bonhoeffer's prison letters will easily recognize this piece of holy plagiarism (at least Bell does reference it in a footnote).

Another, younger, figure who was decisive for the early reception of Bonhoeffer in post-war Britain was the Scottish theologian Ronald Gregor Smith (1913–68).[7] He was a devotee of Buber and Kierkegaard, and in later years a friend of both Karl Barth and Rudolf Bultmann.

While a minister and then an army chaplain during the 1939–45 war he had undergone a spiritual and intellectual crisis. The personal reflections he wrote during the summer of 1944 – like Oldham's statements two years earlier – manifest an uncanny parallel to what Bonhoeffer was writing in prison at exactly the same time: the need for a recovery of God as found in the human Jesus; God as suffering love; and the call for a new kind of church based on honesty, humility and human solidarity. From 1946 to 1948 he was amid the ruins of Germany working for the Allied Control Commission, seeing to the reconstruction of Bonn University and seeing at first hand the challenges facing the rebirth of the nation and its churches. From 1947 he worked for the Student Christian Movement (SCM) Press of which he became editor in 1950, and he used his position to ensure the transmission to the English-speaking world of the most significant recent and contemporary continental thinkers, and none more so than Bonhoeffer.[8] Gregor Smith was himself a brilliant linguist and gifted translator, but as well as publisher his chief role in the transmission of Bonhoeffer was as an interpreter of his thought. This was encouraged by the close friendship that grew between Gregor Smith (with his German wife Käthe) and Eberhard and Renate Bethge on their arrival in London in 1953 when Eberhard took pastoral charge of the German congregation in Sydenham, where Bonhoeffer had ministered 1933–5. Gregor Smith's book *The New Man: Christianity and Man's Coming*

---

6. Ibid., 154.
7. See Keith Clements, *The Theology of Ronald Gregor Smith* (Leiden: E.J. Brill, 1986).
8. *The Cost of Discipleship* (1947), *Life Together* (1954), *Ethics* (1955), *Temptation* (1955) and the chief prize *Letters and Papers from Prison* (1953) were all published in the UK by SCM Press. Gregor Smith could not persuade SCM to take on *Sanctorum Communio* and *Act and Being* but, having translated *Sanctorum Communio* himself, saw to it that both these works were published by Collins after he became Professor of Divinity at Glasgow University in 1956.

of Age⁹ appeared in 1956. With its stress on faith as arising out of history and leading further into new historical responsibility – a concern embodied in his work in post-war Germany – this book can be reckoned the first really serious theological essay in Britain to use constructively, as distinct from simply cite, Bonhoeffer.

Other names that should be mentioned for taking Bonhoeffer seriously in the early 1960s include the Congregational theologian Daniel Jenkins who wrote a positive but not uncritical study of 'religionless Christianity', *Beyond Religion*;[10] and Alec Vidler, the Cambridge historian and editor of the journal *Theology* whose essay 'Religion and the National Church' in the volume of essays *Soundings*[11] warned against any idea of the church being concerned only with the 'religious' department of life.

A sense of historical moment

What did these earlier British recipients and mediators of Bonhoeffer have in common? They were all exercised by public ethics and the need for faith to relate to the social sphere – and indeed in various ways were themselves actively involved in that sphere. Nor is it incidental that they were all known to each other, largely because they were part of the network at the centre of which was J. H. Oldham. In fact Jenkins and Vidler belonged to the 'Moot', the select discussion group on faith and society led by Oldham for nearly ten years from 1938 and which included sociologists of the stature of Karl Mannheim and literary figures including T. S. Eliot.[12] But further, all these figures had a deep sense of the crisis facing Western civilization, brought to the surface by two world wars: a sense of historical moment or *kairos* to use the word now in vogue; of the end of the old Christendom and the impending end of the colonial world; a conviction that a new world had to be in the making, and the need for new tools, new plans, new maps. What appealed to them was Bonhoeffer's perception that faith, far from fleeing from this crisis, should rediscover itself in it; that the crucial issue was not the fate of the church but the future of humanity; and that faith should assist, instead of denying, the coming of age of humankind and take responsibility for the next stage of its history.

Moreover, Bonhoeffer was making an impact beyond the normal church boundaries. For example, in 1961 a lawyer of Jewish background, Peter Benenson,

---

9. London: SCM Press, 1956.

10. Daniel Jenkins, *Beyond Religion: The Truth and Error in 'Religionless Christianity'* (London: SCM Press, 1962).

11. A. R. Vidler (ed.), *Soundings: Essays Concerning Christian Understanding* (Cambridge: Cambridge University Press, 1962).

12. See Keith Clements (ed.), *The Moot Papers: Faith, Freedom and Society* (London: T&T Clark, 2010).

was incensed at reports of ill-treatment of political detainees under Portuguese colonial rule. As a result he founded Amnesty International. Benenson made no secret of the inspirational debt he owed to Bonhoeffer.[13]

Honest to God

In Britain, public awareness of Bonhoeffer went through a major gear shift in 1963 with the appearance of *Honest to God*[14] by John Robinson, at that time bishop of Woolwich. *Honest to God* was the religious publishing sensation of the early 1960s, and Bonhoeffer continued to be invoked in much of the 'secular' theology which ensued in that decade of the 1960s and the early 1970s. But while Bonhoeffer's prison theology continued to excite, or puzzle, it was a somewhat decontextualized Bonhoeffer who was in the spotlight. For this reason, at this point tribute must be paid to the one who from the mid-1960s undertook a lot of the translation of parts of the *Gesammelte Schriften*, the letters, lectures and papers from Bonhoeffer's earlier period, namely Edwin Robertson (1912–2007). Until the appearance of the first English edition of Bethge's biography in 1970 – a translation carried out under Robertson's supervision – these selections[15] were the main sources in English for a more thoroughly grounded view of Bonhoeffer, in terms both of his own development and in the history of his time.

One of the results of the highlighting of the prison writings in *Honest to God* and much of the secular theology was, paradoxically, to create a curiosity about what lay behind them. A number of us whose first encounters with Bonhoeffer had been through the prison letters and *Cost of Discipleship* now found ourselves particularly drawn to the *Ethics*, and I think it fair to say that the bulk of the serious work done in Britain on Bonhoeffer in the past fifty years has been either on the *Ethics* or on the ethical implications of the Bonhoeffer corpus as a whole. I do not think this is simply because, as Karl Barth and others have alleged, we Britons are congenitally Pelagian. But we are pragmatic rather than speculative and it is the concretion of revelation that Bonhoeffer so emphasized, and its bearing on ethical formation, which has appealed so strongly. Certainly a good number of the PhD theses written in Britain have been on Bonhoeffer's ethics, and so too the more significant published studies, in particular Stephen Plant's *Bonhoeffer* (2004).[16] If I may be permitted to mention my own earlier work, *A Patriotism*

---

13. Interestingly, Benenson (1921–2005) as a boy was privately tutored by W. H. Auden, who would later dedicate his poem 'Friday's Child' to the memory of Bonhoeffer.
14. London: SCM Press, 1963.
15. *No Rusty Swords: Letters, Lectures and Notes 1928-36* (London: Collins, 1965); *The Way to Freedom: Letters, Lectures and Notes 1935-39* (London: Collins, 1972); *True Patriotism: Letters, Lectures and Notes 1939-1945* (London: Collins, 1973).
16. Stephen Plant, *Bonhoeffer* (London: Continuum, 2004).

*for Today*¹⁷ (1984), this was an attempt, in the light of Bonhoeffer's career and theology, to rescue the notion of national loyalty from that of unquestioning nationalism and racial ideology, in order to transform it into a mature, clear-headed and critical form of communal responsibility. Because of its publication date, a lot of people have assumed it was written primarily as a reaction to Prime Minister Margaret Thatcher's nationalistic exploitation of the Falklands/Malvinas war of 1982. I have to say, however, that I was well into the writing before that episode. Margaret Thatcher just came along to illustrate my point. Bonhoeffer by then was also important as a theological resource for many of those supporting the South African struggle against apartheid and engaged in the peace movement in the context of the Cold War.¹⁸

More than a statue?

Bonhoeffer as a courageous figure is certainly highly regarded in Britain today. His statue, along with those of nine other twentieth-century martyrs, stands above the great west door of Westminster Abbey. But at the moment we are not sure what to do with him and his theology, beyond obtaining a supply of striking aphorisms. That is because we are not at all sure what to do with ourselves as a nation and a society and as churches, an uncertainty which surfaced in the autumn of 2011 when Britain was convulsed by one of the most bizarre, tragi-comic episodes in our public life: the 'Occupy the City' campaign which, taking its cue from the 'Occupy Wall Street' demonstration in New York, resulted in an encampment of protestors against corporate greed, pitching their tents in front of St Paul's Cathedral in London. There ensued legal measures to evict them, confusion among the cathedral clergy resulting in several resignations, eventual compromises and wide public disbelief that the church could have been so wrong-footed and made to appear more concerned with its health and safety rather than the health and safety of the planet, at this time of global financial crisis.

---

17. 1st edition Bristol: Bristol Baptist College, 1984; 2nd edition London: Collins, 1986. Republished Eugene, OR: Wipf & Stock, 2011.

18. Note should also be taken of the covert influence of Bonhoeffer in the ecumenical programme on Justice, Peace and the Integrity of Creation (JPIC) which during the 1990s in Britain and in other countries had an undoubted influence even at local parish and congregational level. The instigation of the JPIC process, especially in the 'two Germanies' in the 1980s, owed much to the memory of Bonhoeffer's 1934 call for an ecumenical council of all the churches to declare against war. Bonhoeffer's instrumentality was therefore significant in originating the process, but that historical origin was less well-known at the more popular level; nor was JPIC a home-grown British product. Its birth lay at the international ecumenical level, a level in which the British churches have been progressively less interested since the 1990s.

The whole episode, however, merely brought to the surface a deep-seated and long-term malaise in contemporary British society and the churches within it: the lack of any serious, concerted ecumenical attempt, for at least the past decade, at a public theology engaging with the critical issues of the age. I must instantly qualify this by noting, first, that there are various think-tanks, advocacy groups and foundations looking at public ethics, such as *Ecclesia* and *Theos*, although these tend to be marginal to mainstream church life, or mostly ignored by the mainstream. Second, within the UK as a whole Scotland is better served than England, as witnessed by the Centre for Theology and Public Issues in Edinburgh, pioneered by the late Professor Duncan Forrester and others; and by the greater readiness of the Church of Scotland, as compared with the English churches in recent years, to examine sharply issues like poverty, equality and international peace and justice. The situation in Britain has been made drastically worse by the large-scale dismantling in the late 1990s of the ecumenical bodies which, beginning with the British Council of Churches in 1942 and succeeded by the four-nation instruments set up in 1990, had provided an effective forum and platform for the churches' engagement with public and international issues.

Dishonest to God?

In Britain today, while there is a certain anxiety about the future, we do not now have a sense of historical moment, a *kairos* of crisis-and-opportunity, as the first recipients of Bonhoeffer had, and as Bonhoeffer himself had when in the summer of 1944 he began to envision a drastically changed place of religion in Western civilization. Rather, we have to look to such as Bonhoeffer for creating that sense of moment, opening our eyes to the crisis and possibilities. In Britain the post-1945 consensus about Christianity supplying the bedrock morality of our society and civilization has largely gone in the face of a much more pluralist and secular ethos. Indeed a key question facing Britain today is how faith may, if at all, now have a role in the formation of public ethics. The philosopher Mary Warnock (1924–2019), a member of the House of Lords, and one who had been in the forefront of public debates on bioethical issues such as embryo research and euthanasia, in 2010 published a book with a title interestingly twisted from John Robinson's 1963 opus: *Dishonest to God*.[19] Warnock, while not unsympathetic to religion as a source of moral values to the individual, and as supplying a rich vein of cultural enrichment through liturgy and religious art, was highly critical of any corporate role for the church or other religious bodies in the formulation of public policy and its legislative encoding. The danger of any religion, she argued, lies in its claim to absolute immutable moral knowledge which, if justified, would give its adherents a special place or right to instruct others how to behave. 'The only meaning … is that people who *are* religious, who *do* hold the requisite metaphysical or

---

19. London: Continuum, 2010.

supernatural beliefs, should be given special authority over the rest.'[20] Yet this, she asserts, is what the Roman Catholic Church does when it instructs parliaments which side to support on moral issues, 'and it is what the other churches demand too, in offering "guidance" on which way to vote in a general election'. Democracy, she stated, must be alert to every sign of encroaching theocracy. For our purposes we can leave aside the question of whether Warnock is operating with a too narrowly defined understanding of what the democratic process involves, but she is certainly representative of a large body of secular opinion which sees any faith-reference as a threat to the autonomy that is the hallmark of operating in the public forum in a liberal, Western society where reason and its examination of actual experience are the unconditional requirements. On the other hand we have institutional churches, and certain theological movements such as the self-styled 'Radical Orthodoxy' school in Anglicanism, which are overly anxious to demonstrate that there is a secure body of revealed truth, utterly different from anything the world might offer, which alone can supply the basis for a sound and fulfilling human society: the church teaches the way, and itself exemplifies what the world should be like. Caught between these antagonisms, the public realm seems destined to become a battleground between secularists wishing to assert human autonomy, and religious institutions desirous of asserting authority. In between, however, on the street of actual life, there are a lot of people for whom the issue is neither autonomy nor authority, but authenticity: the authentically human, what makes for human fulfilment in community. They are found in local politics, in environmental groups, in ordinary neighbourhood communities, in caring for the homeless, in campaigning for international development – and they were found among those camping on the steps of St Paul's. Such camps are not essentially anti-church. Indeed there is about them something almost akin to the call of the Macedonian, 'Come over and help us!' (Acts 16:9).

An ethic born of love

One voice speaking amid the clamour of 2011 whom I regard as speaking for all such people 'on the street' is that of Rebecca Hickman who in her essay, *In Pursuit of Egalitarianism and Why Social Mobility Cannot Get Us There* (2010),[21] writes,

> To help the most marginalised, and help them gladly, we need an ethic born of love, kindness, sympathy and generosity. *These words currently reside at the outermost fringes of political discourse.* Qualities that we praise and seek in our personal relationships and conduct, we dismiss as sentimental or sources of inefficiency in the design of public services and the organisation of the economy.[22]

---

20. Ibid., 165.
21. Published by Compass – Directions for the Democratic Left (Compassline.org.uk).
22. Ibid., 19. Emphases mine.

There are many in that 'no-man's land', or on the street, who welcome the contribution of faith groups in the struggle to ensure that the language 'born of love, kindness, sympathy and generosity' is *not* marginalized to the fringes of political discourse. They know that such values will not automatically flourish in the supposedly liberal society, prey to so many powerful economic and political interests on the national and the world stage. They have to be stood for, spoken for, struggled for and lived, by whoever believes in them for whatever reason. Since the fracas at St Paul's in 2011 the movements for action on climate change and Black Lives Matter highlight even more the need for, and vulnerability of, those values at every level from the local to the global. What is at issue is not the authority of institutionalized religion but the struggle for the truly human, which is where the church is called to be.

In the penultimate realm

Perhaps, therefore, only now are we at a point where Bonhoeffer's challenge might be felt in full strength: not so much on this or that particular ethical issue but right across the board in a recognition of the significance of what he calls the 'penultimate'.[23] At its most creative, I suggest, a future reception of Bonhoeffer in Britain will, like the early ones, be among those who see that the struggle for authentic humanity and the witness of faith are engaged with the same reality, if not always working from the same point or consciousness. The churches are rightly concerned to retain their identity and calling as witnesses to the gospel of Christ in its specificity and finality. But, unsure of their status in a secular and pluralist society, they are susceptible to two temptations: either to retreat from the world as it is into a self-enclosed space in which the absolute verities can be contemplated and enjoyed in unchallenged fashion; or to seek to impose directly what they regard as these absolute truths on the world around them. Bonhoeffer's full-blown recognition of the ultimate, yet of the rights of the penultimate realm as the place where the coming of the ultimate requires patient preparation, remains crucial for preserving that space in the public realm where faith can be in dialogue with all who seek justice, peace and human fulfilment and dignity.

Bonhoeffer writes in his *Ethics*,

> To give the hungry bread is not yet to proclaim to them the grace of God and justification and to have received bread does not yet mean to stand in faith – The entry of grace is the ultimate. But we must speak of preparing the way, of the penultimate – for the sake of those who have failed with their radicalism that denied penultimate things, and are now in danger themselves of being pushed back behind penultimate things, as well as for the sake of those who remained stuck in penultimate things, who have made themselves comfortable with them,

---

23. See below, 132, 143–54.

and who must now be claimed for the ultimate. In the end, however, perhaps we speak of penultimate things primarily for the sake of those who have never achieved these penultimate things, whom no one has helped to gain them, for whom no one has prepared the way and who now must be helped so that the word of God, the ultimate, grace, can come to them.[24]

That, I suggest, constitutes a basic theological charter for seeking a public ethic for a new generation.

---

24. DBWE 6, 163–4.

Part II

WORLDLY FAITH AND A TRANSCENDENT GOD

Chapter 4

CENTURIES APART YET NEIGHBOURS IN SPIRIT:
THE WORLDLY HOLINESS OF THOMAS TRAHERNE
AND DIETRICH BONHOEFFER

At first it seems an unlikely pairing: a seventeenth-century Anglican who spent much of his adult life in a quiet Herefordshire rectory, and a twentieth-century German Lutheran whose opposition to Nazism and involvement in the actual conspiracy to overthrow Hitler cost him his life. On the one hand, someone whose received image is that of a mystical poet; on the other hand, a modern figure not only embroiled in the political dramas of his age and our recent past but by many seen as a disturbing and controversial theologian, who in prison became the prophet of a 'religionless Christianity'. Surely, it will be thought, these two must be centuries apart not only in time but in thinking.

But we might first of all note some parallels which, if purely incidental, are nevertheless intriguing For a start, both were males who died relatively young and at almost the same age: Traherne in 1674 at about thirty-eight, Bonhoeffer in 1945, just turned thirty-nine. Both were unmarried (though Bonhoeffer was engaged at the time of his death). Both were ordained clergy of their respective churches. Each lived in a turbulent time for his nation and church.

Indeed when Jan Ross in her editorial introduction to the Traherne works says of Traherne, '[His] life spanned less than forty years, a time not only of catastrophic events but also the beginnings of major shifts in religion, philosophy and science, which shook the foundations of authority and belief',[1] virtually the same words could be used of Bonhoeffer. At the time of their deaths both were writing extensive works on Christian ethics. Both of them wrote poetry, though Bonhoeffer came to that only very late in life. Both had published some works in their lifetime, but each has become chiefly known for what has appeared posthumously. Today, in each case, we are now privileged to have published their complete works in a single series: in Traherne's case, the six-volume works edited by Jan Ross; in Bonhoeffer's case, the sixteen volumes of the entire Bonhoeffer corpus, comprising all his known writings whether previously published or not, the English edition

---

Lecture given at the Traherne Association Festival, Credenhill, Hereford, 21 June 2014.

1. Jan Ross (ed.), *The Works of Thomas Traherne*, vol. I (Cambridge: D.S. Brewer, 2005), xiv. Series hereinafter referred to as *Works*.

of which was completed by Fortress Press in 2013. These series reveal that both were figures not only of considerable learning but of unusually independent mind, reflecting the intellectual contexts of their times but also responding to them in highly individual and original ways.

But my main concern is to highlight a striking affinity at a profound level in their thought: what in summary I call their 'worldly holiness'. Both, to a remarkable degree, affirmed this world of creation and human life as the place and means of encounter with God. Their thought challenges that persistent temptation in Christianity to take a negative view of the world. Early Christianity had to fight a battle against the Manichean belief that matter was essentially evil, and against those gnostic cults which saw salvation as consisting in the soul's escape from this messy, sinfully corrupt material world, into the far beyond of the highest heaven of light and purity, where alone God dwells. Right down to the present day, there are versions of Christianity which see the created world as either an unfortunate entanglement for the soul, or a distraction from true religion or at best simply incidental to God's real purpose, the stage setting for the real drama of salvation which is fitting us for heaven to live with God there. According to all such, holiness has to be sought apart from the contaminating world.

Traherne and Bonhoeffer, however, see the world as not just the stage on which the drama of salvation is set, but as itself involved in our salvation, a means of grace, through which God is met and humanity is made whole, or begins to be made whole. The world for them is not just an anteroom of heaven but a place already being colonized by paradise. Only through participating fully in the world do we participate in God, just as only by participating in God do we participate truly in the world. True holiness can only be a worldly holiness. It will, I trust, go without saying that Traherne and Bonhoeffer each provide a rich resource for the development of an ecological theology which is such a pressing contemporary issue in the face of climate change and the degradation of the environment and natural resources.[2]

This parallelism between Traherne and Bonhoeffer is best illustrated simply by placing citations from each side by side. Then we can ask whether their similarity is more than incidental, whether there are significant reasons for it,

---

2. On Bonhoeffer's relevance for ecological concern, see e.g.: Larry Rasmussen, 'Bonhoeffer's Song of Songs and Christianities as Earth Faiths', in *Religion im Erbe: Dietrich Bonhoeffer und die Zukunftsfähigkeit des Christentums*, Christian Gremmels and Wolfgang Huber (eds) (Gütersloh: Gütersloher Verlagshaus, 2002), 186-93; Rasmussen, 'Bonhoeffer: "Ecological Theologian"', in *Bonhoeffer and Interpretive Theory: Essays on Methods and Understanding*, Peter Frick (ed.) (Frankfurt am Main: Peter Lang, 2013), 251–67; Dianne Rayson, *Bonhoeffer and Climate Change: Theology and Ethics for the Anthropocene* (Lanham, MD: Lexington, 2021); Dianne Rayson. *Bonhoeffer and Climate Change: Theology and the Anthropocene* (Lanham, MD: Lexington Books/Fortress Academic, 2021). Lisa Dahill, forthcoming works *One Reality: Bonhoeffer, Non-Dualism, and Wild Life on Earth*; and *Rewilding Life Together: Bonhoeffer, Spirituality, and Interspecies Community*.

which indeed makes them close neighbours in spirit. Let me say at this point that I have found no evidence that Bonhoeffer had ever known of Traherne, let alone read him.³

Instant impressions of an instinctive affinity

Let us begin with instant impressions of an instinctive affinity. On Traherne's side, from his first 'Century of Meditations' these are the words which gripped me when as a student many years ago I first heard them on the radio:

> You never enjoy the world aright, till the sea itself floweth in your veins, till you are clothed with the heavens, and crowned with the stars; and perceive yourself to be the sole heir of the whole world; and more than so, because men are in it who are every one sole heirs, as well as you.⁴
>
> Never was anything in this world loved too much, but many things have been loved in a false way: and all in too short a measure.⁵

And from the young Bonhoeffer, who while a student pastor with the German congregation in Barcelona in 1929 gave an address on Christian ethics and declared,

> The earth remains our mother just as God remains our Father, and only those who remain true to the mother are placed by her into the father's arms. Earth and its distress – that is the Christian's Song of Songs.⁶

Then in 1932 in a lecture in Berlin he states,

> If we are to pray for the coming of the kingdom, we can pray for it only as those wholly on the Earth. 'Thy kingdom come' – this is not the prayer of the pious soul who wants to flee the world ... Rather, this is the prayer only of the church-community of children of the Earth, who do not set themselves apart, who have no special proposals for reforming the world to offer, who are no

---

3. Of course one cannot be absolutely certain and dogmatic here. Traherne is nowhere cited in any of Bonhoeffer's writings, but as the case of Fredrich von Hügel (see Chapter 5) demonstrates, lack of *written* evidence cannot absolutely rule out a possible influence, however unlikely.

4. Version taken from Thomas Traherne, *Poems, Centuries and Three Thanksgivings*, Anne Ridler (ed.) (London: Oxford University Press, 1966), 29. Spelling and orthography modernized by KC.

5. 66th of Second Century, from Ridler version (see n.4), 244.

6. *Dietrich Bonhoeffer Works English Edition* (hereinafter *DBWE*), Vol. 10 Barcelona, Berlin, New York: 1928–1931 (Minneapolis, MN: Fortress Press), 378.

better than the world, but who persevere together in the midst of the world, in its depths, in the daily life and subjugation of the world The earth wants us to take it seriously.[7]

Finally, from one of his prison letters written secretly from prison to his friend Eberhard Bethge in 1944,

> What matters is not the beyond but this world, how it is created and preserved, is given laws, reconciled, and renewed. What is beyond this world is meant, in the gospel, to be there *for* this world.[8]

Creation: Materiality and the body

Traherne in his poetry is famous for recalling his childhood rapture at the created world around him:

The skies in their magnificence,
   The lively, lovely air;
Oh how divine how soft. How sweet, how fair!
   The stars did entertain my sense,
And all the works of GOD so bright and pure,
   So rich and great did seem,
As if they ever must endure,
   In my esteem.[9]

He speaks no less evocatively in his prose of the 'glad tidings of infinite and eternal love' in the world: 'It whispers in every gale of wind, and speaks aloud in thunder. It is templed on the earth and crowns us in the heavens. It burns in the sun, and shines in the stars.'[10]

But Traherne does not just wax lyrical. He manifests a sober delight in the facts of: astronomy, cosmology, zoology and botany, even arithmetic! The ultimately

---

7. DBWE 12, 289–90.
8. DBWE 8, 373.
9. 'The Salutation', from Ridler edition (see n.4).
10. From *The Kingdom of God*, in Works, vol. I, 313. Shortly after, Traherne continues, 'It breathes in the air and communicates the light. It shades like a banner in every cloud, and drops down upon us in every shower.' One cannot but notice the close similarity with the language used over a century later by Robert Grant (1779–1838) in his well-known hymn 'O worship the King', especially the 4th verse: 'Thy bountiful care / What tongue can recite? It breathes in the air, / It shines in the light; / It streams from the hills, / It descends to the plain, / And sweetly distils / In the dew and the rain.' Can this similarity be accounted for solely by a like inspiration from Psalm 104?

minute atom and the antics of the ant fill him with wonder.[1] The kingdom of God is on earth, in all things.

Moreover, nothing is more wonderful to him than the human body in all its materiality as seen in his *Thanksgivings for the Body*:

Thou hast given me a Body,

Wherein the glory of thy power shineth,
Wonderfully composed above the beasts,
Within distinguished into useful parts,
Beautified without many ornaments.
    Limbs rarely poised,
        And made for heaven;
    Arteries filled with celestial spirits:
Veins, wherein blood floweth,
Refreshing all my flesh,
    Like rivers.

Sinews fraught with the mystery
    Of wonderful strength, Stability,
    Feeling.
O blessed be thy glorious name.[12]

He goes on to exult in all that human beings are able to do individually and communally through their bodies. Further, it is through the body that Christ minsters to us in his body. All creation is bodied in its ministering to us. Traherne voices this delight in the body no less rapturously than his *Thanksgiving for the Soul*.

Now to Bonhoeffer. Just like Traherne, Bonhoeffer could, and often did, wax eloquent on the beauties and wonders to be found and enjoyed in the world – he had a love of nature, of all the good things of life and all the human arts, especially music (he was an accomplished pianist). But theologically he also treated the doctrine of creation with great seriousness. As a junior lecturer in the University of Berlin, during the winter semester of 1932–3 he gave a series of lectures based on chs. 1–3 of the book of Genesis, later published under the title *Creation and Fall*. Especially interesting as a parallel to Traherne's vision of human bodiliness in an embodied universe is his exposition of Genesis 2:7, God's fashioning humankind from the dust of the earth and breathing into the man the breath of life

Bonhoeffer emphasizes the thoroughgoing materiality of the biblical narrative:

The human being whom God has created in God's image … is the human being who is taken from the earth. Even Darwin and Feuerbach could not use stronger language than is used here. Humankind is derived from a piece of earth. Its bond with the earth belongs to its essential being. The 'earth is its mother'; it comes

---

11. See especially Traherne, *Commentaries of Heaven* in *Works*, ed. Jan Ross, vols I and II.
12. From Ridler edition (see n.4), 376.

out of her womb ... it is God's earth out of which humankind is taken. From it human beings have their *bodies*. The body belongs to a person's essence. The body is not the prison, the shell, the exterior of a human being: instead a human being is a human body. A human being does not 'have' a body – or 'have' a soul; instead a human being 'is' body and soul. The human being in the beginning really is the body, is one – just as Christ is wholly his body and the church is the body of Christ. People who reject their bodies reject their existence before God the Creator. What is to be taken seriously about human existence is its bond with mother earth, its being as body.[13]

Notice how similar to Traherne's is Bonhoeffer's drawing of the link between our human bodily life and the ministry of Christ through his body. In his particular context, the Berlin winter of 1932–3, Bonhoeffer's exposition takes on a special significance. These were the months immediately preceding Hitler's coming to power at the end of January 1933. Already the tide of Nazi propaganda was in full flood, affecting the churches too and not least certain sections of Protestant theology. In the first place, even to deliver lectures based on the opening chapters of the Hebrew scriptures was to make a powerful statement against the prevailing anti-Jewish mood of the hour. Second, in his emphasis on the earthliness of the biblical narrative of creation Bonhoeffer was attacking the falsely spiritualizing tendency of much religious piety which shied away from what was actually being done to people's bodies, whether on the battlefield or, as was to happen, in the ultimate act of de-creation at Auschwitz. Third, in Nazi Germany there was in fact a good deal of earthy talk about creation, but of a highly questionable kind. Some theologians asserted a divine sanctioning of so-called 'orders of creation' like race and nationhood, which was simply a glorification of the world as it was, in its lust for power. Bonhoeffer is clear that God's creation of humankind is of embodied persons, not the dehumanizing abstractions of the Nazi creed of blood, race and soil which overrode all notions of human personhood and interpersonal relationships. To see the true reality of the world as God intends, it has to be seen in the light of Christ, in and for whom it has been created and in whom creation takes its true form.

To see all things in the light of Christ, Bonhoeffer recognized, means finding a point of detachment from which to view the whole. For all that the world is to be cherished, there can be no direct, self-seeking attachment to the things of this world. There has to be conscious positioning of the believer under the word of God in Christ, if the church is not to be simply co-opted into the interests and ambitions of the world as it is. Bonhoeffer, even before Hitler came to power, for all that he was a Lutheran, believed that Martin Luther would now be calling for a new kind of monasticism in which Christians could learn again what discipleship means. Not that this new monasticism would in itself constitute holiness, but it would prepare people to engage in the fray fully armed for the costly struggle

---

13. DBWE 3, 76–7.

against oppression and injustice. This idea began to be realized by Bonhoeffer from 1935 in the underground theological seminary at Finkenwalde which he directed for the Confessing Church, that is, that section of German Protestantism which resisted the Nazification of the church. His ordinands learnt not only how to preach but how to pray and meditate and confess their own sins before dealing with the sins of the world. This was not to promote a self-enclosed holiness but to prepare future pastors spiritually for the true holiness of engaging with the world in their parish ministries amid a hostile environment, to the point of suffering or even martyrdom.

Traherne similarly recognized the need for a proper still centre for viewing the world if the believer is to live authentically in it. To quote again, 'Never was anything in this world loved too much, but many things have been loved in a false way: and all in too short a measure.'[14] That requires a conscious discipline. Traherne argues for this in his beautiful piece of pastoral theology, *Inducements to Retiredness*. This sounds like an advert for a large pension pot but is in fact a call for periodically disengaging from the everyday world and human society to the point where a person can reflect on everything in the light of eternity: a still centre from where a proper perspective on all things can be found:

> Because eternity is contained in the soul, a man in finding himself findeth eternity; and because in finding himself he findeth eternity, in finding himself he findeth all things ... Since therefore in retirement alone a man findeth himself, in retirement alone a man findeth all things. Nor can there be any rest, till he findeth all things his delights and treasures.[15]

This 'retirement' is not an end in itself. By itself it does not confer holiness. It prepares one for re-engaging with the world: 'In society a man may discourse of excellent things; if the company be excellent; but by retirement, we are fitted for that society.'[16] This, we may well think, was sound advice for a worldly holiness in the society of Restoration England where, after the rigours of the Commonwealth, it could appear that 'anything goes'. Love of creation, for Traherne as for Bonhoeffer, is a qualified love grounded in the love of God.

God and the world: The one kingdom of God

We now approach the most profound level of affinity between seventeenth-century Traherne and twentieth-century Bonhoeffer. Let them speak for themselves. First, Traherne from his treatise *The Kingdom of God*.

---

14. See above n.5.
15. Traherne, *Inducements to Retiredness*, in *Works*, ed. Jan Ross, vol. I, 6.
16. Ibid., 7.

One efficient cause guiding all things in all worlds to one end, makes the kingdom one. God being an infinite and eternal king, in whose sublime and perfect empire, all nations, and kingdoms flourish ... which are all but so many provinces of his care and government: kings themselves being his deputies and vicegerents in their dominions ... Neither is it here upon earth alone, that the kingdom is one: heaven and earth are parts of the same empire.[17]

The celestial city is not far from us, as heaven from the earth, but infinitely more remote, if we neglect it. As on the other side, it is far nearer if we apply our minds to consider it. We may in a moment come unto the gates of heaven, and like lightening penetrate those eternal courts and present ourselves before the throne of God. The distance is not to be measured by the length of spaces, but by the Institution of our lives, and the affections of our minds.[18]

Here we have Bonhoeffer in his *Ethics*, written during the war while engaged in the political conspiracy against Hitler:

Since the beginnings of Christian ethics after New Testament times, the dominant basic conception, consciously or unconsciously determining all ethical thought, has been that two realms [Raüme] bump against each other: one divine, holy, supernatural, and Christian; the other worldly, profane, natural, and unchristian.[19]

This division of the whole of reality into sacred and profane, or Christian and worldly, sectors creates the possibility of existence in only one of these sectors: for instance a spiritual existence that takes no part in worldly existence, and a worldly existence that can make good its claim to autonomy over against the sacred sector.[20]

There are not two realities, but *only one reality*, and that is God's reality revealed in Christ in the reality of the world. Partaking in Christ, we stand at the same time in the reality of God and in the reality of the world. The reality of Christ embraces the reality of the world in itself.[21]

A remarkable parallel between Traherne and Bonhoeffer. Bonhoeffer was reacting in the first instance against what his Lutheran tradition had over the course of four centuries made of Martin Luther's own doctrine of the 'two kingdoms', the spiritual and the secular, which had become hardened into a rigid separation

---

17. Traherne, *The Kingdom of God*, in *Works*, ed. Jan Ross, vol. I, 255.
18. Ibid., 268. Traherne's critique of spatial language to denote the human relation to heaven, to be understood instead in terms of 'the affections of our minds', reads almost like an attempt to 'demythologize' the traditional imagery nearly three centuries before the German theologian Rudolf Bultmann caused controversy by doing so!
19. DBWE 6, 56.
20. Ibid., 57.
21. Ibid., 58.

between church and government, between piety and politics, between duty to God and duty to Caesar, in a way that Luther himself had never intended. But Bonhoeffer points out that this dichotomy also finds expression in pre-Reformation times, and indeed in most versions of Christianity since. In Nazi Germany it suited those happy to give Hitler a free hand in public life while the church closed its eyes in prayer. Bonhoeffer, engaged in the resistance movement, knew he was acting clean counter to that seductive tradition. He was even accepting complicity in a conspiracy that would eventually involve assassination of the head of state. The only holiness he could hope for was a very worldly one. Those who know more about Traherne in his own context may wish to comment on whether Traherne himself either directly or indirectly had a kind of public theology in the making.

For both Traherne and Bonhoeffer, this unity of the kingdom of God, of heaven and earth, of sacred and profane, is based on the great central item of Christian faith, Jesus Christ as God incarnate, God enfleshed. They both write in language saturated with the Bible, and one notable text which they clearly love in common is Colossians 1:17 – '[Christ] himself is before all things, and in him all things hold together.' So Bonhoeffer:

> In Christ we are invited to participate in the reality of God and the reality of the world at the same time, the one not without the other. The reality of God is disclosed only as it places me completely into the reality of the world. But I find the reality of the world always already borne, accepted and reconciled in the reality of God.[22]

And Traherne:

> Duties towards ourselves and neighbour may be united. For infinite goodness hath made us one; no man may hurt or defile himself because he is an object of God's goodness. Verily as ye did it to the least of my brethren saith our Saviour, ye did it unto me.
>
> He that toucheth you, toucheth the apple of mine eye. How great, how infinite, how high, how divine is his love, how perfect and ineffable. He dwelleth infinitely higher than the heavens, yet he condescendeth not only to note such feeble worms, but to raise up the poor out of the dust, and to lift the needy out of the dunghill, to seat him with princes even with the princes of his people. He is so deeply concerned in them, that he is persecuted, imprisoned, wounded, flouted, killed in his servants, which lest we should think it a strain of eloquence and no reality I can assure you, his love is so infinite and its object so tender a part of himself, that had he a body, and did he live here upon earth, he would become our shield to save us, by receiving the wounds himself, that are inflicted on his people, he would be made a curse for us, and die in our places. How great

22. Ibid., 55.

then ought our love to be to all his creatures? ... We must be transformed into his similitude, before we can be blessed.[23]

A principle of holiness within makes him truly free that is full of love, for it is his meat and drink to do all that is commanded. By enlarging his will to the extent of God's own will, it magnifies him endlessly, by causing him to love whatsoever God loves, and nothing else, it inspires him with the divine nature, it unites him to the Lord, and makes him one spirit with God.[24]

And here is Bonhoeffer at the end of his great work *Discipleship*, written in 1937 in the midst of the Church Struggle, and speaking of how the image of God, the form of Christ, is recreated in us and what it leads to:

> Inasmuch as we participate in Christ, the incarnate one, we also have a part in all of humanity, which is borne by him. Since we know ourselves to be accepted and borne within the humanity of Jesus, our new humanity now also consists in bearing the troubles and sins of all others. The incarnate one transforms his disciples into brothers and sisters of all human beings. The 'philanthropy' (Titus 3:4) of God that became evident in the incarnation is the reason for Christians to love every human being on earth as a brother or sister. The form of the incarnate one transforms the church- community into the body of Christ upon which all of humanity's sin and trouble fall, and by which alone these troubles and sins are borne.[25]

Why this parallelism?

I have by no means exhausted the parallels in the thought of Traherne and Bonhoeffer. To do them justice I would have to deal with at least two others: their emphasis on human existence as social; and the significance in both of them, albeit in somewhat different ways, of the child. But to reiterate, the most fundamental likeness is that both see holiness as a human likeness to God which is formed not apart from the world but within it and for it, through a life shared with Christ.

But what common factor may have prompted this impulse in such seemingly different contexts so far apart in time? I suggest that one common factor is the way each was trying to respond, not just to the world as a general reality but each to something particularly new in his contemporary world of learning and experience. Each was recognizing that there was something distinctive in their contemporary contexts which had to be positively received and affirmed as of God. Traherne's world of the late seventeenth century was the world of new and extended knowledge and discovery in almost every branch of knowledge, above

---

23. Traherne, *The Kingdom of God*, in *Works*, ed. Jan Ross, vol. I, 302.
24. Ibid., 305.
25. DBWE 4, 285.

all in the natural sciences, particularly in physics, astronomy and physiology. The Royal Society, founded in 1660, was the great sign and supreme instrument of the new knowledge and its entry into public life. No less in the areas of historical study, legal theory and political economy the developments were dramatic. It was already a very different world from that of the Tudors and Shakespeare. As the historian Gerald Cragg puts it, "Within little more than a generation we pass from an atmosphere still predominately medieval to one which is essentially modern."[26] It was a world in which traditional religion was already becoming ill at ease, as apparent mysteries dissolved before new facts and explanations and God appeared to be less and less necessary for an understanding of the world and human affairs. The question arose: where now is God in all this? A range of answers appeared on the table.

Sheer atheism declared there was no god at all. Deism located God completely outside and beyond this world, at best the clockmaker who has designed and wound up the machine which is now left to tick away by itself. At the other extreme came Spinoza's pantheism, where God is simply nature in its entirety and therewith came a host of new problems about human freedom and personality. What should orthodox religion do? It could look inwards, to the private sphere of the soul where God might still be at work, in ways known only to piety. It might tenaciously hope for miracles confounding nature, special interventions from on high. Or it might shut the door on the new knowledge and bow down before sheer absolute pronouncements from ecclesiastical authority. Traherne takes a rather different path to any of these, and a clue to how he thought of his enterprise is given in an almost throwaway line at the start of his entry on 'All Things' in his *Commentaries of Heaven*. Here he refers to it being 'a new doctrine, and too great to be believed, that a man on earth should be the heir of all things', and which has led to him being accused, as was St Paul by Festus, of having been made mad by much learning.'[27] Traherne was clearly brim-full of excitement at this 'new doctrine' – that a human person is the *heir of all things*. The world as a whole, not peculiar bits of it or sections of experience, is mystery, wonder, miracle. Traherne is not fazed by any of the scientific or philosophical advances of the day. He accepts them all – just look at his encyclopaedic surveys of the natural and human world.[28] *The world as known to us in its entirety* is the gift of God and the means of grace through which God is met, known and served and in so doing human beings find true fulfilment, inheriting God's world. Traherne simply wants to claim this newly being-discovered world as God's world, the means of God's glory and of humanity's true joy. The new knowledge is simply grist to this mill of faith and praise.

---

26. G. R. Cragg, *The Church and the Age of Reason 1648–1789* (London: Penguin Books, 1960), 80.

27. Traherne, *Commentaries of Heaven*, in *Works*, ed. Jan Ross, vol. II, 407.

28. Especially in *Commentaries of Heaven*.

Bonhoeffer, as we have seen, was from his early days eager to assert the worldliness of faith. In 1944, during the second of his two years in prison, he was led to a new and still more positive assessment of his contemporary world, which he describes in his famous and controversial phrase, 'the world come of age'. This resonates uncannily with Traherne's 'new doctrine' of the human person being 'heir of all things' and he takes it still further by implying that humankind is not only heir but is now called to the status of maturity to inherit. It must be said that by a world 'come of age', or 'mature', Bonhoeffer does not mean a morally perfect world, but rather a world in which human beings have to take responsibility for themselves through what they now know of how the world works. Vital to Bonhoeffer's thinking here was his reading, while in prison, of a new book by the scientific philosopher Carl Friedrich von Weizsäcker, *The World View of Physics*.[29] Bonhoeffer comments on its impact upon him:

> It has again brought home to me quite clearly that we shouldn't think of God as the stopgap for the incompleteness of our knowledge, because then ... when the boundaries of knowledge are pushed even further, God too is pushed further away and thus is ever on the retreat, We should find God in what we know, not in what we don't know; God wants to be grasped by us not in unsolved questions but in those that have been solved ... God wants to be recognized in the midst of our lives, in life and not only in dying, in health and strength and not only in suffering, in action and not only in sin.[30]

Also important in his reading while in prison was the nineteenth-century German philosopher Wilhelm Dilthey, with his depiction of the modern human being as one who seeks through experience, education and values to be a wholly integrated person, and to look upon the world as an integrated whole in a unified structure of knowledge. According to Bonhoeffer, if there are any remaining gaps in our knowledge of the world, it is a mistake to assume that *they* are where God is to be looked for. It is also a mistake to think of God as a supernatural power who is called in only when human resources fail, like the deus ex machina of the ancient Greek plays, the god who is finally wheeled in to save the day, the bit-part god, the stop-gap god, the god who is on the boundary and to whom we go only – if at all – when all else fails. Rather, in his words, 'God is the beyond in the midst of our lives.'[31] Like Traherne, Bonhoeffer asks that we accept the world in its entirety as God's gift, created by him, indwelt and reconciled to him in Christ, and entrusted to us for our responsibility in fellowship with him. We do not have to look for God only in spooky little holes of apparent mystery, or to construct elaborate

---

29. The book was recommended to Bonhoeffer by his brother Karl-Friedrich, himself a distinguished physicist.
30. DBWE 8, 405–6.
31. Ibid., 367.

arguments to prove that God exists in a sphere outside this world and beyond our reach. 'Instead, our relationship to God is a new life in "being there for others", through participation in the being of Jesus.'[32]

The crucial phrase here is 'participation in' (the being of Jesus). It is a matter of being drawn into the dynamic of Christ's life, which is God's own love for people, not a religious experience which is some kind of private possession. It's a holiness which is very worldly as it takes us into the world as God loves the world. A number of recent commentators likewise see Traherne as rejecting faith as something static, which one possesses in itself and for oneself, but is rather an opening out into all that is, through *participation* in God who is all, and in all. As Melvyn Matthews says of Traherne, 'He it is who urges us to move out of the prison of our self with a delight in all that is, a delight which enables us to share in the delight that God has in things, and so brings us back to the kingdom from which we have fallen through thoughtlessness.'[33] To be taken out of oneself into relationship with all else through God in Christ in the world is both challenging and liberating in today's environment which is so individualist, self-centred and acquisitive, in religion as in so much else in contemporary life. Taking Traherne and Bonhoeffer together, precisely because they are three centuries apart, shows us that their kind of theology and spirituality can't be dismissed as either a relic of the past or as just a quirky blip on the quirky screen of contemporary Christianity. They are witnessing to something fundamental that lies deep both in the Christian tradition[34] and in the ongoing quest of the human spirit. Our recent and contemporary life throws up examples of how their thinking does resonate on the leading edge of human endeavour.[35] Early in this chapter I referred to our contemporary ecological concerns. Traherne and Bonhoeffer encourage us

---

32. Ibid., 501.

33. Melvyn Matthews, *Awake to God: Explorations in the Mystical Way* (London: SPCK, 2006), 97.

34. Cf. Paula Gooder's succinct biblical study *Heaven* (London: SPCK, 2011), 102. 'Believing in heaven should mean that we carry with us a vision of the world as God intended it to be and strive with everything that we have to bring about that kind of world in the places where we live and work.'

35. Two disparate but telling examples can be cited. Dag Hammarskjöld Secretary-General of the UN from 1953 till his death in a suspicious air crash in 1961, and posthumously awarded the Nobel Peace Prize, wrote, 'In our era, the road to holiness necessarily passes through the world of action.' See his *Markings* (London: Faber & Faber, 1966), 108. John Simpson, World Affairs editor of the BBC, writes,

> But what if ... the point of living isn't to be placid and happy and untouched by the world, but to be deeply, painfully sensitive to it, to see its cruelty and savagery for what they are, and to accept all this as readily as its beauty? To be touched by it, loved by it, hurt by it even, but not to be indifferent to it?

Not Quite World's End: A Traveller's Tales (London: Macmillan, 2007), 460-1.

towards a spirituality integral to that concern, taking us beyond a 'concern for' the created world, to a 'participation in' the world, the world where the sea flows in our veins, which is drawn into our participation with God in Christ.[36]

I would just add a qualifier. While Traherne does speak so much of delight, and of God as answering the search for 'felicity', there is no naïve, one-sided emphasis on joy in Traherne. He knows that to share in Christ means to share in his cross. Equally, while Bonhoeffer writes so powerfully on the cost of grace and discipleship, he knows that the end is joy in God. So let us conclude with two final parallel readings. Here is Traherne:

> O Jesu, thou king of saints, whom all adore; and the holy imitate, I admire the perfection of thy love in every soul! Thou lovest every one wholly as if him alone, whose soul is so great an image of thine eternal Father, that thou camest down from heaven to die for him, and to purchase mankind that they might be his treasures. I admire to see thy cross in every understanding, thy passion in every memory, thy crown of thorns in every eye, and thy bleeding, naked wounded body in every soul. Thy death liveth in every memory, thy crucified person is embalmed in every affection, thy pierced feet are bathed in everyone's tears, thy blood all droppeth on every soul. Thou wholly communicatest thyself to every soul in all kingdoms, and art wholly seen in every saint, and wholly fed upon by every Christian. It is my privilege that I can enter with thee into every soul, and in every living temple of thy manhood and thy Godhead, behold again, and enjoy thy glory.[37]

And here is Bonhoeffer writing with joyous assurance from his prison cell on 21 July 1944, the day after the plot against Hitler had finally failed and he knew what his likely end would be:

> In the last few years I have come to know and understand more and more the profound this-worldliness of Christianity ... I do not mean the shallow and banal this- worldliness of the enlightened, the bustling, the comfortable, or the lascivious, but the profound this-worldliness that shows discipline and includes the ever-present knowledge of death and resurrection ... I am still discovering to this day, that one only learns to have faith by living in the full this-worldliness of life. If one has completely renounced making something of oneself – whether it be a saint or a converted sinner or a church leader (a so-called priestly figure!), a just or an unjust person, a sick or a healthy person – then one throws oneself completely into the arms of God, and this is what I call this-worldliness: living fully in the midst of life's tasks, questions, successes and failures, experiences,

---

36. See e.g. Craig Gardiner, *Melodies of a New Monasticism: Bonhoeffer's Vision, Iona's Witness* (Eugene, OR: Cascade Books, 2018), 274–7; John de Gruchy, *This Monastic Moment* (Eugene, OR: Wipf & Stock, 2020).

37. Traherne, 86th in First Century, Ridler edition (see n.5), 205–6.

and perplexities – then one takes seriously no longer one's own sufferings but rather the sufferings of God in the world. Then one stays awake with Christ in Gethsemane. And I think this is faith; this is *metanoia* [repentance]. And this is how one becomes a human being, a Christian [cf Jer. 45!] How should one become arrogant over successes or shaken by one's failures when one shares God's sufferings in the life of this world? So I am thinking gratefully and with peace of mind about past as well as present things.

Centuries apart but neighbours in their worldly holiness? Traherne and Bonhoeffer both affirmed that the transcendent God is encountered precisely in the this-worldliness of life. It might be going too far to say that Bonhoeffer and Traherne could each have written the other's piece. But we can well imagine Traherne declaring a very Anglican 'Amen' to Bonhoeffer's letter, and in turn Traherne's meditation receiving a hearty *Jawohl!*

Chapter 5

'IF YOU ENGLISH HAD READ HIM YOU WOULD NOT HAVE NEEDED TO READ KARL BARTH': BONHOEFFER ON THE CATHOLIC MODERNIST FRIEDRICH VON HÜGEL

The seed for this essay was sown in my mind just over thirty years ago by the notable Anglican bishop and ecumenist Oliver Tomkins (1908–1992). He had been bishop of Bristol from 1959 to 1975, and it was during his time there that I had first known him, followed by several conversations at ecumenical occasions during his retirement, and in correspondence relating to the ecumenical pioneer J. H. Oldham whom he had known personally. In one of the last exchanges we had, he surprised me by saying that in 1939, while working for the Student Christian Movement (SCM) in London, he had actually met Dietrich Bonhoeffer at a small lunch party attended by several other notable ecumenical figures. Someone in the party had asked Bonhoeffer which English theologian he thought most worth reading, and his reply was 'Friedrich von Hügel', on the grounds that if the English had read him they would not have needed to read Karl Barth!

This was to say the least intriguing. But first, readers who are not already familiar with Friedrich von Hügel (1852–1925) may need convincing that such a Germanic-sounding name belonged to an Englishman. His father was in fact an Austrian baron and diplomat (who had taken a Scottish wife), but Friedrich was brought up and lived almost his entire life in England He regarded himself as English and in fact sought and was granted British nationality on the outbreak of the First World War in 1914. That aside, there were genuine grounds for surprise at this report of Bonhoeffer's choice for approbation, because as far as I knew (and still know) there is absolutely no mention of von Hügel in any of Bonhoeffer's published works or in his preserved unpublished writings. There is less surprise at knowing that von Hügel was a Roman Catholic, since Bonhoeffer, notwithstanding his Lutheran background and allegiance, was from his student days conspicuously drawn to certain aspects of Catholicism and once apparently confessed to briefly thinking of conversion.[1] There is still less surprise when it is recognized that von Hügel was an unusual Catholic for the time. He was a

---

1. A letter in April 1929 from D. Albers, a teacher in Barcelona, where Bonhoeffer was a student pastor during 1928–9, implies this. See DBWE 10, 181.

lay theologian with a major interest in the philosophy of religion, and historical and biblical studies, of independent mind and independent means – he inherited from his father not only the aristocratic title 'baron' but also the financial means to ensure a life of scholarly pursuits entirely of his own choosing. He had no formal education and never held an academic post, but acquired an almost unique intellectual reputation as writer, leading member of several learned societies, guest lecturer at universities and recipient of honorary doctorates from the universities of Oxford and St Andrews. Most telling of all, he became closely associated with the Catholic Modernist movement, the group mostly comprising French and other continental scholars which during the early 1900s sought a rapprochement between traditional Catholic teaching and the areas of modern science and historical research. The movement, officially described by the church authorities as promoting 'the synthesis of all the heresies', was in 1907 condemned by Pope Pius X in his decree *Lamentabili* and his encyclical *Pascendi gregis*. Prominent clerics in the movement, including the French biblical scholar Albert Loisy and the English Jesuit George Tyrell, were excommunicated and anti-modernist oaths were enjoined upon priests suspected of Modernist sympathies, effectively ending the movement by 1911. Von Hügel was central to the thinking of the movement, dubbed by some its 'international bishop' on account of his mediating role at the European level. Being a layman (and moreover, some have drily noted, a baron) he himself was spared censure. Moreover he had always protested an unswerving loyalty to the Church, while believing that the core of Catholic Christianity lay not in its authoritarian institutions but in the inner life of spirituality and voluntary adhesion to belief on the part of its members. Until his death in 1925 he continued to write, to wide acclaim in both academic and popular circles in the English-speaking world, in his chosen fields of philosophy of religion, spirituality and church history. W. R. Inge, dean of St Paul's Cathedral, judged him the ablest Christian apologist of the age.[2]

Von Hügel's works

By the early 1900s, through his public lectures, articles in journals and the press, and voluminous correspondence, von Hügel had certainly acquired a wide reputation, in Britain and beyond, as an immensely erudite yet informative commentator on the place of religion, and Christian belief in particular, in the modern intellectual milieu of scientific method and critical historical investigation. Moreover, quite apart from his involvement with the Catholic Modernists, at a personal level he had acquired a remarkable network of colleagues, correspondents and friends well beyond the Catholic fold. In the opinion of one biographer he did 'more

---

2. For a succinct portrait of von Hügel and his significance on the English scene, see Adrian Hastings, *A History of English Christianity 1920–1985* (London: Collins, 1986), 153–5.

than any man living to bring together the profoundest religious thinkers of the age'.³ His opinion was sought on a wide range of issues, and on every question his approach was holistic and synthetic rather than coldly analytical, still less partisan. Significantly, one of the several intellectual societies he helped to found in London was called 'The Synthetic Society'. His synthetic approach operated at every level. Thus, Western civilization reveals three main forces: Hellenism, the thirst for richness and harmony; Christianity, the revelation of personality and depth; and science, the engagement with fact and law. All three forces are necessary for fullness of human life; none can do without the others. Even Christianity cannot subsist by itself, hence for him scientific and historical criticism must be conducted in freedom – for the good of faith itself. The community of the Church must likewise comprise a blend of the institutional, the dogmatic and the voluntary, the 'mystical' faith element that directly apprehends God. No less, the life of the individual comes to its fullest human and Christian flowering in a synthesis of essential elements: the intellectual, the personal-mystical and the participation in the corporate life of the Church.

Von Hügel's intellectual standing in his generation was decisively established with the publication in 1909 of his massive, two-volume *The Mystical Element of Religion as Studied in Saint Catherine of Genoa and Her Friends*.⁴ In this study the fifteenth- to sixteenth-century saint is not so much the sole focus but the continuing reference point for illustrating and exploring further the threefold synthesis of Hellenism, Christianity and science which von Hügel had made his own. 'Mysticism' for him means not an absorption of the human soul into the divine but the direct encounter of the soul with God who is always transcendent, an encounter which combines with the other elements – historical, rational and institutional – in religious experience and activity. Despite its formidable length and erudition its impact was profound on the British theological scene. William Temple, future archbishop of York and then of Canterbury, and the major Anglican theologian of his generation, hailed it as 'the most important theological work written in the English language during the last half-century', while James Hastings, editor of the *Encyclopaedia of Religion and Ethics*, believed it to be 'the most thorough investigation of the subject that has ever been made'.⁵ Fortunately for the less academic readership, von Hügel was also able to write in more accessible and shorter formats, particularly for example in his collection *Essays and Addresses on the Philosophy of Religion*⁶ and a significant amount of his correspondence.⁷ His death in 1925 did not halt his influence. He had been preparing his Gifford

---

3. M. D. Petre, cited in Michael de la Bedoyere, *The Life of Baron von Hügel* (London: J.M. Dent, 1951), 124.

4. Vol. I. *Interpretation and Biographical* and Vol. II. *Critical* (London: J.M. Dent, 1908).

5. Bedoyere, *Life of Baron von Hügel*, xi.

6. London: J.M. Dent, 1921; 2nd series 1926.

7. See Friedrich von Hügel, *Selected Letters 1896–1924* (London: J.M. Dent, 1928); *Letters from Baron Friedrich von Hügel to a Niece* (London: J.M. Dent, 1928).

Lectures to be given at Edinburgh University during 1924–5 and 1925–6; his unfinished material was published in 1931 as *The Reality of God and Religion and Agnosticism*.[8] He continued to be a familiar source of quotations in British religious writings at both academic and more popular levels up to and beyond the Second World War. The superlative accolade is awarded by Adrian Hastings: 'He stands as an angel at the gate of our period, the great reconciler, seer of a whole new Christianity, overarching the divisions of the medieval and Reformation centuries, but firmly rooted in the transcendent God, the historic incarnation, the Eucharist. Above all, he was a man of prayer.'[9]

Tomkins, Bonhoeffer and von Hügel

Oliver Tomkins died in 1992. I regretted not having had, or made, opportunity to pursue his Bonhoeffer recollection further. In 2001, however, there appeared the biography of Tomkins by the historian Adrian Hastings[10] who was able to draw on Tomkins's personal journal from his days as a theological student in the 1930s at Westcott House, Cambridge, and as a young priest working for the SCM. Hastings not only confirms but also amplifies and sets in context what Tomkins had related to me, in particular how as a student he had been searching for a more profoundly spiritual theology than was evidently on offer from the liberal Cambridge theologians of the day:

> By the end of the year at Westcott [House] this hitherto pretty typical 'Liberal Evangelical' had come to see that the monastic and the mystical mattered a very great deal. Baron Fredrich von Hügel had helped him here. It was at Westcott that he began to read von Hügel. Later he would like to recall that the only time he met Dietrich Bonhoeffer – it was in 1939 on the stairs of the Athenaeum[11] – he had made one remark which he could never forget: 'If you English would read von Hügel, you would not need Karl Barth.' Von Hügel was the totally European English Catholic layman, at once critical and mystical, at once the sympathetic student of all religions and the firm assertor of the transcendence of God and the unicity of Christ, some sort of mysterious amalgam of Troeltsch and Barth – the historical width of the one with the faith of the other. For Oliver, Bonhoeffer 'meant that in von Hügel the sovereign grace of the Eternal God over the proud pretensions of man was so richly expounded by a liberal Roman Catholic that the same message from a conservative biblical Protestant was made redundant.

8. London: J.M. Dent.
9. Hastings, *A History of English Christianity*, 153.
10. Adrian Hastings, *Oliver Tomkins: The Ecumenical Enterprise, 1908–92* (London: SPCK, 2001).
11. The prestigious London club much favoured by bishops, statesmen and senior academics.

From von Hügel I learned an analysis of reality not just of religion, which has never left me.'[12]

Although not mentioned in any other source, Tomkins's vivid recollection of such a meeting is entirely consistent with what we know of Bonhoeffer's whereabouts in March–April 1939,[13] and I am most grateful to the members of Oliver Tomkins's family who have kindly located for me the entry in his journal: his son Stephen Tomkins, his daughter Monica Cleasby and granddaughter Emma Cleasby. On 12 March Bonhoeffer, accompanied by his close friend Eberhard Bethge, arrived in London for a five-week visit to England. He had several objects in view: to discuss with ecumenical contacts, including Bishop George Bell and Canon Leonard Hodgson of Oxford, future relationships between the Confessing Church and the ecumenical movement in view of the formation of the World Council of Churches which was now under way; to confide in George Bell the agonizing personal choices now facing him as war approached, on whether to stay in Hitler's Germany where he was likely to face the military call-up as well as the mounting suspicions of the Nazi authorities; and to visit his twin-sister Sabine, her 'non-Aryan' husband Gerhard Leibholz and their two young daughters. The Leibholzes had got out of Germany the previous year and with George Bell's assistance found refuge in London. Meetings with all these mentioned figures took place during the visit, and are well chronicled as are two others: with W. A. Visser't Hooft who happened to be in London briefly, and with the American theologian Reinhold Niebuhr who was delivering the Gifford Lectures in Edinburgh and came south to meet Bonhoeffer at St Leonards-on-Sea and discussed actual possibilities for him to get away to America at least for a time. But nowhere, not even in Eberhard Bethge's account of these London days, is there a mention of this Athenaeum lunch meeting, or the precise date on which it took place. We cannot even be sure who else was present at it.[14] These uncertainties, and the fact that there is no mention of von Hügel in Bonhoeffer's legacy of writings, need not deter us from exploring

---

12. Hastings, *Oliver Tomkins*, 20.

13. See Eberhard Bethge, *Dietrich Bonhoeffer: A Biography* (Minneapolis, MN: Fortress Press, 2000), 635–48.

14. Oliver Tomkins does not give a precise date but according to his journal it must have been on or about 25 March and in a later reminiscence he thinks that J. H. Oldham and W. A. Visser't Hooft were most likely to have been present also, though the Oldham records do not mention this meeting, and Visser't Hooft recalls meeting Bonhoeffer not at the Athenaeum but at Paddington Station (see W. A. Visser't Hooft, *Memoirs* (Geneva: WCC, 1987), 108–9). These fragments of evidence are not necessarily incompatible. For example, Visser't Hooft states that in his meeting at Paddington, he was surprised at how eager Bonhoeffer was to confide in him, at that time an almost complete stranger, about his difficult personal position in the face of the coming war. If they had previously been together in a larger group at the Athenaeum, Bonhoeffer may well have preferred to wait for a much more discreet tête-à-tête.

further the possible significance of 'the Baron' for Bonhoeffer. It would be sheer presumption to assume that there is nothing whatever to be known about a person or event beyond what is on paper or in print. Even the most incidental piece of oral transmission may prove significant.

Bonhoeffer encountering von Hügel

Just when and where Bonhoeffer first encountered von Hügel's writings, and which of them he actually read, is not known at present, and no more than informed guesses can be made. It is tempting to assume it was during his most extended residence in England, from October 1933 to April 1935, when he was pastor of two of the German congregations in London. But an earlier possibility would be his year as an exchange student at Union Seminary, New York, 1930–1. Among his teachers at Union was the Scotsman John Baillie, professor of systematic theology, with whom Bonhoeffer enjoyed a good and mutually appreciative relationship despite Baillie's reservations about his (as Baillie saw it) extremely Barthian view of grace. In 1934 Baillie returned to Scotland as professor of divinity at Edinburgh, and Bonhoeffer visited him there in 1935. Baillie had a very positive appreciation of von Hügel – in fact for his 'equipoise' in countering what Baillie saw as Barth's one-sided emphasis on transcendence with due recognition of the divine immanence too.[15]

By the time of Bonhoeffer's 1933–5 stay in London von Hügel had been dead for eight years but the interest in him was continuing. The second series of *Essays and Addresses on the Philosophy of Religion* had appeared posthumously in 1926, the two volumes of letters (see note 7) and the incomplete Gifford Lectures *The Reality of God*, 1931.

Bonhoeffer's time in England as well as the visit to John Baillie occasioned meetings with a number of theological figures and visits to theological colleges (Anglican, Baptist and Methodist), together with the local ministers' fraternal meeting in Forest Hill where one of his congregations was located. It would not be surprising if he found interest in von Hügel there. One figure whom Bonhoeffer came to know well was the leading ecumenist J. H. Oldham, secretary of the International Missionary Council and main architect of the 1937 Oxford Conference on Church, Community and State, whose highly popular *Devotional Diary*[16] culled liberally from von Hügel's writings. Then there was the one who became Bonhoeffer's closest English friend, George Bell, bishop of Chichester. In the absence of actual evidence there can only be speculation, but it is hard not to imagine that Bell found a kindred spirit in von Hügel. Back in 1912, in response

---

15. See e.g. John Baillie, *Our Knowledge of God* (Oxford: Oxford University Press, 1939) and its references to von Hügel, 34n, 91–3, 179, 229, 235n, 237–8.

16. London: SCM Press, 1925 (1st edition, revised 1926).

to the controversy that greeted *Foundations*, the collection of essays by liberal-leaning Oxford theologians, Bell had taken a very measured view:

> Of course there must be creed and dogma, the intellectual presentation of the Word. But the Word itself is alive, quick and powerful. To me 'faith' in the New Testament suggests something very living, creative, rather than something settled and deposited once for all Christianity is a life before it is a system and to lay too much stress on the system destroys the life.[17]

This was not von Hügel speaking, but it was very Hügelian in tone, and the emphasis upon the primacy of life over creed and dogma was to mark Bell for life. Bonhoeffer, then, was certainly moving in English circles where von Hügel was appreciated – though to what extent he was actually known may stand further enquiry.

What Bonhoeffer found in von Hügel

Let us suppose that Bonhoeffer opened von Hügel's magnum opus, *The Mystical Element of Religion*. He would have found von Hügel expressing appreciation of a whole gamut of religious and philosophical thinkers of both past and present, the former including St John of the Cross and John Henry Newman, the latter including Ernst Troeltsch and the Scottish advocate of personal idealism A. S. Pringle-Pattison. But Søren Kierkegaard also appears.

First, he is a model for writing '*existentially*, pricked on by the exigencies of actual life, to attempt their expression in terms of that life, and in view of its further spiritual development'.[18] Second, Kierkegaard discomforts idealism with the 'jealousy' of God, saying, 'the Absolute is cruel, for it demands *all*, whilst the Relative continues to demand *some* attention from us'.[19] In Volume II of *The Mystical Element in Religion* von Hügel engages in a complex discussion of asceticism as seen in St John of the Cross, Catherine of Genoa, Blaise Pascal and Kierkegaard. Sufficient for our purpose here is what he says about Kierkegaard, 'who pushed the doctrine of the qualitative, absolute difference between God and all that we ourselves can think, feel, will or be, to lengths beyond even the transcendental element ... in the great Spaniard's [i.e. St John of the Cross] formal teaching'.[20] For Kierkegaard, von Hügel recognizes, the soul's relation to God 'is a relation to a Being absolutely different from Man, who cannot confront him as

---

17. Cited in R. C. D. Jasper, *George Bell: Bishop of Chichester* (London: Oxford University Press, 1967), 16–17.
18. *The Mystical Element* I, xvii.
19. Ibid., 353.
20. *The Mystical Element in Religion* II, 345.

his Superlative or Ideal, and who, nevertheless, is to rule in his inmost soul'.[21] The result is a suffering asceticism.

Von Hügel in these passages was approaching the divine transcendence primarily with an interest in its subjective apprehension by the believer and in its consequent ascetic expression. But in later writings, as seen in the posthumously published *Essays and Addresses* he is clear about the objective reality of the transcendent God being the ultimate focus of belief, above all in his 1921 lecture 'The Facts and Truths Concerning God and the Soul Which Are of Most Importance in the Life of Prayer'. God is a *stupendously rich Reality* at work in creation and redemption. 'But God is God, already apart from His occupation with us. These are the great facts which I believe to be specially revealed to us in the dogma of the Holy Trinity – facts of which we have an especial need in these our times.'[22] *God alone is fully free* in his creative life and his fully incarnate life in Christ. He is the God of prevenient grace in all things. He is not entirely unlike us, else how could we know God or, as the Gospel enjoins, be perfect even as our heavenly Father is perfect?

> Yet God is also *other than man*. Other, because He, God, is a Reality, an Identity, a Consciousness, distinct from the reality, identity, consciousness, of any of His creatures or of the sum-total of them. And God is other, because this His distinct Reality is, by its nature, so much higher and richer, not only in degree but in kind, than is the nature of man or of any other creature. 'Man is made in the image of God.' Yes, but we must not press this as an exhaustive norm, as though God were simply man writ large – man's better and best instincts and conditions on an immense scale.
>
> We shall doubtless be much nearer the facts if we think of God as the living Source and the always previous, always prevenient Realisation, in ways and degrees for us ineffable, of our ideals and ever imperfect achievements – a Realisation which must be taken directly to contain concretely what our conditions and strivings contain ideally.[23]

It might indeed have seemed to anyone acquainted with the early Barth that they were reading what Barth had written in the preface to the second edition of his commentary *The Epistle to the Romans* (1921), namely, that if he had a system it was 'limited to what Kierkegaard called the "infinite qualitative distinction" between time and eternity, and to my regarding this as possessing negative as well as positive significance: "God is in heaven, and thou art on earth."'[24] The insistence on God's transcendence is a note that is sounded also in von Hügel's *The German*

---

21. Ibid.
22. *Essays and Addresses*, 218.
23. Ibid., 222.
24. KarlBarth, *The Epistle to the Romans*. Translated from 6th edition by E. C. Hoskyns (Oxford: Oxford University Press, 1933), 10.

Soul[25] and in his letters to his niece: 'We shall never be God, we shall always be men. He gives: we receive.'[26] The note features no less strongly in his unfinished Gifford Lectures *The Reality of God and Religion and Agnosticism*.

In the course of time the apparent similarity between von Hügel and the early Barth did not go entirely unnoticed by British readers. In introducing his 1945 selection of von Hügel's writings Franklin Chambers[27] includes a citation from Barth on the transitory and the eternal, and in his biographical preface states, 'Von Hügel's effort to bring back Christian theology to the "otherness", the over-againstness of God, has led some to compare him with the Swiss theologian Karl Barth who has done much to turn Protestant theology in the same direction.' Chambers however turns to John Baillie of Edinburgh, whom we have suggested before as a possible conduit of von Hügel to Bonhoeffer, for a more balanced assessment here:

> Great as is the service which Dr Barth has rendered us in weaning us from the enticements of a one-sided immanentism, he has tended to lead us away in his apparent complete rejection of the truth for which immanentism and mysticism alike stand. And probably when the theological excitement of these present years gives place to a period of calmer reflection it will be recognised that von Hügel was here the safer guide.[28]

Nor was von Hügel the only British theologian inviting some comparison with Barth. In 1939 Barth's son Markus (who became a distinguished New Testament scholar), following a year at Mansfield College, Oxford, stated that the British could best get the message his father had to deliver from the Scottish Congregationalist theologian P. T. Forsyth (1848–1921).[29] The notion that Forsyth was a 'Barthian before Barth' has however been disputed, not least by some admirers of Forsyth who feel that the comparison is lacking in respect – to Forsyth.[30]

Bonhoeffer's remark to Oliver Tomkins, that if the English had read von Hügel they would not need Karl Barth, can be interpreted more than one way. It could mean that he thought von Hügel had been grossly neglected or unknown in Britain hitherto, an unlikely scenario given that Bonhoeffer must have known of von

---

25. *The German Soul in Its Attitude towards Ethics and Christianity, the State and War* (London: J.M. Dent, 1916).

26. *Letters from Baron Friedrich von Hügel to a Niece*, xviii.

27. P. Franklin Chambers, *Baron von Hügel. Man of God: An Introductory Anthology Compiled with a Biographical Preface* (London: Geoffrey Bles; Centenary Press, 1945).

28. Baillie, *Our Knowledge of God*, 237.

29. See A. R. Vidler, *The Church in an Age of Revolution* (London: Penguin Books, 1961), 219.

30. See John Thompson, 'Was Forsyth Really a Barthian Before Barth?' in Trevor Hart (ed.), *Justice the True and Only Mercy. Essays on the Life and Theology of Peter Taylor Forsyth* (Edinburgh: T&T Clark, 1995), 237–55.

Hügel's relative and continuing popularity. But it could also imply that Bonhoeffer was aware of how difficult, intimidating or simply baffling even educated Anglo-Saxons often found Barth's language and ideas in English translations, and that Bonhoeffer sensed von Hügel could provide a less intimidating approach to the divine mystery. Or perhaps Bonhoeffer felt that having been allured into reading von Hügel, and then if they *really and thoroughly* read him – beyond those comforting passages assuring them that faith, science and historical criticism could be blended in a harmonious whole – and had dared the rugged crags where he, with Kierkegaard and St John of the Cross, was leading them to face the otherness of God, then indeed they might be excused the Barthian challenge.

As well as all these considerations there is, however, the obvious point: Bonhoeffer believed that 'the English' *ought* to have read and listened to Barth, and that to read the Englishman von Hügel was the next best thing for them.

Background: The reception of Barth in Britain

The reception of Barth in Britain from the early 1920s to the outbreak of war in 1939 was uneven, and indeed the actual process of transmission of Barth's work into Britain was disorderly to say the least. The fullest account of the story is by D. Densil Morgan, *Barth Reception in Britain*.[31]

The initial introduction of Barth onto the British scene was made by the Swiss theologian, ecumenist and humanitarian entrepreneur Adolf Keller who in the 1920s publicized Barth and the 'theology of crisis' in a number of British journals[32] and a few years later in his major work *Karl Barth and Christian Unity*.[33] Barth's own works began to appear in English, starting with *The Word of God and the Word of Man* (1928). The work which had detonated the whole Barthian explosion, his restless, radical and prophetic (or 'extreme' in some eyes) commentary on *Romans*, barbed with Kierkegaard's insistence on the wholly otherness of God, had originally appeared in German in 1918. It, or rather its sixth edition, did not appear in English until 1933, translated by the Cambridge scholar Edwyn C. Hoskyns.[34] By that time Barth had moved on (or 'matured' some would say). In 1938 the *Church Dogmatics* started their journey into English with *The Doctrine of the Word of God*.[35] Barth himself gave the Gifford Lectures at Aberdeen University in 1937 and 1938, published in 1938 as *The Knowledge of God and the Service of*

---

31. London: T&T Clark International, 2010.

32. Ibid., 5–24.

33. Adolf Keller, *Karl Barth and Christian Unity: The Influence of the Barthian Movement Upon the Churches of the World* (London: Lutterworth, 1933). Translation of *Der Weg der dialektischen Theologie durch die Kirchliche Welt* (1931).

34. See n.24.

35. Translation of *Kirchliche Dogmatik* I/1 by G. T. Thomson. Edinburgh: T&T Clark.

God.³⁶ British readers might be asking where the real (or the latest at any rate) Barth was to be found.

But further, Barth's reception was subject to all manner of factors – theological, denominational, national and cultural – within the four-nation British Isles context. The intra-British geographical and religious-cultural factors were certainly important. Scotland, where the Genevan Reformed legacy remained strong, ensured a ready welcome in the divinity faculties. There was at least as much in Welsh Nonconformity, home of vigorous biblical preaching. In England the situation was more complicated. Paradoxically it was the Anglo-Catholic Hoskyns who translated Barth's *Romans* commentary, while Barth sat uncomfortably with the ethos of the Anglican national church and its accommodating tradition of giving full scope to reason as well as revelation. But even among the English Free Churches the Barthian message had for some time to fight for a hearing in the face of the remaining culture of nineteenth-century liberalism and its gospel of progress; it was among the Congregationalists that Barth won his strongest theological support in England. The reception was also affected by which other continental figures called for attention – the Swiss Emil Brunner for instance appeared to many to offer a more straightforward version of the 'theology of crisis' – and by differing perspectives taken towards the unfolding drama of the German Church Struggle in which Barth was so heavily engaged from 1933 onwards.

1939: Bonhoeffer and the theological milieu in Britain

In 1938 the long-awaited report *Doctrine in the Church of England* was published.³⁷ It was the work of a Commission appointed as long before as 1922 by the then Archbishop of Canterbury, Randall Davidson, in response to the continuing disquiet resulting from the *Foundations* debates of 1911 and other controversies, and by such extreme liberalism as expressed by the Modern Churchmen's Union at their Cambridge conference in 1921. Anglo-Catholicism, Modern Churchmen and evangelicalism were represented on the Commission which was to 'consider the nature and grounds of Christian Doctrine with a view to demonstrating the extent of existing agreement within the Church of England and with a view to investigating how far it is possible to remove or diminish existing differences'. Since 1925 it had been chaired by William Temple, who became archbishop of York in 1929. It covered a wide range of topics in Christian doctrine, including the nature of authority, God and Redemption, the Church, Sacraments and eschatology. There was widespread agreement that its work was both comprehensive and thorough. In short, it was a model search for consensus which owed much to the approach of Temple himself, who from the early 1920s until his untimely death

---

36. London: Hodder and Stoughton, 1938.

37. *Doctrine in the Church of England*. The Report of a Commission on Christian Doctrine Appointed by the Archbishops of Canterbury and York in 1925. London: SPCK, 1938.

in 1944 expressed in his own theology the greatest of Anglican strengths, namely its balance and comprehensiveness. When he attained the primacy at Canterbury in 1942, he embodied for a whole generation the Anglican ideal. Indeed, as one historian confesses, it is hard at times not to want the history of English Christianity in the first half of the twentieth century 'to look little more than a history of William Temple'.[38] His theology, centred on the incarnation and infused strongly with philosophical idealism, was expressed in a rational, consensual approach to problems both theological and political.[39] His view on how the church should engage with social issues was in essence, 'The Church must announce Christian principles and point out where the existing social order is in conflict with them. It must then pass on to Christian citizens, acting in their civic capacity, the task of re-shaping the existing order in closer conformity to the principles.' This view had obvious strengths but could at times seem oblivious to the instances where the realities of social life were already destructively impacting on people's lives and where the need was not for principles but for decisions on how to right the all-too-obvious wrongs which did not need 'pointing out' by the church.

Barth's call to recognize the radical otherness of God's word and to reject all forms of natural theology was a severe challenge to the measured, consensual approach of Temple-era Anglicanism. This was recognized by the Anglican who, more than any other, had conveyed the challenge of the early Barth to England, the translator of the *Romans* commentary, the Cambridge Anglo-Catholic E. C. Hoskyns. In 1936 he addressed to Barth a 'Letter from England' which appeared that year in the Festschrift honouring Barth's fiftieth birthday.[40] Hoskyns writes apologetically to account for what must have seemed to Barth the uncertain English response overall, conditioned by 'a real barrier' of difference in language, culture, piety and theological thought-forms. But that was not to deny a real significance to his work. Employing the favourite English device of double negatives, he cautiously wishes to assure Barth,

> You will therefore perhaps understand and forgive me if, for one moment, I break through the reserve that has been imposed upon us, in order to assure you that your work has not been altogether misunderstood in England, and to assure that your purpose in permitting your book to appear in English has not been altogether overlooked.[41]

Hoskyns proceeds effusively to offer gratitude to Barth for redirecting theology back to its biblical roots, and to the centralities of the apostolic and prophetic

---

38. Hastings, *A History of English Christianity*, 254–5.

39. See e.g. his *Mens Creatrix* (1917), *Christus Veritas* (1924) and his Gifford Lectures *Nature, Man and God* (1934).

40. Edwyn C. Hoskyns, 'A Letter from England', in *Theologische Aufsätze Karl Barth zum 50, Geburtstag*, E. Wolf (ed.) (Munich: Chr. Kaiser Verlag, 1936), 525–7.

41. Ibid. See also Morgan, *Barth Reception*, 153.

tradition. Hoskyns' untimely death in 1937 is judged by Densil Morgan to have been a main reason 'for the virtual end of a possible Barthian movement within England's established church'.[42] It must have seemed as if Barth's star was fading, at least as far as the Anglican Church was concerned.

At this point it is apposite to pause momentarily and reflect on the differing but convergent angles along which Barth, von Hügel and Bonhoeffer were approaching the subject of God's transcendence. All were concerned to acknowledge God as the transcendent, wholly other One, all-sufficient in prevenient grace and holiness. Equally, all three (even Barth) were aware that the human encounter with God, or rather our being encountered by God, takes place within the contingencies of earthly, material human existence. At the risk of over-simplification, one might compare von Hügel and Barth by saying that the former leads his readers through the successive layers of human consciousness and experience to the point where God is apprehended as the mystery beyond all other apprehensions, confessed in adoring prayer; whereas Barth (at least the early Barth) *begins* with the wholly otherness of God, who declares judgment on all intellectual and religious exercises purporting to reach God, who can be apprehended only in his self-revelation through his Word, Jesus Christ. Bonhoeffer is usually and rightly recognized as in the Barthian camp – though always a carefully critical follower of the Barthian flag. Always, Bonhoeffer was anxious that Barth might sit loose to the very concrete ethical demands of a faith situated in this world. Bonhoeffer's distinctive apprehension of the transcendent in 1939 was, we shall see, inseparably linked to the crisis of personal *decision* that was now confronting him.

Bonhoeffer, Barth and England 1939

The English milieu as regards Barth which Bonhoeffer would have encountered in London in the spring of 1939 was already well known to him. He knew well enough the 'Anglo-Saxon' (as he called them) susceptibilities through his previous experiences: in his encounters with the British churches and theological colleges during his London pastorate in 1933-5; his friendships and collaborative work with the likes of John Baillie, J. H. Oldham and George Bell; and his participation in the ecumenical organizations, the World Alliance for International Friendship through the Churches and the Life and Work movement. In particular, he had grown to appreciate the Catholic spirituality manifested in the Anglican religious houses and colleges at Cowley, Kelham and Mirfield, and on which he drew in shaping the communal life of his illegal seminary at Finkenwalde. Yet he had never lost hold of the primal, radical, Christocentric theology of the word of God which Barth had given him in his student years and which was the presupposition of all his theology thereafter. If in 1939 he believed that British theology needed to hear the essence of Barth's message no less than before, how might they hear it if

---

42. Ibid., 153.

Barth himself still seemed too extreme, paradoxical and at times baffling – and, as the *Dogmatics* began to roll out, too verbose? Friedrich von Hügel offered real possibilities here. By the time of his death in 1925, he had long been accepted by the English as one of their own. Many of his writings were congenial and made their appeal by their synthetic approach to the otherwise divisive matters of science and religion, biblical truth and historical criticism, ecclesiastical order, authority and the freedom of personal faith.

They pointed to deeper realities than arid controversies could comprehend. In an age when to many minds science and religion were still at loggerheads, ecclesiastical authority was in dispute and the different churches were only at the merest beginnings of ecumenical encounter, he offered a holistic, unifying blend of thought, commitment, ethical action and prayer. Above all they met the hunger of many people for a deeper spiritual life of meditation, prayer and sacramental communion – to those who had known him intimately the most telling image they retained of von Hügel was of this immensely erudite man of many words kneeling in wordless adoration of the sacrament.

But – and it is a very large but – one could read much of von Hügel and be enriched by all he had to say about the need for synthesis of the different elements of human life and religion, without facing fully what he also has to say about the transcendence, the otherness of the God who is not man, with all that this means for an ascetic of *suffering* in the face of the all-holy God. Von Hügel does not lessen the Kierkegaardian discontinuity between God and humankind, between heaven and earth. This discontinuity brings the ultimate disturbance to the synthetic life, jealously confronting the beautiful synthesis of relative relations with what lies beyond yet seeks to claim it *absolutely*. In the context of prayer this leads von Hügel, with the aid of St Augustine, to be as brusque as Barth in opposing the sentimental, easy-going familiarity between the human and divine which had marked much recent religious thought:

> All we have so far said implies or leads up to the great fact and truth: *that we men need God much more than, and very differently from, the way and degree in which God needs us men*. God is the Absolute Cause, the Ultimate Reason, the Sole True End and Determiner of our existence, of our persistence, of our nature, of our essential calls and requirements. God is all these things for man. Man is not one of these things for God. Man comes to his true self by loving God. God is the very ocean of Himself – of Love – apart from all creation. Thus the positions between God and Man, and between Man and God, are entirely uninterchangeable. Hence the most fundamental need, duty, honour and happiness of man, is not petition, nor even contrition, nor again even thanksgiving; these three kinds of prayer which, indeed, must never disappear out of our spiritual lives; but *adoration*. Probably the greatest doctor and the greatest practiser among souls well known to us in these respects, of such overwhelmingly adoring prayer, is St Augustine. Never, in spite of his tenderly anthropomorphic devotion, does the great African forget this profound non-equality, this non-interchangeable relation between God and man. Our prayer will greatly deepen and widen out,

if we also develop such a sense – a sense which is now continually exposed to the subtle testing and sapping of the pure immanentisms and the sentimental anthropocentrisms which fill the air.[43]

We can well imagine Barth giving at least one or two nods in agreement here, and Bonhoeffer adding to any British readers: 'See, that's not too difficult. Where's the problem? Read on!' It is not the *technique* of prayer – the preoccupation of much devotional literature and courses in spirituality – but the *object* of prayer, which von Hügel here emphasizes. The goal of the subjective journey through the synthesis of the relativities that make up human consciousness – that which so appealed to many of von Hügel's readers – is the encounter with the transcendent God. This God who does not fit into any prearranged philosophical or theological system ('the system is hospitable', says Kierkegaard, likening the idealist philosopher to a well-to-do but naïve burgher who is happy for any Tom, Dick or Harry to accompany him in his carriage[44]) but arises in the mystery of God's own selfhood and cannot be explained in terms of what is other than God. That, we might judge Bonhoeffer to be wishing, is what Christian faith is centred upon from start to finish. It is the mystery, the present, not far-off mystery, of God's own being and claim which does not extend our understanding but demands faith and obedience – *decision*.

Bonhoeffer himself expresses the divine transcendence in terms of mystery. Indeed the necessity to acknowledge mystery runs like a palimpsest throughout Bonhoeffer's theology, at times so carefully woven into the fabric of his thought as to be overlooked, at other points thrust into the gaze of the reader or hearer. It is his persistent refusal to try and explain God by what is not God. A striking instance is his sermon preached in London on Trinity Sunday, 27 May 1934,[45] perhaps not coincidentally for Bonhoeffer just two days before the momentous Free Synod of Barmen met to draw up the Theological Declaration, largely inspired by Karl Barth, which effectively launched the Confessing Church. Bonhoeffer bases his sermon on 1 Corinthians 2:7-10: 'But we speak God's wisdom, secret and hidden, which God decreed before the ages for our glory.' He begins by asserting that mystery is an essential part of life. To live without mystery means 'passing by that which is hidden within ourselves, other people, and the world, staying on the surface, taking the world seriously only to the extent to which it can be *calculated* and *exploited*, never looking for what is behind the world of calculation and of gain'. Trees grow in the dark depths of the earth; life comes from the dark, secret place of the womb. The roots of everything clear and obvious lie in mystery. Mystery always eludes our grasp. We cannot explain it by dissecting it; thereby we only kill it. But, *mystery does not mean simply not knowing something*. 'The greatest mystery is not the most distant star: to the contrary, the closest something is to us,

---

43. *Essays and Addresses*, 223–4.
44. Søren Kierkegaard, *Concluding Unscientific Postscript*, David F. Svenson (trans.) (London: Oxford University Press, 1941), 223–4.
45. DBWE 13, 360–3.

the better we know it, the more mysterious it becomes to us.' The same applies to persons. It is not the person furthest from us who is the most mysterious to us, but our neighbour and the more we find out about him or her the more mysterious they become to us. The very deepest mystery is when two persons grow so close that they *love* each other. Only within love is there true understanding, and the mystery is not thereby dispelled but grows even deeper. So too, there is no way to understanding the doctrine of the Holy Trinity except as mystery:

> God lives in mystery. To us, God's very being is mystery, from everlasting to everlasting: a mystery because it speaks of a home in which we cannot – not yet – be at home. All the thoughts that we can ever think about God should never be for the purpose of solving this mystery, making God easily understandable and no longer mysterious for everyone. Instead, all our thinking about God must serve only to make us see how completely beyond us and how *mysterious* God is, to makes us glimpse the mysterious and hidden wisdom of God in all its mystery and hiddenness, rather than making it less so – and thus perhaps give us a glimpse of the mystery of that home from which it comes. Every dogma of the church only points to the mystery of God.[46]

The fully mysterious God is revealed to us in the cross of Christ, which is why the world is blind to his glory.

> That is the unrecognized mystery of God in this world: that this Jesus of Nazareth, the carpenter, was the Lord of glory in person, that was the mystery of God. A mystery, because here on earth God became poor and lowly, small and weak, out of love for humankind; because God became a human being like us, so that we might become divine.[47]

This is the mystery of God, Father, Son and Holy Spirit, whose self-glorification is seen in the divine love which embraces the whole world.

The palimpsest is conspicuous also in the prison letters: the need for 'respect for mystery'[48] and an 'arcane discipline' through which the mysteries of the Christian faith are sheltered. But this mystery is not to be equated with an obscurity set in place by the limitations of human knowledge and power. It is the mystery of the God who is both very present and refuses to be any other than the God who will be what he will be. In exploring what a 'religionless Christianity' might look like Bonhoeffer objects to the religious positing of God beyond our reach and the limits of our knowing: 'God's "beyond" is not what is beyond our cognition! Epistemological transcendence has nothing to do with God's transcendence. God is the beyond in the midst of our lives.'[49] The Old Testament, which speaks of the

---

46. Ibid., 362.
47. Ibid.
48. DBWE 8, 215, 216.
49. Ibid., 367.

unutterability of the name of God who is in the midst of human life, comes to the fore in Bonhoeffer's mind again.

Von Hügel knew well, as did Kierkegaard, that encounter with the Absolute does not lead to a monistic absorption of the human into the divine but to a hearing of the call to act obediently to the divine amid the multiple responsibilities of creaturely, human existence.[50] There can be no smoothing away of the discontinuity between human existence and divinity, nor between human aspirations to goodness and the blunt realities of human behaviour, by an idealism, Hegelian or otherwise, which finds a place and explanation for everything and removes all need for decision-making, risk and sheer venturing in faith. Bonhoeffer would have detected resonances here. Both of them laid stress on the concrete forms of social life and engagement within which faith operates, and to which Christian community gives rise (von Hügel's daughter Thekla became a Carmelite nun). This is not to deny significant differences between the two figures. Bonhoeffer found more attraction in Catholicism than von Hügel did in Lutheranism, which von Hügel reproached for its thinness and 'glaciality' in comparison with the rich spirituality and doctrinal breadth of his Catholic heritage.[51] Nor was von Hügel enamoured with the notion of a suffering God, the concept which was central to Bonhoeffer.[52]

March–April 1939: A troubled Bonhoeffer

It is fully understandable, therefore, that Bonhoeffer would have commended von Hügel to his friends in London as a surrogate Barth to counter the still-prevailing idealism pervading theology (at least in the Anglican Church). There is a very specific and existential reason, however, why he might have felt constrained to do this in March–April 1939. His visit to London was prompted by severe anxieties for the future of the Confessing Church and for himself, and some of his experiences during the visit increased those anxieties still further. As stated earlier, he had been assigned by the leadership of the Confessing Church the task of exploring what place might be found for the Church in the structures of the ecumenical movement. In conjunction with the world conferences of the Life and Work and Faith and Order movements in 1937, at Oxford and Edinburgh, respectively, plans had been laid for the formation of a World Council of Churches. Moreover its constitution had been laid down and agreed at a conference at Utrecht in 1938, a provisional committee appointed, and also a general secretary, the Dutchman Willem Visser't Hooft. But the Confessing Church was in danger of becoming marginalized, if not absent altogether, from this major new initiative. There had been no German delegates at either Oxford or Edinburgh (apart from a tiny, and

---

50. See *The Mystical Element of Religion*, 353–61.
51. See *Essays and Addresses*, 99.
52. Ibid., 167–216.

pro-Nazi, group from the Free Churches) since the German authorities had refused travel permits, and moreover the Confessing Church had resolved not to attend Oxford since representatives from the official Reich Church were to be invited also. Since its formation in 1934 this issue had embroiled the Confessing Church in controversy with the secretariat of Life and Work in Geneva and also with Faith and Order. The Confessing Church maintained that since at the Barmen Synod it had declared itself against the racial and nationalistic heresies of the so-called German Christian Movement, the Confessing Church alone should be recognized as having a rightful place at the ecumenical table.

Bonhoeffer had taken a rigorous line on this since the inception of the Confessing Church in 1934. In 1935 he received an invitation from the noted Anglican theologian Leonard Hodgson, secretary of the Faith and Order movement, to a meeting in Denmark of the committee preparing the 1937 Faith and Order Conference. On learning that Theodor Heckel, head of the foreign relations department of the Reich Church, would also be attending, he refused. If the meeting was to comprise representatives of churches which 'accept our Lord Jesus Christ as God and Saviour', he declared, it would be impossible for a Confessing Church representative to attend, since the Reich Church, as shown by its teachings and practice, did *not* recognize Christ as its head.[53] Rather, the Reich Church government was 'an instrument of the Antichrist' and should be judged accordingly by the ecumenical conference. In a frank exchange of correspondence, Hodgson stated and repeated that according to its statutes Faith and Order was obliged to invite 'all branches of the Christian Church' to the meeting. This of course did not meet Bonhoeffer's claim that the Reich Church was *not* part of the Christian Church. The matter ended in stalemate.

Now, four years after that exchange, the situation had changed somewhat. The Confessing Church leadership, evidently feeling that continuing to make an exclusive claim to ecumenical participation had to be weighed against the dangers of total isolation from the ecumenical movement and the emerging World Council, deputed Bonhoeffer to see if there might at least be *a* place for a Confessing German either as a staff person or a member on one of the governing bodies. Accordingly, while in London Bonhoeffer secured a meeting with Leonard Hodgson in his rooms at Christ Church, Oxford, on 29 March.[54] It was a long, fraught and fruitless meeting in the course of which, Hodgson reported later, Bonhoeffer grew very heated. Hodgson was adamant, his position no different from that of 1935. First, according to the Faith and Order rules, only those churches actually present at the 1937 Edinburgh Faith and Order Conference were entitled to claim a place on its continuation committee. Second, while that committee could co-opt other representatives to attend, this would require the Germans to apply to Faith and Order via a central German body having the confidence of all the 'groups' within

---

53. Keith Clements, *Dietrich Bonhoeffer's Ecumenical Quest* (Geneva: WCC, 2015), 166.
54. Ibid., 195–7. For the Bonhoeffer–Hodgson correspondence see DBWE 15, 154–5, 157–9. See also Bethge, *Dietrich Bonhoeffer*, 641–4.

the German Evangelical Church, and there was not of course any such body in Germany. Hodgson's mind was as far removed as could be imagined from the situation that Bonhoeffer believed the Confessing Church, and he himself, to be in: a battle to the point of suffering for the truth of the gospel, not an academic discussion or a game of inter-church politics. It was not a matter of being fair to all 'groups' but of acknowledging which was the true, as distinct from heretical, church in Germany. Bonhoeffer was yet again meeting a refusal to see the issue as one of truthful witness in Germany. He returned to London dispirited and frustrated. The official ecumenical leadership's stated wish to act 'impartially' was once again simply playing into the hands of the Reich Church. He would no doubt have been even angrier had he known that William Temple, chair of the WCC Provisional Committee, on receiving Hodgson's report on the meeting strongly agreed with the line he had taken. The desire for inclusivity and impartiality at all costs was shielding the ecumenical bodies from taking a *decision* about what was happening to the gospel in Germany. English (or at any rate Anglican) reasonableness and a framework of philosophical idealism were fine when the path to be plotted lay through green pastures and beside still waters. But in 1939 Bonhoeffer and his cohorts in Germany were on a steep and rugged pathway where there were no clear maps to guide, with hazardous ravines to negotiate or leap across, and before long a perilous descent into a valley as dark as death. He was not wanting easy answers but had hoped at least for recognition of the plight of those making the costly witness in Germany. He did not find it in Oxford.

He did find that recognition in his closest English friend, George Bell, to whom he wrote while in London with similar ideas to those he put to Hodgson, and whom he visited at Chichester. Bell was now on the provisional committee of the WCC though no longer with any official standing in Life and Work. But to Bell Bonhoeffer also wanted to unburden himself of his most pressing personal dilemma: whether to leave Germany or not. Bell's wife Henrietta noticed the change in Bonhoeffer since she had seen him during 1933–5: 'He was much quieter, much more serious and labouring under great personal strain. He wanted to stay in his own country … and he wasn't sure of his whole attitude to war.'[55] The only alternative to conscription or conscientious protest would be service outside Germany, or perhaps on behalf of the Confessing Church within the ecumenical movement, or maybe with one of the British missionary societies. But would not this be flight rather than fight? Bell evidently invited him to relax his scruples on this point and, like the good counsellor he was, simply let him talk. Afterwards Bonhoeffer wrote gratefully to the bishop, thanking him 'for the great help you gave me in our talk at Chichester. I do not know what will be the outcome of it all, but it means much to me to realize that you see the great conscientious difficulties with we are faced.'[56] He also found recognition in his unexpected encounter with

---

55. BBC radio interview. See Keith Clements, *Bonhoeffer and Britain* (London: CTBI, 2006), 100.

56. DBWE 15, 160.

Willem Visser't Hooft.[57] Then there was the meeting with Reinhold Niebuhr at St Leonard's on Sea, from which arose the invitation for Bonhoeffer to go to the United States in the summer, a visit which led him into even more heart-searching and his eventual, fateful decision to return to Germany for good.

It was, then, a troubled Bonhoeffer who was in London in March and April 1939, less in need of a comprehensive understanding of the world situation (he knew that well enough already) than of grace in making drastic decisions. Four years earlier in his London vicarage, he had written to his brother Karl-Friedrich on the need for a new Christianity based on the Sermon on the Mount and uncompromising discipleship: 'Things do exist that are worth standing for without compromise. To me it seems that peace and social justice are such things, as is Christ himself.'[58] Now in London again, he was in search of a community which recognized this challenge, and wanted to direct his English friends to listen to one who, from within their own midst, had pointed to the overriding claim of the transcendent God and face the ultimate point, the beyond in the midst, where personal faith and public responsibility meet in the hour of crisis. Besides that, nothing else mattered.

We can therefore readily imagine Bonhoeffer approving of von Hügel's embrace of the whole sweep of human experience and engagement, aesthetic, social and scientific as well as religious, as the domain of faith. Moreover, Bonhoeffer, like von Hügel (and Kierkegaard), knew that this encounter with the ultimate, whenever it takes place in the course of a life, entails *decision*. Indeed, as we have seen, during those fraught months in 1939 Bonhoeffer was already in a very dark valley of inescapable decision. It did not sit easily within the kind of comprehensive, idealistic framework that was still permeating the thinking of what he called the 'Anglo-Saxons'. Von Hügel, Bonhoeffer evidently believed, offered the pragmatic, empirically minded English – apt to be intimidated by the astringencies of Barth – an exposure to the transcendent; or, to use the phrase he was to coin in his prison writings, the Beyond in the midst of our lives.

57. See note 13.
58. DBWE 13, 285.

Chapter 6

BETWEEN A CONFESSING CHURCH AND
CONTEXTUAL ETHICS: BONHOEFFER, THE CRISIS
OF 1934 AND THE CONTINUING ECUMENICAL
QUEST FOR A PUBLIC THEOLOGY

The context—

In September 1934 a very small conference of young British and German theologians, under the leadership of Dietrich Bonhoeffer, met in Bruay-en-Artois, France, to reflect on 'The Task of the Church Today'. This meeting took place very soon after the ecumenical conference on the Danish island of Fanø 24–30 August, at which the Universal Council for Life and Work met concurrently with the Ecumenical Youth Commission. The Fanø conference was a landmark event for the ecumenical movement in its relation to the German Church Struggle, as it was the first significant such meeting since the emergence of the Confessing Church, founded upon the Barmen Theological Declaration in late May that year; the Fanø conference overwhelmingly identified itself with the Confessing Church. It was also at Fanø that Bonhoeffer made his striking appeal for 'the one great Ecumenical Council of the Holy Church of Christ over all the world' to declare against war and to summon the nations of the world to peace.

Bruay: A Youthful Project

Meeting in Paris in early 1934, the Ecumenical Youth Commission, of which Dietrich Bonhoeffer was a member, resolved on holding a conference for young theologians from Germany, France and Britain, to take place in Luxembourg in September that year. Its theme would be 'A Theological Word from the Ecumenical Youth on the Task of the Church Today'. Bonhoeffer was charged with the

Paper presented at the XIth International Bonhoeffer Congress, Sigtuna, Sweden, 27 June–1 July 2012, published in Kirsten Busch Nielsen and Ralf K. Wüstenberg (eds), *A Spoke in the Wheel. The Political in the Theology of Dietrich Bonhoeffer* (Gütersloh: Gütersloher Verlagshaus, 2013), 109–19.

organization, which logistically proved very difficult. Late in the day Luxembourg became impossible as a venue and, by invitation of Bonhoeffer's French friend Pasteur Jean Lasserre, the conference was relocated to Lasserre's parish at Bruay-en-Artois in northern France, just inland from the port of Calais: a small coal mining town marked chiefly by industrial grime and poverty. This change of venue however was only the start of problems. Apart from Lasserre (who only acted as host and took very little part on proceedings) and Bonhoeffer himself, only five participants arrived on the appointed day (4 September): two Germans, two English and the wife of one of the English. To Bonhoeffer's bafflement and extreme annoyance, no French came at all. No wonder Lasserre in later years in some embarrassment described Bruay as having 'failed somewhat'.[1] It would be easy therefore to dismiss such a tiny, four-day gathering and its very brief report written by Bonhoeffer[2] as of little theological or historic significance. But the subject – the task of the church today – had been given an added urgency quite unforeseen when the conference was proposed seven months earlier thanks to the formation of the Confessing Church, and the Fanø conference. While very disappointed in the absence of the French, characteristically, as at Fanø, Bonhoeffer at Bruay was more concerned in having a decisive word said than in how many said it.

He could be sure of the support of all the participants. The two Germans, Winfried Maechler and Jürgen Winterhager, had been among Bonhoeffer's students at Berlin University during 1932-3, and Winterhager was also an active member of the World Alliance for International Friendship through the Churches.[3] Of the English, Trevor Kilborn was an Anglican priest and a travelling secretary of the Student Christian Movement based in London. He had attended the ecumenical youth meeting in Gland, Switzerland, the previous year. His wife Elizabeth was at Bruay as a guest. Cyril Blackman was a Congregational ordinand, at that time studying at Marburg and destined to become a scholar of high repute in New Testament and early church history.[4] Two points should be noted about the participants. First, all had been at Fanø, and conspicuously involved in the youth conference.[5] Kilborn had made a presentation on church–state relations in

---

1. G. B. Kelly, 'Interview with Jean Lasserre', *Union Seminary Quarterly Review* 27 (3 Spring 1972), 157. Lasserre gives an interesting account of Bonhoeffer and the other participants sharing in 'street preaching' in Bruay, but unfortunately – and to his later regret – did not attend any of the actual discussions in the conference.

2. 'Report on the Theological Conference in Bruay-en-Artois, September 15, 1934', DBWE 13, 10–313 (hereinafter 'Bruay Report').

3. Bonhoeffer himself had been a travelling youth secretary of the World Alliance since 1931. The Youth Commission was a joint committee of the World Alliance and the Universal Christian Council for Life and Work, with a shared secretariat in Geneva.

4. Cf. his widely influential *Marcion and His Influence* (London: SPCK, 1948).

5. The Fanø conference (22–29 August 1934) in fact comprised two gatherings: the Universal Christian Council for Life and Work, and the Youth Conference organized by

England; Maechler gave a paper on 'Christian and State according to the Bible'; and Blackman was both involved in the drafting of the youth resolutions and in presenting them to the 'senior' conference of the Council of Life and Work.[6] Second, as well as Bonhoeffer, the two Germans Winterhager and Maechler were competent in English, Winterhager especially so as he had spent two terms at Cambridge; while Blackman, fresh from Marburg, had German. Whatever differences in theological approach and cultural background, therefore, there would have been no real need for the conference to divide into separate language groups for purposes of discussion, and that is important for imagining the dynamic of the meeting.

The message from Bruay?

The 'theological statement' produced by the Bruay conference ran:

> The Church, although it cannot enter into the political struggle in an official capacity ought, however, through its members to study social and political questions with a view to action on their part either individually or in groups. Such an action should be based upon the responsibility of the church members for the social order according to the Will of God. The aim of this action should be building up of a State where there is entire freedom for the Christian life (the guidance of which should clearly be recognised in such Scripture passages as Matthew 5-7, Acts 5:29, etc.). Further there are many ways in which the

---

the Ecumenical Youth Commission. The youth delegates attended a number of the Life and Work sessions and presented their own resolutions there. Bonhoeffer was co-opted to the Life and Work Council at this meeting. See 'Report of the International Youth Conference, held at Fanø (Denmark) August 22-29th, 1934', Fanø Fellowship No. 1 (Geneva Archives Box 432.022). Sections of this report are to be found in DBWE 13, 201-9.

6. Blackman also wrote an informative account, 'The Youth Conference at Fanø', The *Churches in Action* News Letter (Ecumenical Youth Commission, No. 6, November 1934), 7-8, including the perceptive comment:

> The difficult position of our German friends became more and more apparent. Naturally their very presence, the situation in their country being what it is, considerably heightened the interest of the Conference. They were very careful in stating their case and in defending themselves against any possible misrepresentation. A casual observer might have received the impression that the German delegation had set itself to oppose every statement coming from the French and English parties. The falseness of such an impression became obvious as time went on, however. There was no rift, but only an anxious desire to leave no aspect of the situation unnoticed and emphasised. As might have been expected, the German delegation seemed more deeply concerned with the whole problem of the relation of the Church to the State.

Church, *within its own membership*, can and should reproduce the Christian life to-day, e.g., church unity, community living, settlement of disputes between church members without going to law, liberal education. As representing and proclaiming the voice of Christ ever remains the primary task of the Church throughout the world, the Church should not neglect its obligation to point out and to criticize those attainments of human society which are not in accordance with the Will of God as revealed in the Bible.[7] (Emphases original)

Some elementary source-criticism makes quite clear where parts of this statement come from. The first three sentences ('The Church … Acts 5:29 e') reproduce virtually verbatim paragraph (b) of the resolution on church and state from the Fanø youth conference. Commenting on this report, Victoria Barnett is therefore right to say that Bruay was essentially affirmative of Fanø while at the same time, remarkably, carrying no hint either of Bonhoeffer's outspoken presentation at Fanø on the church's calling to peace, or of the strong stand taken by the youth delegates on pacifism, conscientious objection and the universality of the church.[8] Bruay was indeed focusing, as Barnett states, 'on church and state, justice and love'.[9] But there is another element in the Bruay statement, which distinguishes it quite markedly from the Fanø proceedings. The second half of the extract beginning 'Further, there are many ways in which the Church …' provides a list of quite modest but concrete examples of obedient action in Christian community, while the final sentence in indicating the church's obligation to criticize social developments and policies leaves very open just what will need to be said in any particular context. While, therefore, the dramatic post-Barmen, post-Fanø context is very apparent, at Bruay there is a certain change, not in commitment or direction but in application. The high electrical voltage generated at Barmen and Fanø is passing through a step-down transformer in the attempt to provide a current which can be used in the domestic appliances of everyday living, what we might call a contextual ethic of responsibility.

Germans and Anglo-Saxons: One conference, two approaches?

Preceding this theological statement, Bonhoeffer's report on the Bruay conference deals with its background, including the organizational problems, the absence of the French, the participation of the group in Lasserre's in parish mission, and then states,

> The discussions took place on the content of the Christian Gospel and on *the ultimate authority for us Christians in proclaiming the Gospel.*

---

7. Bruay Report, DBWE 13, 313.

8. V. J. Barnett, 'Introduction' to the Bruay Report as first published in Barnett, Kirsten Busch Nielson, Ralf K. Wüstenberg and Jens Zimmermann (eds) *Dietrich Bonhoeffer Jahrbuch 2 2005/2006* (Gütersloh: Gütersloh Verlagshaus, 2005), 89–91.

9. Ibid., 90.

One group affirmed the truth of Article 9 of Dr Oldham's Fanø Theses on Church and State that the essence of the Christian Gospel was the *supremacy of the personal*; that the origin and authority are ultimately to be found in the mind of the Christian community which may or may not be at any given time the organized Christian Church. Another group affirmed the ultimate authority to be the Word of God as revealed in the Old and New Testaments.

Because of these two different affirmations the relations between Church and State were also viewed in different ways.

The first group was inclined to make no final separation between Church and State, since the supremacy of the personal could be concerned in either.

The other group drew a sharp distinction between the Church as really being the living body of Christ (in the full meaning attached to it in the New Testament) and the State as being only God's institution for preserving his fallen creation from chaos.[10] (Emphases original)

It is of course tempting to see these two different approaches as simply representing, on the one hand, the liberal pragmatism we might expect from the English, and on the other hand the more rigorously Lutheran or Confessing stance of Bonhoeffer and his students – and indeed the second approach strongly echoes the paper presented by Maechler at Fanø.[11] If we admit as much, then for that reason alone Bruay is interesting as a microcosm of encounter between the entire thought-worlds of Anglo-Saxon and Continental Protestantism. But there is more to it than that. The first group, we note, is affirming what J. H. Oldham, the leading British ecumenist and social ethicist,[12] had presented at Fanø in the ninth of his theses on 'Church and State'.[13] Oldham's thesis reads in full:

The foremost task of the Church in the present historical situation is, in the light and in the power of faith in God and the Father of our Lord Jesus Christ, who calls us through his living Word to a life in personal responsibility, to promote and to proclaim unremittingly the *supremacy* [*Vorrang*] *of the personal*.[14] (Emphases in original)

We should note first of all that Oldham, no less than the Barmen Declaration, locates the authority in Jesus Christ as Word of God, and the authorization of

---

10. Bruay Report, 312.

11. Maechler's paper is summarized in the Fanø Report (see n.5), 5–6, based on notes taken by Dorothy Watson (England); in Geneva Archives Box 4232.003.

12. On Oldham, see Keith Clements, *Faith on the Frontier: A Life of J.H. Oldham* (Edinburgh: T&T Clark; Geneva: WCC, 1999).

13. Published as J. H. Oldham, 'Die Kirche und der Staat', in *Die Kirche und das Staatsproblem in der Gegenwart* (Geneva: Forschungsabteilung des Ökumenisches Rates für Praktisches Christentum, 1935), 214–16. English translation here by K. Clements.

14. Ibid., 215.

faith as lying in the call of that Word. Second, Oldham's term 'a life in personal responsibility' [in German *zu einem Leben in persönlicher Verantwortung*] has a quite specific reference. Victoria Barnett rightly paraphrases Oldham's term 'the supremacy of the personal' as 'the centrality of personal faith as the basis for Christian community and the preaching of the Gospel'. But it would be misleading to see Oldham's emphasis on 'the personal' as meaning a purely private, individual inwardness in distinction from the public social and political sphere. It is personal *responsibility* (*Verantwortung*) which Oldham emphasizes, and by this he means not an individual's private subjectivity of faith or inward feeling but the answerability of a person to another person – a highly social concept. For the past three years or more, Oldham had been drawing upon a whole range of continental thinkers who were affirming human sociality and encounter, the significance of 'the Other': they included Martin Buber and Emil Brunner but above all the philosopher Eberhard Grisebach.[15] For Grisebach, real existence lay not in abstract ethical thought, nor in inwardness, nor in scientific mastery of the world around us, but in the challenging encounters with other persons: 'Only in this world of the contradiction of living persons is there real responsibility'[16] is Oldham's summary of Grisebach. Oldham therefore is not saying that the personal is one area of life set over against other realms such as the political, but that it is the essential component of a truly human existence in *every* realm of life: state, no less than church.[17] I would therefore hesitate to say, with Barnett, that the group following this view would allow the church to 'yield to the state's authority on "social" and worldly issues'.[18]

Confessing and responsibility: The ecumenical calling

At Bruay there were indeed two rather different approaches to understanding the relation between church and state: on the one hand the continental confessional approach which, sharpened immeasurably by Barmen, wished to affirm on the basis of the ultimate authority being the Word of God in Scripture the utterly distinct nature of the church as the living body of Christ, as against the state which at most was God's preservative against chaos; on the other hand the Oldham line which was not in fact a simple 'Anglo-Saxon' one but was informed by much continental personalist thought, of a common calling to responsibility in both

---

15. See Clements, *Faith on the Frontier*, 270–9. Grisebach's *Gegenwart* (1928) made an especial impact on Oldham.

16. J. H. Oldham, 'The Dilemma of Western Civilisation', *Student World* 25, no. 3 (3rd Quarter 1932), 193.

17. In fact Oldham's tenth Fanø thesis emphasizes that witness to the 'supremacy of the personal' has to acknowledge (without being overridden by) such factors as economic conditions (as noted by Marxism), a biological understanding of life and the differences between group and individual relations in political life.

18. Barnett, 'Introduction', 91.

church and state. But perhaps the most significant statement in the whole of Bonhoeffer's Bruay report is the remark,

> These different views did not represent final differences as between the groups, since individual members found a measure of agreement although they could not find adequate language to express that agreement fully.

This admission of need to find the underlying agreement is arguably the real significance of Bruay, and in retrospect we can place the Bruay discussion on two major trajectories of thought.

The first trajectory is that followed by ecumenical social thought leading up to the landmark 1937 Oxford Conference on Church, Community and State; and thence, following the interruption of the Second World War, to the inauguration of the World Council of Churches (WCC) and the development of its early programmes on church and society. At Oxford 1937 Oldham was the pre-eminent influence, and even into old age his thought still carried weight. Oxford 1937 was, one could almost say, a struggle with the Bruay questions writ large, although for well-known reasons there were hardly any Germans present. In its section on 'The Church and Community' the Oxford report at one point virtually repeats the options described at Bruay – with some added.[19] In 1948, the newly formed WCC adopted the term 'The Responsible Society' to describe the concept of a right ordering of society, and it was Oldham who suggested this phraseology to W. A. Visser't Hooft, first general secretary of the WCC.[20] It remained the key ecumenical term effectively till the fourth assembly at Uppsala in 1968 (or, more precisely, until the 1966 Geneva conference on 'Christians in the Technical and Social Revolutions of Our Time') when 'revolution' and 'rapid social change' became the dominant terms. The notion of the state as primarily God's last bastion against chaos has not by and large been a serious player in ecumenical discussion. What *has* become more of a challenge since 1945 is the concept of a confessing church, and the recognition of certain major social ethical issues presenting a *status confessionis*: most notably, from the 1970s onwards, racism, nuclear warfare and, more recently, the global market economy.[21]

The second trajectory is that of Bonhoeffer himself. He was evidently concerned to keep open the issue between the two approaches represented at Bruay and to search for a more basic and unitive perspective. He certainly was not happy with a sheer polarization between church and state as unrelated areas of Christian responsibility. In the Bruay resolution and especially its final sentence – on the

---

19. J. H. Oldham (ed.) *The Churches Survey Their Task: The Report of the Conference at Oxford, July 1937, on Church, Community and State* (London: George Allen and Unwin, 1937), 237.

20. W. A. Visser't Hooft, *Memoirs* (Geneva: WCC, 1987), 205.

21. Keith Clements, 'Barmen and the Ecumenical Movement', *Ecumenical Review* 61, no. 1 (March 2009), 6–16. For a general survey and discussion of 'confessing' situations see R. W. Bertram, *A Time for Confessing* (Grand Rapids, MI: Eerdmans, 2008).

need for a critical examination of features of human society not in accord with the Will of God as revealed in the Bible – we can recognize the one who the previous year in his Berlin paper 'The Church and the Jewish Question', had pointed to the calling of the church to question policies of the state, and possibly even to 'put a spoke in the wheel'. But the whole tenor of his Bruay report can be seen as also pointing forwards, through *Discipleship* towards *Ethics* and the prison writings. In the later chapters of *Discipleship* we see affirmed both the distinctiveness of the church as a community and – especially in the final chapter 'The Image of Christ' – the declaration that those who are 'in Christ' are thereby bound in his solidarity with the needs of all people and especially those who suffer.[22] In *Ethics* we see a determined attack on 'two realms' thinking, 'There are not two realities, *but only one reality*, and that is God's reality revealed in Christ in the reality of the world.'[23] There is a resonance here with the Oldhamite refusal to make a final separation between church and state since in both the 'supremacy of the personal' must be maintained, although of course in Bonhoeffer there is a rather different theological rationale. But notice, too, how much effort Bonhoeffer in *Ethics* devotes to 'The Structure of Responsible Life', 'The Place of Responsibility', 'Love and Responsibility'.[24] 'The structure of responsible life is determined in a twofold manner, namely, by life's bond to human beings and to God, and by the freedom of one's own life. Without this bond and without this freedom there can be no responsibility.'[25] Therewith Bonhoeffer proceeds to give Christological grounding to responsibility with his concept of *Stellvertretung*, vicarious representative action, of which the incarnate Christ is the enabler and supreme exemplar.[26] Equally, both church and government, along with work and marriage, are identified as 'divine mandates', divinely imposed tasks 'through Christ, toward Christ, and in Christ'.[27] One could say that all along the line Bonhoeffer was taking up the unitive Oldhamite approach but giving it a Christological framework. Moreover as time went on Bonhoeffer was also seeing the danger of a two-realms mentality arising even out of a confessing church, as we see in the prison writings. The Confessing Church was essential, and no one was more committed to it than Bonhoeffer. Yet, he writes in his *Outline for a Book*: 'Confessing Church: revelation theology; a *dos moi pou stō* standing against the world … Generally in the Confessing Church: Standing up for the "cause" and so on, but little personal faith in Christ.'[28]

Such a church, Bonhoeffer is saying, is defending a great principle against the totalitarian state but is doing little to help people in their actual faith and moreover their actual *living* day by day in the world. It will have to teach, but more

22. DBWE 4, 285.
23. DBWE 6, 58.
24. Ibid., 246–98.
25. Ibid., 257.
26. See Chapters 1 and 2.
27. DBWE 6, 69.
28. DBWE 8, 501.

importantly learn for itself, what it means to live in 'moderation, authenticity, trust, steadfastness, patience, discipline, humility, modesty, contentment'.[29] Or, we might say: less of the rhetoric and more of actually helping other people. I would like to juxtapose with Bonhoeffer's words here what was written sometime later in a commentary on the Letter of James and in particular the letter's final verses which speak about bringing back a wandering sinner (James 5:19–20)

The comment reads:

> What a beautiful passage this is at the end! It conjures up the picture of the Church as a band of brethren who really care for one another and bear one another's burdens. Not the glorious company of the Apostles: not a company that professes to be the Body of Christ or claims many gifts of the Spirit; not perhaps a church whose meetings attracted many in from the street or struck intellectuals as having much significance. But surely a body of people who showed a moving concern for one another in life's ups and downs.

If those words resonate with what the Bruay statement says about the calling of the church both to critique society and, humbly, to manifest true community among its own membership that may not be accidental, since the writer is Cyril Blackman.[30] Bruay had recognized the need for community living and concrete ethical guidance in all spheres of life, as well as the distinctness of the church as a body placed under the authoritative Word of God. It is pertinent to ask what part the very physical context of Bruay, its poverty and deprivation, and the experience of preaching in its grimy streets – so different from the conferences rooms, sand-dunes and beach-huts of Fanø! – may have played here. Shortly after the conference Bonhoeffer wrote to his Swiss friend Erwin Sutz: 'It was the first time I have seen a *totally* working-class congregation. The surrounding area with war-memorial tourist sites and cemeteries and the terrible poverty of these mining towns make a dark background for preaching the gospel.'[31]

So too Bonhoeffer in prison looks not only for a church courageous enough to say 'no' to the false claims of the powers of this world but for a church humble enough itself to learn, and then to teach – and for its members to practise – forms of obedience in their particular worldly contexts. The church is always situated in the creative tension between being a confessing community and a contextual experiment of responsibility. In ecumenical terminology, this is expressed as the relation between ecclesiology and ethics, to which the WCC gave renewed attention from 1994 onwards. Highly important here have been the WCC's 1993 text *Costly Unity: Koinonia, Justice, Peace and Creation*,[32] and the responses to that text in

---

29. Ibid., 503.
30. E. C. Blackman, *The Epistle of James: Introduction and Commentary* (London: SCM Press, 1957), 159–60.
31. Letter of 11.09.34, DBWE 13 217.
32. T. F. Best and W. Granberg-Michaelson (eds) (Geneva: WCC Units I and II, 1993).

the report *Costly Commitment*,[33] and the summary of much of the study process *Ecclesiology and Ethics* (1997).[34] We may note the Bonhoefferian echoes in both titles, and also the leading role in this study process of Bonhoeffer scholar Larry Rasmussen who was co-moderator of the WCC programme unit on Justice, Peace and Creation. In his chapter in *Costly Commitment* he summarizes the testing questions that need to be put to each church in every age and in every context: 'What is the moral substance of the church and how does it play out as the means of moral formation of members and their worlds? How does it fashion character and conduct in accord with the claims and nature of the church? What concretely is being embodied and communicated, from a moral point of view, by church practices?'[35]

Those sorts of questions no less have to be put to a confessing church, which is not absolved of its ethical responsibility simply by declaring itself to be on the side of the angels against the totalitarian state, or the racist regime, or nuclear weaponry, or the global market economy. For example, to declare the global economy a *status confessionis* is but the beginning of responsibility.[36] It requires something to be done about it, and not just at the church's corporate level in its engagement with governments, multinational companies and financial institutions but at the level of individual citizen and church member, and in their being *enabled* so to act. In Bonhoeffer's words in prison, 'The church must participate in the worldly tasks of life in the community – not dominating but helping and serving. It must tell people in every calling [*Beruf*] what a life with Christ means, what it means "to be there for others."'[37]

The relationship between being the church distinctively under the Word of God and the defining of ethical responsibility within society as a whole will never be easy. At Bruay Bonhoeffer and his young colleagues effectively identified the ecumenical task for the coming decades right down to today: to find language adequate to express what is intuitively felt must be a fundamental agreement between those who start with the distinct nature of the church in contrast to the state and world in general, and those who start with a sense of human responsibility in both spheres. The question is: does Bonhoeffer's own developing theology, setting everything within a Christological framework, of overcoming thinking in two realms, of all life structured for responsibility and of divine mandates covering responsibilities in government as well as in church help us find that essential agreement and the language within which to express it?

33. T. F. Best and M. Robra (eds) (Geneva: WCC Units I and III, 1995).

34. T. F. Best and M. Robra (eds), *Ecclesiology and Ethics: Ecumenical Engagement, Moral Formation and the Nature of the Church* (Geneva: WCC, 1997).

35. Larry Rasmussen, 'Moral Community and Moral Formation', in *Costly Commitment* (see n.33), 60.

36. As an example of an attempt to move from a 'confessing' to a concrete ethical stance see P. Pavlovic (ed.), *Poverty, Wealth and Ecology in Europe: Call for Climate Justice* (Brussels: Church and Society Commission of Conference of European Churches, 2011), a report arising out of dialogue between the Latin American Council of Churches and the Conference of European Churches as a contribution to the Global Ecumenical Discussion.

37. DBWE 13, 503.

Chapter 7

'WHAT DOES IT MEAN TO TELL THE TRUTH?' THE CHURCH AND THE ALLEGATION OF 2015 AGAINST BISHOP GEORGE BELL IN THE LIGHT OF BONHOEFFER'S 1943 PRISON ESSAY

In late 1943, during his confinement in Tegel prison, Dietrich Bonhoeffer was working on an essay, 'What Does It Mean to Tell the Truth?'[1] That question is of course a universally relevant one for humanity, and from his personal situation as a prisoner preparing to face interrogation by the Gestapo, Bonhoeffer advances his enquiry into the different levels and contexts in which the question of truth-telling arises, and the varied relationships, responsibilities and limitations which have to be recognized as the realities of human life. This chapter draws upon some of the insights into the essay while examining a recent British episode where the issue of public truth-telling came to the fore. With tragic irony, this concerned allegations against Bonhoeffer's closest English friend, Bishop George Bell.

George Bell and the allegation against him

George Bell (1883–1958) needs little introduction to any who know the Bonhoeffer story. He was the Anglican bishop of Chichester from 1929 till the year he died, 1958. A leader of the ecumenical movement in the 1930s, he was the unswerving advocate of the German Confessing Church, a commitment embodied in his friendship with Dietrich Bonhoeffer to whom he became a trusted confidante. In England he worked tirelessly for 'non-Aryan' and other refugees from Nazi Germany. During the Second World War he spoke out courageously against the area bombing of civilian populations by the Allies. In 1942 he and Bonhoeffer had their remarkable clandestine meeting in neutral Sweden at which Bonhoeffer on behalf of the German resistance gave Bell full details of the conspiracy against Hitler, to be passed to the British government; and in April 1945 Bonhoeffer's last recorded words before being taken to Flossenbürg Concentration Camp for

---

Paper presented at the XIIIth International Bonhoeffer Congress, Stellenbosch, South Africa, 19–23 January 2020.

1. DBWE 16, 601–8.

trial and execution included a personal message for Bell, a message of gratitude and hope. Bell was a founding figure of the World Council of Churches and after the war was foremost in the work of reconciliation. After his death he was accorded virtual sainthood within the Anglican Communion, with his own day of remembrance in the church calendar, and his name has been revered throughout the worldwide ecumenical family. His life is summed up in the inscription on his memorial tablet in Chichester Cathedral: A TRUE PASTOR, POET AND PATRON OF THE ARTS, CHAMPION OF THE OPPRESSED, AND TIRELESS WORKER FOR CHRISTIAN UNITY.

It was therefore a shock on 23 October 2015 to read in the English press headlines such as 'Eminent bishop was paedophile, admits Church'.[2] The Church of England Media Centre had the previous day released a statement to the effect that the present bishop of Chichester, Dr Martin Warner, had made a public apology to someone who had alleged that they had been sexually abused over a period of time in the 1940s and 1950s, by George Bell. In his statement the bishop said, 'We face with shame the story of abuse of a child.' It transpired that a sum of money had been paid to the complainant by the Church. Overnight, the reputation of George Bell as a figure of courage and integrity became that of a child-molesting monster, with the church hierarchy and officialdom taking immediate steps to erase his image from public esteem: literally so, insofar as his portrait was removed from Chichester City council chamber; George Bell House, a small conference centre close by the cathedral, was no longer so named, likewise the George Bell School in Chichester. Guides conducting visitors around the cathedral received instructions that those viewing Bell's memorial tablet were to be assured that the Church of England took child abuse with the utmost seriousness. It was even being mooted that Bell's name might be removed from the Church of England's liturgical commemoration of venerated figures.

At this point it must be recognized that in the background to such reactions is the shameful record of abuse of minors within churches of all traditions that is only now coming into the full light of day, in the Church of England as in other churches: a disgrace matched only by the habitual attempts of church authorities to cover up such crimes. Moreover, the diocese of Chichester had itself been found gravely at fault in this respect over episodes involving even senior clergy from the 1970s onwards. The immediate impression created by the church's announcement was that the Bell case was yet another incident in that dark history but one which was at least being faced publicly and with due, if belated, contrition by the church.

This view of the matter, however, was challenged almost immediately, and not only by those who instinctively believed that all they knew of Bell's character rendered him most unlikely to have perpetrated such abuse. The church's announcement was subjected to intense scrutiny by those versed in legal, historical and ethical issues. While the church authorities had claimed that the Safeguarding Committee's investigation had been thorough and objective, some of the church's

---

2. *Times*, 23 October 2015.

public pronouncements were to say the least ill-considered: for example, the statement of 22 October saying that the Sussex Police had confirmed in 2013 that 'the information obtained "would have justified, had he still been alive, Bishop Bell's arrest and interview, on suspicion of serious sexual offences"'. This was highly misleading, since it is standard police procedure to question anyone against whom allegations are made, but without prejudice to any further process which would be a matter not for the police but for the Crown Prosecution Service. The church seemed content to operate with a peculiar mix of bold public assertion and studied secrecy. For a while even the gender of the claimant was not stated, still less was any indication given of the nature of the evidence on which the Safeguarding Group's decision was based. While Bishop Warner had stated that the investigation into the reliability of the complainant's testimony had been undertaken by 'people who command the respect of all parties' no information was given as to who these people or parties were. As Judge Alan Pardoe stated in a letter to the *Church Times*, 'It is incomprehensible why the Church in its Media Centre's statement has almost casually lent its authority to the utter destruction of the reputation of George Bell, arguably one of the greatest bishops of the Church of England.'[3] Another letter to the *Church Times*, by the Cambridge theologian Dr Jeremy Morris and other concerned academics, challenged the church's secretiveness, which was all the more surprising given that the church had previously been rightly accused of cover-ups: 'The Church's only defence of this position is "You must trust us".'[4] The letter's suggestion that at least some of the actual evidence, suitably redacted to preserve the anonymity of the claimant, should be made public was ignored.

What did eventually emerge was that the claimant was a woman, now in her seventies, to be known by the pseudonym 'Carol'; that her testimony of what had allegedly taken place over sixty years earlier, and totally uncorroborated, was the only evidence on which the church's decision was based; and apparently that no enquiries had been made of any people still living who had been contemporaries of the alleged events in Chichester and who had known Bell. Moreover, it was found that the group investigating the allegations did not include anyone appointed to represent the interests of Bell or his family (none of whose surviving members had been informed of the allegations until the press statement was released).

In response to this situation, the George Bell Group was formed, including senior lawyers, academics, clergy, parliamentarians and journalists. It was coordinated by Dr Andrew Chandler, the modern church historian and greatest present-day authority on Bell, himself based in Chichester, and well-known in Bonhoeffer study circles, whose new biography of Bell was going to press just when the church's announcement was made.[5] I was pleased to be a member of the Group, and was impressed not just by the serious concern of such a wide range of people on behalf

---

3. Letter, *Church Times*, 13 November 2015.
4. Letter, *Church Times*, 20 November 2015.
5. See Andrew Chandler, *George Bell, Bishop of Chichester: Church, State and Resistance in the Age of Dictatorship* (Grand Rapids, MI: Eerdmans, 2016).

of the memory of Bell but above all by the professionalism of the legal experts who scrutinized objectively and forensically the statements and actions of the Church.[6] We were not seeking at all costs to safeguard Bell's reputation as a 'saint' but to ensure that a proper regard for truth and justice was being observed. Nor were we in any doubt as to the seriousness of the accusation against Bell, and of the whole issue of abuse within the Church as in society as a whole. (Speaking for myself, I can say that some thirty-five years ago my wife and I, with other parents, had to take concerted action over perceived dangers to our children in a church institution, and encountered the inertia of the church authorities who were in evident denial about what was taking place.) The Bell Group met at regular intervals over the four years from late 2015. As well as our meetings in London, the work involved a good deal of advocacy in widening the public support for Bell's case, both in the UK and abroad, for example, by letters to the press and recruiting signatories, and not least informing members of the International Bonhoeffer Society worldwide. Not everyone was as concerned as we were, and on one occasion a member of the Group was told by one church official that as we had no connexion either with Bell or the complainant, it was none of our business – an astonishing view to be voiced in a democratic society under the rule of law where any apparent miscarriage of justice is surely a legitimate concern of any citizen. I myself believed moreover that a common loyalty to both Bell and his German friend Bonhoeffer, and what they had stood for together, needed to be energized here. That Bell, who in his lifetime had laboured so selflessly for victims of injustice, should have his own claim on justice treated so casually would surely have angered Bonhoeffer.

In the days following the Church statement in October 2015, the official wall of secretiveness did not prevent further puzzling features from emerging. For example, Carol and her solicitor made several statements to the media in the Chichester area giving some details of the abuse she claimed to have suffered. These appeared to be inconsistent both with each other and with what was known of the domestic arrangements and physical layout of the bishop's palace at the time. In this regard a serious failing in the view of the Bell Group was that no attempt had been made to consult the person who knew more than anyone else still living of life in the Bell household, namely his chaplain at the time, Adrian Carey.[7] Carey was utterly certain that what Carol described in her statements simply could not have happened in the way she described, given how the bishop's household and office, for both of which he was doorkeeper, were run.

Meanwhile confusion continued on the status and exact meaning of the church's initial announcements. It was never clear whether the sum (£16,800) paid to the claimant was to be regarded as compensation for the alleged abuse or for the fact that, as she claimed, Dr Warner's immediate predecessor as bishop of Chichester

---

6. In particular, Mr Desmond Browne, Queen's Council, and Judge Alan Pardoe.

7. Carey died in July 2017, aged ninety-six. He had been able to make a testimony earlier that year, in regard to the allegation against Bell.

had not taken adequate action when the allegations had first been made several years earlier. Then on the one hand the Bishop of Durham on behalf of the Church's Safeguarding Committee told the House of Lords in January 2016 that if their lordships read very carefully what had been put out 'they will see that there has been no declaration that we are **convinced** that this [abuse] took place' (emphasis original). On the other hand the Archbishop of Canterbury Dr Justin Welby in a BBC local radio broadcast on Good Friday, 25 March 2016, defended the church's action, stating, 'it seemed clear to us after *a very thorough investigation* that that [action] was correct and so we paid compensation and gave a profound and deeply felt apology' (my emphases). It was evident to the George Bell Group that only confusion and unwarranted statements about Bell were abroad, and therefore the Group took the lead in calling for an independent review of how the church had dealt with the case. A petition, launched in 2016 (independently of the George Bell Group), acquired over 2,000 signatories in the UK and abroad. Eventually, in November 2016, the Church of England announced the commissioning of an independent review to be undertaken by a senior barrister, Lord Alex Carlile QC (Queen's Counsel), a former Liberal Democrat member of the House of Commons and now a member of the House of Lords. His investigation occupied the best part of a year and included interviews with all parties in the investigation including the claimant Carol herself, Archbishop Welby, Bishop Warner of Chichester and others including Bell's chaplain Adrian Carey, as well as receiving information from other quarters.

The 'Carlile Report, published in December 2017,[8] ran to seventy-four pages and constituted a severe criticism of the whole process employed by the church and its Safeguarding Team. It catalogued shortcomings varying from the failure to seek evidence from such as Adrian Carey, or to contact Bell's surviving family members and others who could have been key witnesses of events sixty and more years ago,[9] to an apparent failure even to maintain consistent attendance at meetings

---

8. 'Bishop George Bell. The Independent Review by Lord Carlile of Berriew, CBE, QC.' Published 15 December 2017. The Review is accessible online by link at the George Bell Group website www.georgebellgroup.org/.

9. Twice, former boy choristers of Chichester cathedral wrote to the *Times* (6 November 2015, 22 January 2018) protesting at the allegations against Bishop Bell whom as children they had known, admired and revered. A woman ('Pauline') whose adoptive mother had worked as a cook in the Bishop's Palace when she herself was a young child in the 1940s, and was now living in the United States, wrote to Carlile and met with him while visiting the UK, conveying a wholly positive recollection of Bell and his attitudes to children: she had herself no recollection of 'Carol'. Carlile makes the point that while these observations cannot in themselves be said to *contradict* Carol's claims, if the Safeguarding Group investigators had known of them a more cautionary approach to her testimony might have been taken. There were also at the time many refugee children of the *Kindertransport* from Nazi Europe, housed around the palace at Chichester. No suggestion of improper behaviour has emanated from that quarter.

of the core Safeguarding Team, together with the making of misleading claims to confirmation by psychological experts as to the reliability of Carol as a witness (in fact Carlile discovered that the credentials and opinions of those who encouraged credence to Carol's story had *not* been examined impartially). Most seriously of all, the process was 'a rush to judgement' violating the most basic principle of English law, namely the presumption of innocence of the accused until proved guilty. Moreover, Carlile was astonished that if the Church was indeed hesitant about explicitly affirming Bell's guilt, full confidentiality had not been applied to the case. 'For Bishop Bell's reputation to be catastrophically affected in the way that occurred was just wrong.'[10]

In short, the church's treatment of the Bell case was exposed as wrong on two levels: first, the quality of the investigation itself; second, those statements by the church media office and the church hierarchy which conveyed an impression of certainty not justified by the actual findings. While it was not within Carlile's brief in his report to comment on the truthfulness or otherwise of the claimant's allegations, and therewith the guilt or innocence of Bell, elsewhere he has made it clear that in his view the charges should not have been brought, that Bell should be exonerated and his reputation restored. That restoration has to a great extent now been effected in the public mind. The Archbishop of Canterbury, however, while admitting that lessons had been learned about the process of investigation, and offering an apology to Bell's surviving family member, did not retract his view that the investigation had been serious and thorough, and maintained that 'a significant cloud' was left over Bell's name. In a letter to a member of the Bell Group the archbishop said he supported the statement of Bishop Warner in response to the Carlile Report, that 'we cannot favour the famous against the unknown; both deserve respect'.[11]

With that, surely no one would disagree. But it is hard to imagine how simply calling for justice – a fair hearing – for Bell was in any sense a 'favouring' of him.[12]

'What does it mean to tell the truth?' Bonhoeffer's essay

Though short (in fact incomplete in the version that has survived), Bonhoeffer's essay is swift-moving and very compact in its argument, and full justice cannot be done to it here. Does truth-telling mean simply saying 'What is strictly in accordance with the facts?' No, says Bonhoeffer, the precise nature of truthfulness

---

10. Carlile Report, 68, para. 268.
11. Letter to Keith Clements, 19 January 2018.
12. On 29 January 2018 it was announced that a second allegation against Bell had been made and would be investigated. The Safeguarding Team at first appointed a person to the committee to represent the Bell family's interests but without consultation with the family. At the request of the family Douglas Browne QC (a member of the George Bell Group) was appointed instead. The Safeguarding Team soon decided the allegation was without foundation.

depends on the conditions in which the discourse takes place, and especially on the status and inter-relationships of those who are speaking and listening. We have to recognize the several levels and circles on and in which we as humans live out our relationships, and the realities *and boundaries* that exist, if we are to speak and act truthfully. Conscious of this, Bonhoeffer warns against 'the increasing profligacy of public discourse' in the media: 'Chatter has replaced authentic words.'[13]

Bonhoeffer states that truth requires insight into what it means to be truly responsible to others and to God in specific and concrete instances of life. In the face of God who is not an abstract general principle but is the living God, who in Jesus came into the world, the requirement is 'how to bring into effect in my concrete life, with its manifold relationships, the truthful speech I owe to God'.[14] Echoing much of what he had written in his *Ethics* about *reality* he states that truthful speech is that which accords with the reality of the situation, first of all the human reality of relationships and ultimately the living God who 'has placed me in a life that is fully alive and within this life demands my service'.[15]

On the one hand Bonhoeffer considers the situation of someone who is in a highly vulnerable position, under severe pressure to speak in response to sharp and intimidating questions from people in authority, such as a child who at school is asked by his teacher in front of the class if his father often comes home drunk. Even if this is factually the case the child denies it. This is the situation of one who is weak and vulnerable in the face of power and authority. But no less Bonhoeffer addresses the matter of the authority of the one in power. The teacher, says Bonhoeffer, has put the child in an impossible position by requiring him to speak publicly about matters which belong within the circle of the family, not the school. In lying, the child 'acted rightly according to the measure of his perception. Yet it is the teacher alone who is guilty of the lie.'[16] He has ridden roughshod over the boundaries that must be observed in truthful discourse, which is always discourse not just about certain things but between persons. It is the teacher's question that is untruthful, in failing to observe the proper boundary of authentic discourse between teacher and child, a boundary which belongs to the reality of life as willed by God. Here Bonhoeffer is exposing the sin of *presumption*, the attitude which, based upon 'freedom of speech' as an absolute value in itself, assumes the right to speak to or about people without regard to their circumstances. Crucial for Bonhoeffer here is his concept of *authorization*, as distinct from 'authority':

> Who or what authorizes or calls on me to speak? Whoever speaks without authorization or without being called upon is a windbag [*Schwätzer*] ... The claim that you are also allowed to say what you are thinking does not in itself authorize you to do so. Speaking includes the authorization and call given to the

---

13. 'What Does It Mean to Tell the Truth?', 605.
14. Ibid., 602.
15. Ibid., 603.
16. Ibid., 606.

other person. ... The justification for speech always lies within the boundaries of the concrete office that I fill. If these boundaries are crossed, the word becomes intrusive, arrogant, and, whether scolding or praising, harmful.[17]

Bonhoeffer's clear distinction between 'authority' and 'authorization' was of course immensely significant for life in the totalitarian context of his time. In that context, authority had become virtually synonymous with the immediate exercise of power over others and so provided its own authorization. For Bonhoeffer, authorization comes through the awareness that all human speaking must reflect the way in which God speaks: God the ultimate authority, the Creator in whom all human life is grounded, whose word in Jesus Christ is the ultimately and wholly true speech, the word of his love. That distinction however is valid and pertinent for all situations. 'Speaking,' says Bonhoeffer, 'includes the authorization and call given to the other person.' Bonhoeffer typically sees human life, reflecting the image of its Creator, as relational; and therewith all truthful speaking is dialogical. Whoever, in their zeal for the 'truth' come what may, does not recognize this, 'destroys the living truth between persons'.[18] We cannot speak justly about another person without acknowledging *that person's* calling to address *us* out of his or her situation especially if that situation is one of weakness and vulnerability. We might add, too, that the over-readiness to expose and accuse, whether through a zeal for righteousness or an unremitting cynicism about human nature at large, is corrosive of that degree of trust which is foundational for any form of human society.

Sadly, the behaviour of the church to the long-deceased Bell was a prime case of presumption by an institution disregarding the reality of the situation, and the boundary to be respected. In this case the reality was of one who, long dead, was in the ultimate vulnerability of not being able to speak for himself, and for whom no representation on his behalf was invited onto the investigating committee. In effect the church assumed the right to speak as an authority without the authorization of Bell himself, so denying what was always central to Bonhoeffer, the innate, God-given relationality of human life; or, if one prefers apostolic authorization, 'Let all of us speak the truth to our neighbours, for we are members of one another' (Ephesians 4:25). Or, as the Carlile Report states, 'the church feeling that it should be both supportive of the complainant and transparent in its dealings, failed to engage in a process which would also give proper consideration to the rights of the bishop. Such rights should not be treated as having been extinguished by death'. The church had crossed a clear boundary. Instead of an authorized and authorizing dialogue, for the sake of so-called transparency the church launched into a self-justifying monologue which damaged its credibility.

In the opinion of the Carlile Report, the church's rush to judgment was motivated by a desire to enhance the public image of the church as implementing a rigorous, transparent zero-tolerance policy towards child abuse. The hasty, severely flawed

---

17. Ibid., 608.
18. Ibid., 604.

investigation of the Bell case by the church authorities, and, no less, their slipshod and confusing public statements about it, illustrate all too well how prescient for our digital age was Bonhoeffer's comment in his prison essay. To repeat, 'As a result of the increasing profligacy of public discourse in the newspapers and the radio, the nature and limits of different words are no longer clearly perceived ... Chatter has replaced authentic words. Words no longer have any weight. There is too much talking.'[19] In the Bell case, chatter replaced authentic words, and the drive to be transparent resulted in the darkening of counsel. It can now be reported, however, that in a more recent public statement on 17 November 2021, Archbishop Justin Welby retracted, and apologized for, his remark made in 2019 that a significant cloud remains over Bell's name: 'What I say today that is new and should have been said earlier is this: I do not consider there to be a "significant cloud" over Bishop Bell's name. Previously I refused to retract that statement and I was wrong to do so.'[20]

Churches of course are not the only institutions susceptible to self-serving reactions and accusations.[21] What does it mean to tell the truth? In the digital age especially, when it is ever easier to pour forth words into the public arena, powerful corporations (no less than church bodies) must be held to account especially as regards their recourse to litigation employed more for the sake of their public image than respect for truth. Bonhoeffer alerts us to the proper boundaries and procedures that must be observed to safeguard human life against presumption, intrusion and unauthorized speaking, and to promote truthful speaking in our communities. As he says, there must be recognition that 'speaking itself stands under certain conditions, that it does not accompany the natural course of one's life in a perpetual flow but has its own place, time, and mission, and therewith its limits.'[22] Or, one might say, in the face of the ultimate authority of the transcendent God there must be a reverence for truth which does not by default submit to the immanent interests of the institution, whether secular or religious.

---

19. Ibid., 605.
20. *Church Times*, 17 November 2021 (online).
21. One thinks, for example, of the recent long-running case in the UK, of the Post Office litigation against local postmasters and postmistresses for alleged fraud, financial theft and false accounting, pursued despite all the evidence that a faulty computer system was largely to blame. Eventually in 2019 the Post Office agreed to pay compensation to the victims of this miscarriage of justice. The judge in charge of the first High Court hearing on behalf of the staff stated that the Post Office had pursued its litigation 'with impunity and oppressively', presenting misleading evidence '*slanted more towards public relations consumption than factual accuracy*' (my emphases). For the full judgment see the website www.judiciary.uk Bates v. Post Office.
22. 'What Does It Mean to Tell the Truth?', 605.

Part III

PEACE, COMMUNITY AND RECONCILIATION: THE COSTLY WAY

Chapter 8

FROM EAST AND WEST, FROM NORTH AND SOUTH: THE GOSPEL SUBVERTING TRIBALISM

And they shall come from the east, and from the west, and from the north, and from the south, and shall sit down in the kingdom of God.

(Luke 13:29)

Just over 100 years ago, in May 1908, a minor sensation occurred in this very chapel of King's College. A party of representatives of the churches of Germany was visiting England: some 120 pastors, priests, bishops, professors of divinity, court chaplains and the like. They spent a day in Cambridge and of course were brought to see King's. Standing here in the choir they were so entranced by what they saw around them and above them that quite spontaneously and with one voice they burst into song: a lusty rendering of the hymn *Grosser Gott, wir loben dich!* 'Great God, we praise thee'. Quite what the dean or chapel clerk made of this behaviour is not known, but in the official records it was accounted as one of the great highlights of the whole week the Germans spent in England, summing up the spirit of friendship which the visit was intended to foster. It was the first of a series of exchanges between the British and German churches during that time of growing rivalry and tension between the two nations, as each competed for the final imperial carve-up of Africa, as each tried to outdo the other in building ever bigger battleships and as the jingoistic press on both sides of the North Sea fanned the flames of hostility. But on both sides there were people who saw the need to counter this bellicosity. In 1909 a return visit was made by the British churches to Germany. Soon there was formed a joint council of the churches of both countries, and within a short time there grew a still larger movement drawing in the churches of other European countries and North America; and in 1914, on the very eve of the outbreak of the 'Great War', there was formed the 'World Alliance for Promoting International Friendship through the Churches'.

No, it did not stop the war, but despite all the hatred and bitterness that ensued, the war did not stop *it*. When the four years of carnage were over the World

---

Sermon preached at Mattins in King's College Chapel, Cambridge, 9 October 2011. King's Chapel is famed for the beauty of its architecture and stained glass, and for its choir which every Christmas Eve broadcasts to the world the 'Festival of Nine Lessons and Carols'.

Alliance set up meetings where Christians and others from the formerly belligerent countries could encounter each other and seek reconciliation. It grew in strength, drawing in participants from around the globe including Asia and the Far East. In 1931 the World Alliance held one of its largest international conferences here in Cambridge. It was a tributary into that ecumenical stream which, after the next war, issued in the formation of the World Council of Churches, still with us, still growing today.

This story is significant if only because in some quarters today religion is virtually equated with conflict. But in the Christian churches, as in all the great world faiths, for all the blots on our histories there is another story: the prophetic call to seek peace, peace being of the essence of faith in the one God who is God for all people. For Christians this stems from Jesus himself who says that people 'will come from east and west, from north and south, and will sit down to eat in the kingdom of God'. In our reading from the Gospel of Luke, Jesus has been asked how many will get into God's kingdom, that glorious fulfilment of life in union with himself which God promises. He brushes that question aside because he has something more important to say: 'Don't presume that you will be admitted to the feast of the kingdom just because of your race, your nationality or your religious affiliation. Don't even count on an entry ticket because you claim to come where I'm from, that we were at school together in Nazareth. And if you do find yourself seated at the banquet, don't assume that everyone there will be like you, from your place, your culture, your religious tradition. People will come not just from Judea and Galilee, but from far away, east and west, north and south, and will feast together in the kingdom of God.' The open reach of God's kingdom subverts every tribalism.

For that reason, paradoxically, peacemakers are often troublemakers. They challenge the assumed claims to loyalty made by the powers of this world, by state and nation, race and sect, especially when these usurp the claim that can truly be made only by God. Among the Germans who came to Cambridge for the World Alliance conference in 1931 was a young Lutheran pastor and theologian, at that time almost unknown but whose name today is honoured throughout the world, not just as one of the foremost Christian thinkers of his generation but as a martyr for truth and righteousness: Dietrich Bonhoeffer. Cambridge 1931 marked his entry into the ecumenical peace movement, and a journey which eventually led him into the resistance and conspiracy against Hitler, and finally to a barbarically cruel death at Flossenbürg barely a month before the Second World War ended. In that fearfully grim situation, he knew what it means to be one who, as the prophet says in our first lesson, 'walks in the darkness and has no light', yet dares to 'trust in the name of the Lord, and stay upon his God'.[1]

To believe in a Christian fellowship transcending all national and racial boundaries for the sake of the universal family of mankind was dangerous during the Third Reich. It's challenging to declare for today, in a globalized world with

---

1. Isaiah 50:10.

growing competition for the earth's diminishing resources. Do we really believe that people from east and west, north and south, are equally welcome at the table? The Arab writer Amin Malouf puts it starkly, 'What has had its day and now must end is the tribal phase of human history ... the prehistory of mankind ... made up of all our identity-based tensions, all our blinding ethnocentricity, and a selfishness which is held to be sacred, whether based on country, community, culture, ideology.'[2] That is a mighty challenge; it requires a leap of faith to believe that another world is possible. But to faith it is a possibility because God is there already, preparing his banquet for all peoples. It's the kind of faith Bonhoeffer himself called for, when he declared, 'There is no way to peace along the way of safety. For peace must be dared. It is the great venture.'[3]

Bonhoeffer undertook many kinds of risky ventures on his fateful journey. In wartime Nazi Germany, it was a seriously punishable offence if caught by the Gestapo listening in to foreign broadcasts. But Bonhoeffer habitually did so. Moreover as his friend Eberhard Bethge once told me, during the three wartime years before he was imprisoned, each Christmas Eve he would ensure he was within reach of a wireless that could tune in to the BBC Overseas Service, to hear what, for reasons of security, was coyly announced as 'A Service of Lessons and Carols from an English College Chapel'. No doubt he appreciated the music, for he was himself an accomplished musician. But perhaps even more, there was the assurance that even in war, and from the other side of the battle lines, there could still be heard singing about peace on earth and mercy mild, and a voice reciting the promise that 'the earth shall be filled with the knowledge of the Lord, as the waters cover the sea'.[4] Here was an antidote to the tribalism that had led to war and was fed by war. So it is with all worship. Whether it is a spontaneous outburst of singing *Grosser Gott, wir loben dich*, or a carefully prepared choral service, or any act of worship in which the one God of all-embracing love is praised, we are challenging and subverting the world as it is on behalf of the world that God wills and promises. We are conspiring for that great day when from east and west, north and south, people will come and sit and eat in the kingdom of God. To that one God, Father, Son and Holy Spirit, in all languages, be praise and honour and glory, now and for ever. Amen.

2. Amin Malouf, *Disordered World: Setting a New Course for the Twenty-first Century*, George Miller (trans.) (London: Bloomsbury, 2011), 241.

3. From his speech at the Fanø conference, 1934. See 114 below and DBWE 13, 308–9.

4. Isaiah 11:9, in the fourth of the 'Nine Lessons' read on Christmas Eve. One might also make an apposite reference to the altarpiece in King's Chapel, *The Adoration of the Magi* by Peter Paul Rubens (1577–1640), which depicts the 'three wise men' as comprising an Arab, an African and a European.

Chapter 9

LIFE TOGETHER, LIFE FOR OTHERS: DIETRICH BONHOEFFER'S WISDOM FOR MINISTRY IN A POST-CHRISTIAN WORLD

This day, 4 February, is a fitting date on which to speak about Dietrich Bonhoeffer, for it is his birthday. It is not however his actual birth in 1906 that I suggest we first commemorate; rather, his thirtieth birthday party, on 4 February 1936. This took place in a village called Finkenwalde close to the Baltic coast of north-east Germany. There, an old school was now home to an illegal, underground seminary for training pastors for the Confessing Church, that is, that section of German Protestantism which was resisting the takeover of the Church as an instrument of the Nazi state. The seminary had been formed the previous year, 1935, and Dietrich Bonhoeffer – not yet thirty years old – had been appointed its director.

Life in the seminary at such a grim time in Germany was obviously a serious affair. But it was not all work and no play. Ball games of various kinds were encouraged at Finkenwalde; and also on the lighter side birthday celebrations were highlights. So it was on this particular evening, as the students and their director gathered around the fire for a time of music-making, games and friendly chat. But the high point of this party came when one of the students, knowing that the director had many contacts abroad thanks to his ecumenical activities, asked if as a birthday present for him the seminary could make a visit to Sweden. The Lutheran Church of Sweden was taking a big interest in the Church Struggle going on in Germany and the idea was greeted with acclamation, strongly supported by the director himself. The visit, taking in Denmark en route and lasting ten days, took place just a few weeks later, in March.

Life together and the quest for peace

This birthday incident and its aftermath might seem rather trivial in the total context of Dietrich Bonhoeffer's career, which combined profound theological and ethical thinking, costly engagement in the church's witness in the Nazi state and eventual involvement in the political conspiracy against Hitler, which led to

A public lecture given on 4 February 2019 at Whitley College, Melbourne, Australia.

his execution at Flossenbürg execution camp in April 1945, just before the war in Europe ended. There are however two features of this story which point up essential features of how Bonhoeffer saw church, running counter to certain strongly held notions of the time in Germany. First, the very informality of that birthday party and other like occasions at Finkenwalde signalled a rather unusual view of community in academic and clerical circles for that time. Dietrich Bonhoeffer was indeed officially designated director of the seminary, entitled to be addressed as *Herr Direktor*. But from the outset he insisted that on a par with all the students he be styled *Bruder Bonhoeffer* – Brother Bonhoeffer. Life at Finkenwalde really would be life together: not hierarchical but mutual. Second, for five years and more Bonhoeffer had been deeply involved in the international peace movement of the churches. He passionately believed that the church of Jesus Christ was inherently transnational, a single fellowship transcending all national boundaries and loyalties, a sign and instrument of God's command of peace to all peoples. In backing and leading the seminary's visit to Denmark and Sweden he knew what he was doing. He was cocking a snook at the nationalism of the official Reich Church which wanted to control all such contacts itself. The Reich Church regarded international ecumenism as un-German, indeed dangerous to German interests. When the Foreign Ministry of the church found out about the visit there was fury, especially as Bonhoeffer had secured an official invitation for it from the Swedish archbishop, Erling Eidem. Bonhoeffer was landed in deep trouble, incurring warnings that his influence 'was not conducive to German interests'[1] and that he was liable to the accusation of being 'a pacifist and an enemy of the state'.[2] He may well have taken these as compliments.

Finkenwalde and its underlying theology in context

Bonhoeffer's seminary was already arousing suspicions even in some Confessing Church circles. It was rumoured that life at Finkenwalde resembled a Catholic monastery rather than a Lutheran preachers' seminary: as well as rigorous lectures in theology and classes in pastoralia, there was a disciplined daily life of communal prayer and private meditation; and even, it was said, private confession of sins one to another. So what had led this brilliant young theologian to take charge of what was at first sight a most un-Lutheran experiment in training future pastors? In a nutshell, Bonhoeffer believed that German Protestants no longer had any real understanding of what 'church' was all about, no idea of church as a *community* of people. If you went to church it was a basically individual affair of going to Sunday worship for your personal weekly dose of spiritual uplift, with no sense of being brought into active relationship with the others who were involved. Indeed,

---

1. See Eberhard Bethge, *Dietrich Bonhoeffer: A Biography*, revised and edited by Victoria J. Barnett (Minneapolis, MN: Fortress Press, 2000), 510.
2. Ibid., 512.

many thought that such individualism was the hallmark of good Protestantism as against Catholicism. This individualism proved fatally weak in the face of Hitler's advent to power in 1933. But while Bonhoeffer from the start was deeply committed to the Confessing Church, he believed that resistance to the dark spell of Nazism required more than the finest theology or even the magnificent confession of faith set out in the famous Barmen Theological Declaration of 1934. It needed a renewal of community at the heart of the church's life, to counter the appeal of the fake community of racism and militarism, and to stiffen the resolve of those being tempted to retreat even further into an individualist, escapist piety. For that, the church needed adequately trained clergy, and an essential part of their formation would be the experience of living together, in shared learning and spiritual discipline. It needed, he dared to say, a new monasticism, not like the old but adequate to the present challenges. The Finkenwalde experiment lasted two years, during which time some 110 students passed through, until the seminary was closed down by the Gestapo in 1937. But in a dispersed and even more clandestine way the work continued for three more years.

Underlying all that Bonhoeffer was writing and teaching at Finkenwalde was not just a concern to meet the immediate needs of the hour in the Church Struggle but a very definite theology of Christ and the church. He had worked this out long before the Nazi takeover and the onset of the Church Struggle. Indeed, it hails from his doctoral thesis which he completed in 1927 at the outrageously young age of twenty-one. The subject of his thesis was the church, and its title was the Latin *Sanctorum Communio* (The Communion of Saints).[3] In his phrase, the church (i.e. the community or congregation which listens to God's word) is *Christ existing as community*. God in Christ becomes knowable in the community of his people. Revelation lands here on earth in a flesh and blood community, Christ existing as church-community. In saying this he claims that the church-community is not a 'religious association', a kind of society or club of people with a like-minded religious interest. It is actually the body of Christ, as Paul states, its members sharing in the life of Christ and therefore members of one another. It's not a religious society; it's nothing less than the new humanity, God's new creation in Christ: a very 'high' view of the church.

Vicarious representative action

At this point we must reacquaint ourselves with the German term *Stellvertretung*, 'vicarious representative action', which we encountered in the first chapter of this volume[4] and which runs like a stream, sometimes on the surface and sometimes underground, through all Bonhoeffer's thinking, right to his last days in prison. In *Sanctorum Communio* it describes how Christ establishes the church as his body,

---

3. Published as *Sanctorum Communio: A Theological Study of the Sociology of the Church*. DBWE 1.

4. See above, viii, 7–9.

and constitutes how its members relate to one another. It means taking another person's place to the point of sharing his or her suffering, representing that person in their need before others and speaking on his or her behalf. (In not very serious vein, I recall a somewhat scurrilous instance of a plea for *Stellvertretung* during my first visit to Australia thirteen years ago. My wife and I were in a café in Apollo Bay, when a man walked in and quite publicly addressed his friends with a request: he had just received notice of a fine and penalty points from the Melbourne police for going through a red light a few days before. Would someone be willing to say that they had been driving his car that day and collect the points on his behalf? I don't think he found any takers. They obviously don't believe in that form of *Stellvertretung* in Apollo Bay.)

For Bonhoeffer, *Stellvertretung* is most fully exemplified by Jesus Christ himself who did take our place as sinners on the cross, and who always exists as the love shown in that *Stellvertretung*. Equally it defines how members of the body of Christ are called and enabled to relate to one another, to be Christ to one another as Luther said, a forgiven and forgiving people. Bonhoeffer takes the traditional evangelical gospel and transmutes it into entirely relational terms. He moved on from *Sanctorum Communio*, but *Stellvertretung* remained a key concept for him, marking the trajectory of his life and thought, in a stream that acquired widening and deepening significance as it flowed onwards. The church is founded by, and lives by, *Stellvertretung* in its life together as a community of ministry.

Two books from Finkenwalde: Discipleship *and* Life Together

Two of Bonhoeffer's best-known and best-loved books were written out of his time at Finkenwalde. *Discipleship*[5] (still perhaps known to many under the title given to its first English translation, *The Cost of Discipleship*) is based mainly on his seminary lectures on the gospel accounts of the calling of the first disciples and the Sermon on the Mount, and on the Apostle Paul's teaching on the church as the body of Christ. Some of Bonhoeffer's most memorable phrases are found here: 'Cheap grace is the mortal enemy of our church. Our struggle today is for costly grace.'[6] 'Whenever Christ calls us, his call leads us to death.'[7] Bonhoeffer relentlessly etches Christian life as pursuing the narrow way of a relationship focussed exclusively on Jesus Christ himself, come what may. In the context of the time when so many were tempted to follow the broad way, the populist way, of easy conformity to the world and the powers that be, shouting '*Sieg Heil!*', its significance is clear. *Life Together*[8] is a much shorter book but no less challenging,

---

5. DBWE 4.

6. Ibid., 43.

7. Ibid., 87. The earlier translation (*Cost of Discipleship*) ran 'When Christ calls a man, he bids him come and die.'

8. DBWE 5.

and it is not surprising that the Finkenwalde experiment continues to inspire further ventures and thinking on Christian community.[9]

Surprises meet us at almost every page-turn in *Life Together*. If we expect eulogies on the wonder and beauty of Christian fellowship we are in for a rude shock. Indeed, several times Bonhoeffer warns us *off* forming or joining a community, especially if we have idealistic notions about it. The sooner we are disillusioned the better, he says, for community in Christ – whether in a seminary, a congregation or household or whatever – is not based on our visions however pious or romantic as to what it should be, but on the uncomfortable reality of its members as all-too-human people living by the forgiveness of sins. Here he puts flesh on *Stellvertretung*. Part of that life together, he says, is that of service, ministry to one another. He is very practical:

> [Thus] it is a good idea that all members receive a definite task to perform for the community, so that they may know in times of doubt that they too are not useless and incapable of doing anything. Every Christian community must know that not only do the weak need the strong, but also that the strong cannot exist without the weak. The elimination of the weak is the death of the community.[10]

In the sinister context of the Nazi programmes to eliminate mental and physical 'defectives', the resonances of the last sentence in this citation are clear. As so often, what Bonhoeffer says about the church is not *just* about the church. For him the church as community in Christ is called to exhibit God's new creation of *humanity* as a whole. How members of the body of Christ relate to one another will typically be counter-cultural, especially where the prevailing culture is one of authoritarian, hectoring demands for obedience. Pastors, for instance, notes Bonhoeffer, assume that everyone wants to hear them speak, but the first service one owes to others in the community is that of *listening*: 'We should listen with the ears of God, so that we can speak the Word of God.'[11] Then there is the ministry of active helpfulness, even in minor external matters. 'Nobody is too good for the lowest service.'[12] Third, and most important, there is the service of *bearing with others*, in accordance with Paul's injunction, 'Bear one another's burdens, and in this way, you will fulfil the law of Christ' (Galatians 6:2). Forbearance with others' sins means the burden of suffering. 'The burden of human beings was even for God so heavy that God had to go to the cross suffering under it.'[13] Hence, too, the service of hearing another's confession and, in all humility, of speaking and hearing the Word of God one with another. This view of community goes much further than conventional

---

9. See e.g.: Craig Gardiner, *Melodies of a New Monasticism* (Eugene, OR: Cascade Books, 2018); John de Gruchy, *This Monastic Moment* (Eugene, OR: Cascade Books, 2021).
10. DBWE 5, 96.
11. Ibid., 99.
12. Ibid.
13. Ibid., 100.

superficialities about 'fellowship'. Bonhoeffer's views on ministry, as I have already indicated, are in marked contrast to the Nazified ethos of *Führerprinzip*, leadership based solely on power and sheer assertion of authority and the dubious adulation of mass popularity. Pastors are not called to cajole or manipulate people, or force them into their own mould, but to let Christ be formed in the community. We find no expositions of management techniques in the church, and all the accompanying jargon of secular corporate life and decision-making which some church circles are tempted to adopt (at the same time, ironically, as they are being questioned in corporate business life). Still less does Bonhoeffer give houseroom to personality cults and the worst excesses of the celebrity culture: 'The community of faith does not need brilliant personalities but faithful servants of Jesus Christ and of one another. It does not lack the former but the latter.'[14]

Indeed, we find in Bonhoeffer a repeated emphasis on a *shared* ministry. In his classes at Finkenwalde he has some very interesting things to say about preaching, for example, including remarks under the heading 'The How of Evangelisation' as a shared enterprise.

> The bringer of [God's word] should be not an individual but a church-community, that is, several people as a small church-community, as a brotherhood living together under the word ... early Christian proclamation, even that of Paul, who was called alone, was not solitary. To what extent does that also apply to the pastoral office, namely, that the one-man system actually represents an accommodation to secular vocations?[15]

This 'core group' should be a community of prayer with the pastor. It is thus a shared ministry. We hear some striking admonitions, for example: 'Being completely exhausted after a sermon is a bad sign; it derives from an improper disposition. It is not the pastor who is to deplete himself in the pulpit but rather God.'[16]

What about the world?

Bonhoeffer's time at Finkenwalde, and shortly afterwards, might seem indeed to have been a monastic phase of his life, insulated from the world outside, and people sometimes contrast what he wrote in *Discipleship* and *Life Together* with what he went on to write in his wartime *Ethics* and above all in his prison letters, about faith's responsibility in the world and the 'worldliness' of Christianity. But I do not see any sudden breaks in the course of Bonhoeffer's thinking – sharp turns yes, but always with definite continuities. Bonhoeffer concludes *Discipleship* by summarizing the whole of the scriptural witness to God's purpose with humankind

---

14. Ibid., 107.
15. DBWE 14, 521.
16. Ibid., 530.

as the creation of the image of Christ, the restoration of the divine image, in us. Our goal as human beings is to be shaped into the form of the incarnate, crucified and transfigured Christ. Then comes this remarkable passage, one of the most remarkable Bonhoeffer ever wrote, and crucial for understanding the way his mind was moving, just as life was becoming more difficult for him under the increasingly oppressive grip of the regime:

> Christ has taken on this *human form*. He became a human being like us. In his humanity and lowliness we recognize our own form. He became like human beings, so that we would be like him. In Christ's incarnation all of humanity regains the dignity of bearing the image of God. Whoever from now on attacks the least of the people attacks Christ, who took on human form and who in himself has restored the image of God for all who bear a human countenance. In community with the incarnate one, we are once again given our true humanity. With it, we are delivered from the isolation caused by sin, and at the same time restored to the whole of humanity.
>
> Inasmuch as we participate in Christ, the incarnate one, we also have a part in all of humanity, which is borne by him. Since we know ourselves to be accepted and borne within the humanity of Jesus, our new humanity now also consists in bearing the troubles and sins of all others. The incarnate one transforms his disciples into brothers and sisters of all human beings. The 'philanthropy' of God (Titus 3:4) that became evident in the incarnation of Christ is the reason for Christians to love every human being on earth as a brother or sister. The form of the incarnate one transforms the church-community into the body of Christ upon which all of humanity's sin and trouble fall, and by which alone these troubles and sins are borne.[17]

Notice the language of 'bearing' in this passage. This is about ministry as *Stellvertretung* at a new level. One feels here that the whole of *Discipleship* has been leading us along a very narrow defile, focussed entirely on the way of Christ, Christ and his way alone, Christ leading us to the cross. Then all of a sudden, this narrow defile along which we have been walking opens out onto a panorama of the whole world. The Christ whom we have been following to the exclusion of all others turns out to be the one who identifies himself with all people in their suffering and need, and so our faith likewise is called to embrace all humanity without barriers; thereby we allow the image of God to be recreated in us. So Bonhoeffer here is taking up his early notion of the church being Christ-existing-as-community and now placing it in the wider context of that church being Christ-existing-as-community in *Stellvertretung* for the whole world. He himself had in effect already pointed this out four years earlier in 1933, during the early persecutions of the Jews, in his paper 'The Church and the Jewish Question' in which he stated, 'The church has an unconditional obligation toward the victims of any societal order, even if they

---

17. DBWE 4, 285.

do not belong to the Christian community.'[18] That precept is now grounded in his incarnational doctrine of Christ and human community, in which *Stellvertretung* is central. Bonhoeffer's notion of our communion with Christ restoring in us the image of God (an understanding which owes much to the second-century church father Irenaeus) also assumes a notion of salvation somewhat at odds with certain brands of evangelical preaching. Bonhoeffer always affirmed that 'Christ died for our sins', but not in a way that portrays Christ as paying a price external to us, a salvation to which we relate by accepting a bargain which merely imputes to us a righteousness we do not really have. Rather, for Bonhoeffer we are actually drawn into Christ's righteousness in communion with him, and thereby also into his solidarity with all humanity. The implications for our understanding of mission and evangelization are immense, not least their costliness.

Into dark places

This understanding of Jesus Christ as the supreme embodiment of *Stellvertretung* is what accompanied Bonhoeffer into the following tumultuous years of the war, during which he entered into the political conspiracy against Hitler. Now he devoted his writing time to his *Ethics*, which is much occupied with the question of what it means to act responsibly in society. Reading between the lines of the *Ethics* we can see how the context of resistance and conspiracy was pressing upon his mind. All the complexities and ambiguities of involvement in a plot which would eventually require an attempt at assassination of the head of state, and the outcome of which could not be wholly foreseen, brought him face to face with the question of guilt, and of whether in such a situation of massive politicized evil manifest on the scale of the Holocaust, one could ever be guilt-free. Bonhoeffer's guiding light here is again Jesus as the supreme embodiment of vicarious representative action. Jesus, he says, is not 'the individual who seeks to attain his own ethical perfection. Instead, he lives only as the one who in himself has taken on and bears the selves of all human beings including their guilt.'[19] Jesus does not come teaching love as the ethical ideal; he actually loves real human beings. Such love cannot be regulated by any law. 'Jesus does not want to be considered the only perfect one, to look down on a humanity perishing under its guilt … Love for real human beings leads into the solidarity of human guilt.'[20] Responsible action, if it is motivated by love for real people, as was Jesus, will lead to solidarity with their guilt and indeed will be prepared to become guilty for their sake, rather than preserve one's own supposed innocence. This is *Stellvertretung* at its most profound. It accompanied

---

18. DBWE 12, 365. It is in this paper that Bonhoeffer makes his remark that eventually the church may have to consider 'putting a spoke' in the wheel rather than just bandaging up the victims.
19. DBWE 6, 231.
20. Ibid., 233.

Bonhoeffer the conspirator into some very dark places. Bonhoeffer's great friend and biographer, Eberhard Bethge, once told me of a winter's evening early in the war, when he and Bonhoeffer were staying in the country home of Bonhoeffer's brother-in-law Hans von Dohnanyi, who was one of the masterminds on the civilian wing of the conspiracy. The three of them were talking by the fireside, and Dohnanyi asked Dietrich, 'What about the saying of Jesus, "Whoever takes the sword will perish by the sword". Does that mean us? We are taking up the sword?' Dietrich answered, 'Yes, that's true. That word is still valid for us now. The time needs exactly those people who do that, and let Jesus' saying be true. We take the sword and are prepared to perish by it. Taking up guilt means accepting the consequences of it. Maybe God will save us but' – a long pause – 'first of all you must be prepared to accept the consequences.'[21] That was indeed a dark place to be in, but as well as illuminating that extreme situation, Bonhoeffer also uses *Stellvertretung* as a lens to view how all true human social relationships, whether in the family, or the world of work, or education or whatever, in some way manifest elements of vicarious representative action, the kind of action consummated by Christ.[22] That is a sign of the lordship of Christ over all things and all people.

In a world without religion?

Stellvertretung therefore marks the trajectory which Bonhoeffer's thinking, and indeed so much of his activity, took onwards from his first years as a theologian. But what about his latest phase, from his imprisonment in April 1943 to his execution at Flossenbürg concentration camp two years later? Did *Stellvertretung* really survive that time during which, especially from end April 1944, he penned to Eberhard Bethge those startling letters[23] exploring what a 'religionless Christianity' in a 'world come of age' might look like, a world in which we have to live 'as if God was not there'? In those letters, Bonhoeffer described what he saw as a long historical process now coming to completion, of the end of 'religion'. By 'religion' he means, quite specifically, thinking which is 'metaphysical', confining God to a realm outside this visible world of time and space; thinking which is individualistic, concerned with *my* salvation; and thinking which sees that salvation only in a realm the other side of death. What survives as 'religion' today is in Bonhoeffer's mind always something partial, a sacred sector of life, whereas it is our life as a whole which is claimed and transformed by God: 'Jesus calls not to a

---

21. Keith Clements, *What Freedom? The Persistent Challenge of Dietrich Bonhoeffer* (Bristol: Bristol Baptist College, 1990), 37.

22. Note also in Australia, for example, Victoria's own experiences of the instinctive, spontaneous outpourings of communal solidarity in the wake of the 'Black Saturday' bushfires of 2009, and in February 2019 the public vigils for the murdered Arab-Israeli student Aiia Maasarwe in Melbourne.

23. DBWE 8.

new religion but to life.'[24] Religion means thinking of God as a being who is outside and beyond our life in this world, and who is only called in from outside when our human powers fall short. That God of religion is fading away from human life today. But in any case, such a God has very little to do with the one the Bible calls God, whose kingdom is the transformation of this world into a community with God in righteousness and peace.

There has been huge discussion, continuing still today from our vantage point nearly seventy-five years after his death, on whether Bonhoeffer got it wrong. After all, religion in some shape or form, good or bad, is very much alive in our world today. But he was surely right in perceiving that a major shift was under way, in the Western world at any rate, in relation to traditional religion and expressions of faith. Faith is no longer the assumed default position in the societies you and I live in – you only have to read our daily newspapers (even, or perhaps especially, *The Age*[25]) to be struck by how far daily and public affairs are pursued without any reference to God, church or religion of any sort. The American philosopher and historian Charles Taylor was surely right in seeing that a sea change in Western culture became evident in the 1960s. It was not so much a new philosophy that came about but a new way in which people felt and perceived themselves to be in relation to the big dimensions of life: 'That each one of us has his/her own way of realising our humanity, that it is important to find and live out one's own, as against surrendering to conformity with a model imposed on us from outside, or the previous generation, or religious or political authority.'[26] This might seem to be sanctioning the very kind of individualism that Bonhoeffer and others warn against, but that is not necessarily so. A communal form of faith is still very much an essential feature of Christianity today: but it is an *option*, to be embraced in freedom. It cannot be assumed, nor imposed from above. In that sense, we are in a post-Christian world or, perhaps better expressed, a post-Christendom world, a world no longer under assumed Christian institutional dominance, and in a culture no longer of unquestioned Christian values. In fact, Taylor's insight resonates with the criticism that Bonhoeffer in his prison writings makes of his great mentor Karl Barth who, Bonhoeffer says, now comes across as presenting people with a 'take it or leave it' attitude to Christianity as a fixed body of beliefs to be swallowed whole. But if the world is post-Christian or post-Christendom it is not post-*Christ*. Bonhoeffer is absolutely sure of that. This is the main thrust of these prison writings, which focus not just on what is happening to the world but how and where Christ is in it as a transformative presence with us; the place where God is rediscovered not as a remote being beyond this world but the beyond in the midst, the truly transcendent

---

24. Ibid., 482.

25. A long-established daily newspaper published in Melbourne, also serving Australian states other than Victoria.

26. Charles Taylor, *A Secular Age* (Cambridge, MA: Belknap, 2011), 475. See also the extensive discussion of Taylor in James Gerard McEvoy, *Leaving Christendom for Good: Church-World Dialogue in a Secular Age* (Plymouth: Lexington Books, 2014).

one at the centre of life. As his fateful time in prison drew on, in August 1944 he wrote an 'Outline for a Book', which included these notes:

> Encounter with Jesus Christ. Experience that here is a reversal of all human existence, in the very fact that Jesus only 'is there for others'. Jesus's 'being-for-others' is the experience of transcendence! ... Faith is participating in this being of Jesus ... Our relationship to God is a new life in 'being there for others', through participation in the being of Jesus. The transcendent is not the infinite, unattainable tasks, but the neighbour within reach in any given situation.[27]

This leads to the conclusion:

> The church is church only when it is there for others. The church must participate in the worldly tasks of life in the community – not dominating but helping and serving. It must tell people in every calling what a life with Christ is, what it means 'to be there for others'.[28]

This is Bonhoeffer's basic guideline for ministry today: to take part in the transformative life of Christ in the world. While the term *Stellvertretung* does not occur explicitly in those letters, its meaning comes to the full flower of significance for Bonhoeffer, and for us too if we are looking for his guidelines for ministry in the 'post-Christian world', where religion tends to flourish only as a tool for those who want to use it for their own purposes of power and prestige, divisively and destructively. As noted earlier,[29] we see this wisdom poignantly set out in his poem 'The Death of Moses', penned in September 1944 after the failure of the 20 July attempt on Hitler's life, and aware what his own fate was now likely to be, he writes:

> To punish sin, to forgive you are moved;
> O God, this people have I truly loved.
>
> That I bore its shame and sacrifices
> And saw its salvation – that suffices.[30]

That is *Stellvertretung*, life with others, life for others.

Transformation for maturity

The fundamental wisdom that Bonhoeffer sets out for ministry in our world is thus a ministry which serves the transformative growth of people becoming

---

27. DBWE 8, 501.
28. Ibid., 503.
29. See above, 107.
30. DBWE 5, 240–1.

not religious but fully human after the manner of Jesus Christ, to be 'there for others'. It means nurturing church-communities of persons who grow, in the words of the Apostle Paul, 'to *maturity*, to the measure if the full stature of Christ' (Ephesians 4:13); that is, ready for all the responsibilities of *Stellvertretung*, life with and for others, with all its joys and risks, and especially in solidarity with those who suffer and are not reckoned to count in society. In 1939, at the start of the Second World War, one of Bonhoeffer's British friends in the ecumenical movement, the Scottish lay theologian and ecumenist J. H. Oldham, launched his fortnightly *Christian Newsletter*. Throughout the war and after it was a means of information and sharing of views on how Christians and all concerned people could respond to face the dreadful realities of war and all the challenges it would bring for those concerned for the future social order. In the opening number of the *Newsletter* Oldham showed himself to be instinctively on the same track as Bonhoeffer in addressing the subject of fear: 'What holds us back more than anything else is fear – fear not only of death but of life.'[31] Mature life means making decisions, shouldering responsibilities and taking risks, and acting even when we cannot be sure of the outcome. It is the way of faith, hope and love. It is, in fact, *Stellvertretung*. It is a very worldly ministry but does not conform to what either the powers that be or popular opinion expects or wants of religion. We can list certain points at which it challenges our personal and cultural mores, and our churchly assumptions too.

Stellvertretung connotes not an idea but an action, an intensely loving action, divine and human. Bonhoeffer emphatically warns against pure verbalizing of the gospel of Christ.

Words alone, he warns, however theological religious or pious, no longer convey who Christ is today: 'The church's word gains weight and power not through concepts but by example.'[32] Many of us can testify to that, I am sure. I like to collect illustrations of the very point Bonhoeffer makes. One example from the UK is the BBC World Affairs Editor John Simpson, who has spent many years knocking around the world and covering some of the most terrible scenes of conflict (twenty years ago I met him in a Belgrade hotel breakfast bar during the NATO bombing of Belgrade). He tells how his own Christian faith, which he thought he had outgrown decades before, came alive again when in South Africa, through witnessing at first hand the ending of apartheid and especially the role of people like Desmond Tutu as agents of reconciliation. Contradicting the current cultural assumption that life is about protecting yourself from whatever discomforts us, he writes in his memoir,

> But what if ... the point of living isn't to be placid and happy and untouched by the world, but to be deeply, painfully sensitive to it, to see its cruelty and savagery for what they are, and accept all this as readily as we accept

---

31. J. H. Oldham, *Christian News-Letter*, No. 0 (18 October 1939).
32. DBWE 8, 504.

its beauty? To be touched by it, loved by it, hurt by it even, but not to be indifferent to it?[33]

That's a rather good expression of 'religionless Christianity'; or rather 'Christ-full life in the world'.

Stellvertretung involves a spirituality of movement. An essential part of life together as taught by Bonhoeffer at Finkenwalde, and of life for others as he practised it in prison, is intercessory prayer. Intercession is apt to become a cheap matter of simply ticking off the known needs of individuals or communities or nations, job done. For Bonhoeffer it was a more serious matter: 'Once we were told that some Roman Catholic congregations prayed for the imprisoned and persecuted members of the Confessing Church; when some of us did not see anything remarkable in this, Bonhoeffer reacted sharply, saying: "I am not indifferent to somebody praying for me." '[34] The verb 'to intercede' derives from two Latin words, *inter* (between) and *cedere* (to move). In intercessory prayer we don't just 'remember' or 'think about' certain people or situations: we *move ourselves* in spirit (and then, if possible, in body) to where they are, ponder what they are going through, try to identify with it, and then *move* again to God and face God with what we have taken upon ourselves. There is no more profound example of intercessory prayer than the long poem Bonhoeffer wrote in Tegel prison, 'Night Voices',[35] where he makes his own what he imagines his fellow-prisoners – not political prisoners like himself but mostly soldiers who have fallen foul of military law – are muttering in their uneasy sleep, sinners and sinned against, anxious, guilty and fearful of what awaits them.

The way of *Stellvertretung* runs counter to every form of self-enclosed life which regards any claim of what is outside of us as intrusive and a violation of our personal freedom, a threat to our well-being. *Stellvertretung* challenges the self-drawn boundaries of communal identity that claim quasi-sacred significance. The supreme exemplar of *Stellvertretung*, Jesus Christ, took the place of all people before God, and represented God to all people, the Jew and the gentile alike, even to the cross. *Stellvertretung*, vicarious representative action, challenges all our tendencies to erect self-made barriers around ourselves. What is responsible action cannot be determined or limited by the boundaries of race, class nation or gender. In our time, nationalism is rampant again, and moreover co-opting religion into its armoury, as in Prime Minister Narendra Modi's India, President Vladimir Putin's Russia, President Tayyip Erdoğan's Turkey and former President Donald Trump's United States, and you yourselves may have comments to make on the Australian scene. What people glibly call patriotism is itself becoming a new religion.

---

33. John Simpson, *Not Quite World's End: A Traveller's Tales* (London: Macmillan, 2007), 460–1.

34. Julius Rieger, 'Contacts with London', in W.-D. Zimmermann and R. Gregor Smith (eds), *I Knew Dietrich Bonhoeffer* (London: Collins, 1966), 96.

35. DBWE 8, 462–70.

Bonhoeffer's theologically based critique of all forms of nationalism during the 1930s, and his insistence that the ecumenical fellowship of Jesus Christ stands for a totally different order of human solidarity, needs to be revisited and claimed as an essential part of the church's ministry today. This belief never left Bonhoeffer. Among his last known words, the day before he was executed, is a message to his English friend Bishop George Bell: 'Tell him, that with him I believe in the reality of our international Christian fellowship which rises above all national interests and conflicts, and that our victory is certain.'[36] I should add that in Britain today, in the midst of our confusion over our relations with the rest of Europe, we as much as any other people are desperately in need of a mature vision of what it means to be part of the wider family of people. To adapt a famous English poem,[37] no *nation* is an island, entire of itself, every nation is a piece of the continent, a part of the main.

Stellvertretung means calling government, and all power and authority, to account on behalf of those who, it is claimed, will benefit from policies for the common good. We shall identify with refugees and asylum seekers because at the table of our Lord, when we reach out for the bread and wine, we know ourselves to be refugees and asylum seekers yearning for grace and thankful for it. Vicarious representative action does not shrink from but seeks responsible use of the God-given resources of science, technology and all human wisdom. In our day, more than in Bonhoeffer's time, we are coming to recognize that this includes representation on behalf of the whole created order of the earth threatened by climate change and environmental degradation.[38] It means continually asking, are you aware of the consequences for others, of your decisions and actions? Who is likely to be hurt by your actions, or non-actions? It is a question both for pastors and congregations: What kind of Christ is it who we want to be existing as our communities? The fake Christ whom we want to bolster our differences and sense of importance, or the Christ who calls us to share his costly intercession for each and all? What kind of persons are we hoping to nurture through our worship and life together: persons who want to be safely marked out by their virtue, or those who are joyously thankful for grace and so dare to eat with tax collectors and sinners? What kind of impact upon society do we want to make? To restore the old Christendom where church and state went hand in glove, where institutional Christianity dominated everything or do we want to seek embodiments of vicarious representative action wherever and by whomever they enhance justice and promote peace in the world? As disciples (not owners!) of Jesus Christ we shall affirm and uphold appearances of *Stellvertretung* wherever we encounter them in the world, and this is very pertinent to interfaith relations in the common search for human welfare.[39]

36. Bethge, *Dietrich Bonhoeffer*, 1022 n.54.
37. John Donne (1577–1631), 'No Man Is an Island'.
38. See Chapter 4, 47–8.
39. For an instance in the writer's own experience of inter-religious dialogue in the Balkans, see Keith Clements, *Look Back in Hope: An Ecumenical Life* (Eugene, OR: Resource, 2017), 309–10.

Still discovering: Christ in this world

We can describe our world in various ways: the post-religious world, the post-Christian world, the post-Christendom world, the postcolonial world. But it is still the world in which Christ comes to live fully and to bring life in its fullness, by his vicarious representative action, and calls us to be with him there. *Stellvertretung* remains, and will ever be, the way of Christ in the midst of the world, and our way of ministry with him, the way to the truly human fullness of life. John Matthews, Lutheran pastor and Bonhoeffer scholar in Minnesota, United States, sums up Bonhoeffer's guidelines for us better than any I know.

> In a world and church where pain and suffering are seen as God's curse or absence, the disciples of Jesus Christ are called to live in solidarity with those who suffer, in the knowledge that God suffers and calls people to share in God's suffering; in a world and church where fear of God and anxiety for the future cause people to assume a position of immature dependence before the Almighty, Jesus Christ calls disciples to trust the love of God and accept the role of stewarding the world in a mature and interdependent manner.[40]

The temptation is always for us to try and locate God in a different world from that which we are actually experiencing; rather like the Chinese emperor who, so the story goes, became so unpopular with his people that he eventually asked his advisers to find him another and more amenable people to rule over. Ministry means sticking with this world where we are now, even the post-Christian world, not the imagined world of yesterday nor the dreamt-of world of tomorrow, but this very same world where God often seems absent or forgotten, as the world where we find and serve Christ the *Stellvertreter*. One time when I was with Eberhard Bethge in his study I asked him where the original prison letters that he received from Bonhoeffer were now kept. 'Oh, he said,' pointing to his desk, "in here! Would you like to see any of them? Which one in particular?' Without hesitation I asked to see the one he wrote on 21 July 1944, the day after the failure of the plot against Hitler. A moment later it was in my hand. It felt almost like holding the original of one of Paul's epistles. It begins, '*Heute*' – 'today', in other words *this* especially fearful and fateful day – and then goes on with his marvellous statement of faith, in which he reviews his life, now surely with its end in sight, and what he has learnt on the way:

> I discovered, and am still discovering to this day, that one only learns to have faith by living in the full this-worldliness of life … living fully in the midst of life's tasks, successes and failures, experiences, and perplexities then one takes seriously not one's own sufferings but rather the sufferings of God in the world. Then one stands awake with Christ in Gethsemane … And this is how one

---

40. John Matthews, *Anxious Souls Will Ask: The Christ-Centered Spirituality of Dietrich Bonhoeffer* (Grand Rapids, MI: Eerdmans, 2005), 67.

becomes a human being, a Christian. How should one become arrogant over successes or shaken by one's failures when one shares in God's suffering in the life of the world?[41]

'I discovered, and am still discovering to this day.' I wonder, when he was writing these lines, did his mind go back to that birthday party at Finkenwalde eight years earlier? That birthday party was one significant point on his journey of discovery. We too are all invited to make that journey from where we are now. It is a journey to which we are called by Christ: not to religion but to life in all its dimensions, life with others, life for others. The post-Christian world is still Christ's world, and must be inhabited in Christ's way. That is Bonhoeffer's basic wisdom for ministry today.

41. DBWE 8, 486.

Chapter 10

BELONGING WHOLLY TO THE WORLD: THE STILL UNREALIZED ECUMENICAL CALLING

The word 'ecumenical' comes from the Greek *oikoumene*, 'the whole inhabited world'. The great councils of the early church such as those at Nicea and Constantinople in the fourth century were 'ecumenical councils' because they brought together bishops from the churches throughout the *oikoumene*, the whole inhabited earth as known at that time to the people of the Roman Empire. They saw it as an *oikoumene* which was being embraced by the purpose of God in Christ. But we should notice that 'the inhabited earth' refers in a holistic fashion not just to the inhabitants of the earth but to the earth they inhabit as well. The root word of *oikoumene* is *oikos*, 'house, or household', denoting a family or community living together under one roof. Furthermore, from the root *oikos* come words like 'economy' and 'ecology': the household of humankind and the whole environment. The ecumenical movement, in broadest terms, means being caught up into what St Paul in the Letter to the Ephesians describes as God's purpose in Christ, 'a plan for the fullness of time, to gather up all things in him, things in heaven and things on earth (Ephesians 1:10). It may begin with the church, but it certainly does not end there.

What is distinctive about Dietrich Bonhoeffer is that for him the ecumenical vision as far as it concerned the churches should have most concrete and immediate consequences possible. Looking back in later life to the time (1931) when he became actively involved in the ecumenical movement, on his return to Germany from a year's study as an exchange student in the United States, he said that this was the time when he moved 'from the phraseological to the real', from ideas to concrete action.[1]

A youthful entry – and challenge

That entry into ecumenical engagement in 1931 came at the eighth international conference in Cambridge, England, of the World Alliance for Friendship through

---

Paper presented at the seminar 'Bonhoeffer's Theological Legacy', at Volmoed, South Africa, September 2014.

1. DBWE 8, 358.

the Churches, when he was appointed an honorary Youth Secretary for Europe. The main purpose of the World Alliance, as its name implies, was to work for peace, and it was this which was the prime attraction of the organization for Bonhoeffer. For him ecumenism and peace were two sides of the same coin.[2] The church, being the community of Jesus Christ, was the sign and instrument of God's peace in the world. This was one of the two main foci of Bonhoeffer's ecumenical commitment, which reached its highest point at the ecumenical conference at Fanø, Denmark, in 1934 when he made his most outspoken declaration: 'There is no way to peace along the way of safety. For peace must be dared. It is the great venture'[3] and called on that meeting to take on the role of the great ecumenical council and challenge the churches to forbid war. The other focus arose out of the German Church Struggle. Bonhoeffer was not only totally committed to the cause of the Confessing Church within Germany but pressed the case of the Confessing Church in the international ecumenical movement, insisting that since the Confessing Church was the church which had rejected the heresies of Nazified Christianity in Germany, it and it alone had a right to represent German Protestantism at the international ecumenical table. That posed a mighty challenge to the ecumenical movement itself. Was the ecumenical fellowship just a talking shop for dialogue and cooperation on certain issues, or was it more than that: a body which could pronounce authoritatively on the issue of truth, and on the concrete course of right action? In fact, as Bonhoeffer asked at least twice during 1934–5, 'Is the ecumenical movement church?'[4] Closely associated with this question was Bonhoeffer's repeated complaint that 'There is no theology of the ecumenical movement.'[5] By this he did not mean that there were no theologians attending ecumenical meetings (there were plenty); nor that theological issues were never discussed at meetings either of the World Alliance, or of the Universal Christian Council for Life and Work, or of the Faith and Order movement. Of course they were. But what Bonhoeffer was looking for was a theological understanding of the ecumenical movement itself, its status in relation to the nature and purpose of the church.[6] Were the ecumenical bodies just functional organizations for promoting theological dialogue and cooperation, or were they a manifestation of the church itself, the church which is the one body of Christ in all nations, and as such a sign and embodiment of the new humanity in Christ? This for him was a choice between phraseology and reality.

2. For an overall account of Bonhoeffer's ecumenical involvement, see Keith Clements, *Dietrich Bonhoeffer's Ecumenical Quest* (Geneva: WCC, 2015); also Clements, chapter 6 'Bonhoeffer and Ecumenism', in Michael Mawson and Philip Ziegler (eds), *The Oxford Handbook of Dietrich Bonhoeffer* (Oxford: Oxford University Press, 2019), 77–90.

3. DBWE 13, 308–9.

4. In his paper given at the Fanø conference in 1934 (DBWE 13, 304), and in his 1935 essay 'The Confessing Church and the Ecumenical Movement' (DBWE 14, 399).

5. See Bonhoeffer's lecture 'On the Theological Foundation of the Work of the World Alliance' given to the ecumenical youth conference at Ciernohorské Kúpele, 1932 (DBWE 11, 355–69).

6. Ibid., 356.

A theological basis?

In asking whether the ecumenical movement had itself a theological basis, Bonhoeffer was not offering to supply what is often termed an 'ecumenical theology' or a 'theology of ecumenism'. This was for the simple reason that he himself did not have a 'theology of ecumenism' apart from his own distinctive theology of the church. His ecumenical theology was just his ecclesiology writ large. In his earliest work, his doctoral thesis of 1927, *Sanctorum Communio*, he had spelled out his understanding of the church as 'Christ existing as church-community',[7] a community of persons in the relationship of being-with and being-for one another under the word of Christ. It is a community manifesting the work of Christ expressed in the term *Stellvertretung*, 'vicarious representative action'.[8] It means that the church is identified as a community which, under the word of Christ, comprises relationships with the quality of vicarious representative action and mutual service, stemming from Jesus Christ himself, and therefore at its most profound are found in the forgiveness of sins.[9] This was of immense ecumenical significance for Bonhoeffer. It means he was prepared to find the authentic church wherever this quality of relational community is found, be it in his own Lutheran parish, or in a Roman Catholic confessional, or in the Black Baptist Abyssinian church in Harlem. It is a concept of church which relativized for him so many of the confessional distinctions of Christendom. It also meant that when the Church Struggle burst in Germany in 1933, he was ready-armed with tools to combat the so-called German Christian heresy of a purely German church, a non-Jewish church, a church conforming to the Nazi ideals of authoritarian leadership, the *Führerprinzip*, all of which ran clean counter to his concept of church as a community solely under the word of Christ and formed according to Christ's pattern of vicarious servanthood. A church which, for example, introduced a racial criterion of membership was no longer the church of Jesus Christ.

This also meant, however, that he took with him into ecumenical activity a definite concept of what the ecumenical movement should be and how it should behave. A gathering of people from the churches of the world, gathered in service under the word of its common Lord and in solidarity with one another, should regard itself as church in nature, precisely and above all because it was a manifestation of the universality, the catholicity of the church existing in and beyond all national and racial differences. So at the ecumenical meeting of Life and Work and the World Alliance at Fanø in 1934 he could even dare to claim, 'The Ecumenical Council is in session; it can send out to all believers this radical call to peace. The nations are waiting for it in the East and in the West.'[10] Why is this so? It is because 'The World Alliance is a Church so long as its fundamental principles lie in obediently listening

---

7. DBWE 1, 190.
8. See Chapter 1, 7–8.
9. DBWE 1, 180–2.
10. DBWE 13, 309.

to and preaching the Word of God.'[11] If Bonhoeffer was ever challenged as to how he could dare to claim this on behalf of such a motley collection of people, not all of whom had been officially mandated by their churches to act in the way he was calling for, he might well have said something like,

> Well, you tell me: where else is anything resembling the Ecumenical Council meeting just now? If we remain silent, and the world is destroyed by war tomorrow, what are we going to say before the judgment seat of God? Are we going to say, 'Sorry, Lord, but we hadn't had time to get the truly great Ecumenical Council organised?' Won't the Lord say something like, 'All right, if you hadn't got the ideal shouldn't you have at least tried the next, or second or third best thing however unsatisfactory – just as the servant given only one talent shouldn't have left it in the ground but done *something* with it in the market?'

Bonhoeffer was always critical of the ecumenical movement for its slowness and hesitancy. But he never gave up on it, not even after resigning from the Ecumenical Youth Commission in 1937.[12] In 1935, writing on how the ecumenical movement and the Confessing Church needed each other, he speaks about the hopes for an Ecumenical Council: 'It is not an ideal that has been set up but a commandment and a promise – it is not high-handed implementation of one's own goals that is required but obedience.'[13] The promise therefore remains on the ecumenical movement, despite all its often disappointing outcomes, its ambiguities and seeming failures. The vision of ecumenism as the manifestation of the new humanity in Christ in the catholicity of the church remained with Bonhoeffer right to the end. His last recorded words, the day before he was executed at Flossenbürg, were a message to his closest and most trusted ecumenical friend, George Bell, bishop of Chichester: 'Tell him, that with him I believe in the principle of our universal Christian brotherhood which rises above all national interests, and that our victory is certain.'[14]

Belonging to the world: Church for others in a world of many 'others'

Between those earlier statements of 1934–5 and that last statement on the eve of his death, however, certain developments had taken place in Bonhoeffer's thinking which do not contradict or replace his earlier thought but reorientate

---

11. Ibid., 304.

12. The issue was the selection of German youth delegates to the 1937 Oxford Conference on Church, Community and State, over which Bonhoeffer was in sharp disagreement with the Life and Work office in Geneva. See Clements, *Dietrich Bonhoeffer's Ecumenical Quest*, 177–8.

13. DBWE 14, 412.

14. See E. Bethge, *Dietrich Bonhoeffer: A Biography* (Minneapolis, MN: Fortress Press, 2000), 926–7.

them in significant ways. Particularly in mind here are his prison writings and his call for a non-religious interpretation of Christianity with which to address a 'world come of age'. Central to this orientation towards a worldly understanding of Christian faith was a new emphasis in his understanding of the church, summed up in his sentence: 'The church is church only when it is there for others.'[15] This can be seen as an extension of his earlier ecclesiological understanding of 'Christ existing as community', a community structured by vicarious representative action, *Stellvertretung*, towards a corporate vicarious representative action of the church-community for the world in which it is set. I believe that Bonhoeffer, if he had survived Hitler's revenge, would also want the same extension to be applied to the ecumenical movement – as indeed he had already in effect done at Fanø in 1934. In relation to this extension, I want to bring in another citation from Bonhoeffer's prison letters, as when he writes to Eberhard Bethge: 'How do we go about being "religionless-worldly" Christians, how can we be, those who are called out, without understanding ourselves religiously as privileged, but instead seeing ourselves as belonging wholly to the world?'[16] Note that here Bonhoeffer connects religion with 'privilege', targeting the assumed role of churches as guardians of the entrance to another, superior world beyond this one – and therefore claiming privileges in relation to each other also, bearing in mind their competing claims to have identified the heavenly portals of truth. But if the faith they profess to proclaim is not about the correct exit to another world but the entrance into this world of the kingdom of God in righteousness and peace, then it is not privilege towards which they should be aspiring but authentic discipleship of the crucified and risen anointed one in this very world, the way to authentic humanity.

Bonhoeffer's posthumous influence on the ecumenical movement has been immense but his rejection of what he calls privilege and his advocacy of belonging wholly to the world constitute a challenging element of Bonhoeffer's legacy still to be fully claimed, or perhaps rather faced, by the ecumenical movement today. I would like to point up three issues of current ecumenical concern.

The first is the long-running debate, virtually as old as the modern ecumenical movement itself, on the relationship between the institutional churches and the movement towards visible Christian unity, and in particular the organizations created to further the movement. This might seem to be a very mundane matter of churchly bureaucracy but in fact has very wide theological ramifications. At root it is about how we evaluate theologically what is happening beyond the boundaries of official church structures. So for a moment please excuse what may seem a somewhat drab piece of ecumenical storytelling.

The World Council of Churches (WCC) was formally constituted at its first assembly in 1948, in Amsterdam. Almost immediately fears were being expressed among some of its member churches that what was coming into being was some kind of super church claiming an authority over the member churches. In 1950

---

15. DBWE 8, 503.
16. Ibid., 364.

at its meeting in Toronto, Canada, the WCC Central Committee after lengthy and often heated debate agreed on a statement which allayed such fears and ever since has been regarded almost as the holy writ of ecumenism.[17] According to the Toronto Statement, not only does the WCC claim no authority over its constituent churches, but membership of the WCC does not commit any church to agree with the ecclesiology of any other member church, and does not imply any ecclesiological preference by the WCC. This certainly met the fears about the imposition of any one theological understanding of the church. But this was at the price of leaving other questions unanswered. For the Toronto Statement can be interpreted in a very minimalist way, to mean that the WCC itself, or indeed any other ecumenical body, is devoid of any ecclesial significance whatever: that it is a purely functional mechanism by which churches enter into dialogue with one another and into certain inter-church cooperative projects. This issue underlay the discussions in the Special Commission on Orthodox Participation in the WCC, set up following the WCC Assembly in Harare, 1998. The problem is that if ecclesial reality resides only in the institutional churches and their governing bodies, what actually is happening when their representatives meet together and share common prayer for the Holy Spirit's guidance, and enter into any kind of joint decision-making? If there is no *ecclesiological* significance here, is there not at least a *pneumatological* reality? Further, how do we come to terms with the fact that vital to the ecumenical movement have been the witness and activity of what might be called para-church movements, especially among the youth and laity? Indeed, was it not largely out of the Christian youth and student movements of the late nineteenth century that the modern ecumenical movement was born? Bonhoeffer's point remains: we need a theology which recognizes as *significantly church* any place wherever and however the catholicity, the universality, of community in Christ is emerging and being confessed, as a sign of the new humanity in the midst of the old order of division and death, and wherever and whenever a decisive word is spoken to the world for justice, peace and reconciliation. Much is spoken of in various quarters today of the need for the institutional churches to 'own' the ecumenical movement. But does 'owning' mean 'controlling'? This I believe is bound up with a wrongly conceived contemporary obsession with 'identity'. So long as churches are unwilling to be pulled out of their isolation and self-sufficiency into a wider movement of belonging, they can never be manifestations of the new humanity in Christ.[18] For this they do not, here and now, need to be in total theological agreement nor structurally or organically one (though it may be better if they

---

17. See 'The Church, the Churches and the World Council of Churches, WCC Central Committee, Toronto, 1950', in M. Kinnamon and B. E. Cope (eds), *The Ecumenical Movement: An Anthology of Key Texts and Voices* (Geneva: WCC, 1977; Grand Rapids, MI: Eerdmans, 1977), 463–8.

18. Cf. the discussions in N. Sagovsky, *Ecumenism, Christian Origins and the Practice of Communion* (Cambridge: Cambridge University Press, 2000), 194–208; Keith Clements, *Ecumenical Dynamic: Living in More Than One Place at Once* (Geneva: WCC, 2013), 194–213.

were), but at least they need to be counter-signs to the divisions and disintegrating forces running amok in the *oikoumene* at large. To repeat again Bonhoeffer's view, the ecumenical fellowship is not an ideal but – under God – a commandment and a promise.

Second, we are surely all aware that today the ecumenical task has to be negotiated in a multifaith world, a world moreover which is not only one of religious plurality but of social and political conflicts in which religion is often a factor. Hence the frequent contemporary question: Is inter-religious dialogue the new ecumenism? This is one expression of the basic question, of how any one particular religious tradition can claim a universal significance for the whole human community – and indeed for the whole created order on our planet. In fact, awareness of other faiths within the *oikoumene*, and – increasingly – actual dialogue with other faiths – has long been part of what some call the old ecumenism. That this has been so, however, is due to the ecumenical movement always taking seriously the *oikoumene* as a whole, of which other faiths are a part. Unfortunately, one thing which the ecumenical movement, like other human projects, suffers from is fairly short-term amnesia. Over thirty years ago, the WCC Faith and Order Commission ran a study programme, 'The Unity of the Church and the Renewal of Human Community', a study which appears to be largely forgotten but still bears on our concerns today.[19] It is about how we maintain the specificity of the church as the body of Christ together with the universality of the hope given to the whole *oikoumene*, without playing off one against the other but maintaining the necessary and creative tension between them. A firm consensus emerged in the programme that the church is not itself the kingdom of God but a prophetic sign and instrument of the kingdom. It does not itself realize the kingdom in its fullness, but surrenders itself to God in the power of the Spirit to be a kind of first fruits of that kingdom, a sign of it upon the earth. As such it must manifest in its own life what it means to be a community of mutual acceptance, forgiven and forgiving, free in its diversity and one in all its differentiations. But equally it identifies with the whole of the *oikoumene* without reservation. From my own time on the Faith and Order Commission I especially remember a presentation made to its plenary meeting in Stavanger, Norway, in 1985 by Frieda Haddad, a Lebanese lay theologian of the Greek Orthodox Patriarchate of Antioch. I say 'presentation' but in fact she was not herself able to be present in Stavanger – Lebanon was still enmeshed in its terrible civil war, the road to Beirut airport was one of the most dangerous in the world and so her paper was read on her behalf. It was titled 'The Christian community as sign and instrument for the renewal of human community: a Lebanese perspective'. She described how Lebanon had inherited from both Ottoman and French rule a system of government which preserved the *millet* system, whereby limitations

---

19. See especially G. Limouris (ed.), *Church Kingdom World: The Church as Mystery and Prophetic Sign*, Faith and Order Paper No. 120 (Geneva: WCC, 1986).

and rights of each religious community were carefully set out, including the proportions to which they were entitled in representative government. This sought to provide checks and balances against any one community becoming either too dominant or too marginalized and oppressed – a precarious balance, as Lebanon's history shows all too well. But Haddad argued that from her faith perspective this was inadequate for an understanding either of how she understood her church or what it meant to be a member of Lebanese society. It reduced the understanding of human community to legally defined association. So she asked what does it mean to be 'church' in Lebanon, and what does it mean to be Christian in Lebanon. In a powerful and moving way, given the fearful nature of her context there and then, she protested against all thinking in primarily legal and institutional terms, whether of church, society or nation. She goes on:

> He who takes his citizenship seriously works earnestly for the advent of a renewed human community where the 'other' lives, for he cannot legitimately share in the communal reality of the body politic without sharing in the reality of the other, he cannot conceive of himself as answerable to state laws without answering at the same time for the other. In simple and direct terms this means, for instance, that the unbearable living conditions of the displaced, no matter what their religious affiliations are, are unbearable to me personally. Their uprooting from their villages and towns is my personal uprooting. This involvement with the other rules out any theological formulations what would consider the other as 'unholy', or as incapable of being hallowed? I cannot look at him as being part of the *human* community whereas I am part of the 'Christian' community. My life and his life are interwoven in the body politic. My hope of salvation, my way to the infinite passes through the other, through our fulfilled finitude.[20]

For Frieda Haddad, then, being church in the awful context of Lebanon meant an unconditional identification with the *whole* of her society as a human community and its crying needs, a commitment transcending all demarcations and assumed tribal loyalties. She wants to speak not so much about 'Christian witness and mission' in a majority Muslim society but about social education for the elimination of authoritarian legal structures, a revolution in the understanding of what it means to be human in community. Her conclusion is, 'The Christian community is not a minority group seeking to elaborate for itself a defensive standpoint over and against the yearnings of the human community in which it is called to live. It rather seeks to nurture in its bosom a genuine openness to the common heritage

---

20. Frieda Haddad, 'The Christian Community as Sign and Instrument for the Renewal of Human Community: A Lebanese Perspective', in T. F. Best (ed.), *Faith and Renewal: Reports and Documents of the Commission on Faith and Order Stavanger 1985, Norway* (Geneva: WCC, 1986), 187.

that binds Christians and Muslims together.'[21] It takes as its point of reference the whole life of the *polis*, the body politic, the human community and seeks to discern the signs of hope for its future. She recognizes the danger that this might drift just into ethical pragmatism, but she maintains the Godward dimension to the Christian's responsibility, a responsibility that may include suffering, perhaps a suffering with the body politic but not abandoning him- or herself blindly to any of its movements or ideologies

On behalf of the oikoumene

While Haddad nowhere mentions Bonhoeffer, this I think is a good example of what Bonhoeffer was striving for: a view of church which, without privilege, vicariously exists for the sake of the *oikoumene* before God. Those who stand under and receive the word of Christ, the church-community, are not some separate species from the *oikoumene*, the inhabited world. Says Bonhoeffer in his *Ethics*: 'It means that there are human beings who allow themselves to receive what, from God's perspective, all human beings should actually receive: it means that there are human beings who stand vicariously in the place [*stellvertretend dastehen*] of all other human beings, of the whole world.'[22] There is thus an ultimate solidarity here with the whole human family. Our approach to other faiths can only be on this basis: they too are part with us of the *oikoumene* – as too are the people of no faith, no religion. In this last respect we do well to heed the words of Lesslie Newbigin, speaking of rejoicing in the light wherever we find it:

> Here I am thinking ... not only of the evidences of light in the religious life of non-Christians, the steadfastness and costliness of the devotion which so often puts Christians to shame; I am thinking also of the no less manifest evidences of the shining of the light in the lives of atheists, humanists, Marxists and others who have explicitly rejected the message of the fellowship of the church. 'The light' is not to be identified with the religious life of men; religion is in fact too often the sphere of darkness, Christian religion not excluded. The parable of the Good Samaritan is a sharp and constantly needed reminder to the godly of all faiths that the boundary between religion and its absence is by no means to be construed as the boundary between light and darkness.[23]

The *oikoumene* includes, because it is bigger than, other faiths. It would be ironic if our concern for inter-religious dialogue in fact led to a narrowing of our

---

21. Ibid., 190.
22. Dietrich Bonhoeffer, *Ethics*, Dietrich Bonhoeffer Works, volume 6 (Minneapolis, MN: Fortress Press, 2005), 403.
23. Lesslie Newbigin, *The Open Secret: Sketches for a Missionary Theology* (Grand Rapids, MI: Eerdmans, 1978), 198.

understanding of the *oikoumene*. Inter-religious dialogue must not create another band of privilege, a religious federation over against the non-religious world. As said at the beginning of this chapter, the *oikos*, the household of which the *oikoumene* is part, embraces the whole created order.

This leads to the third point where current ecumenism is facing a real challenge, which I would summarize as the need to provide not just calls for action but a spirituality of action in the world. Recalling what was learnt in the struggle against apartheid, the South African theologian Nico Koopman believes that 'Bonhoeffer challenges us to a spirituality and a life of prayer that enhance the dawning of a life of human dignity and human rights'[24] and sums up all that Bonhoeffer offers us in inspiration and guidance for responsible living in society: 'He shows the way to a threefold action of firstly prayer, which includes spiritual and moral formation, secondly concrete obedience, and lastly active hoping and waiting upon God.'[25] Here is where I think the modern ecumenical movement, which rightly claims to have been inspired by prayer and spirituality, needs to take a fresh look at whether it really is resourcing people to engage with the *oikoumene* as the prime object and goal of God's own engagement, in other words, providing a spirituality for true worldliness.

I return to Bonhoeffer's question from prison: 'How can we be εκ-κλησία, those who are called out, without understanding ourselves religiously as privileged, but instead seeing ourselves as belonging wholly to the world?'[26] His question has not in fact been adequately answered thus far even in the ecumenical community. There can be much talk about a worldly or world-oriented or secular understanding of mission, but Bonhoeffer was asking first not about what Christians and churches should *do* but what, or who, they *are*, and to what or where they belong, a sense of self out of which their action arises. The recent ecumenical statement on the church *The Church: Towards a Common Vision*,[27] building on earlier studies, states well in its final chapter 'The Church: In and for the World' the biblical vision of the inclusive purpose of God's love for all people and all creation: 'The Church was intended by God, not for its own sake, but to serve the divine plan for the transformation of the world.'[28] Moreover, 'The Church does not stand in isolation from the moral struggles of humankind as a whole. Together with the adherents of other religions as well as with all persons of good will, Christians must promote.'[29] Christian communities cannot 'stand idly by' in the face of human suffering and

---

24. Nico Koopman, 'How Do We Live Responsibly? Bonhoeffer and the Fulfilment of Dignity in Democratic South Africa', in Kirsten Busch Nielsen, Kirsten Busch Nielsen, Ralf K. Wüstenberg and Jens Zimmermann (eds), *A Spoke in the Wheel: The Political in the Theology of Dietrich Bonhoeffer* (Gütersloh: Gütersloher Verlagshaus, 2013), 429.

25. Ibid., 431.

26. DBWE 8, 364.

27. *The Church: Towards a Common Vision*, Faith and Order Paper No. 214 (Geneva: WCC, 2013).

28. Ibid., 33.

29. Ibid., 35.

the plight of creation. 'The world that "God so loved" is scarred with problems and tragedies which cry out for the compassionate engagement of Christians.'[30] Prophetic engagement with the abuse of power, if necessary to the point of persecution and even martyrdom, is called for.

All this is well and very clearly stated as the conclusion to the whole document, which is set in the perspective of God's purpose being to establish *koinonia* between himself and all that he has made. Perhaps however it is the very fact of this being the final chapter of the document which lends a sense that such statements just have to be made, if not as an afterthought, then attached for the sake of completeness and theological correctness. The presupposition of the document seems to be not just that church and world are distinct entities (which of course they are) but that they are related only from one side, that of the church. It is a one-way bridge from church to world. The world is the object of the church's action, it is the world that has to be actively transformed by the church's witness, and it is the world's plight that calls for Christian compassion. In all this still lurks the tendency to what Bonhoeffer calls 'privilege' on the part of Christians. It is the church that rides to the rescue of the imperilled world. One recalls the popular ecumenical slogan of the 1960s, 'Let the world write the agenda!' which sounds very world-oriented but in fact implies that once the agenda is set out, it will be the church that graciously deals with it and, moreover, always knows in advance what is to be done.[31] It is the perspective of the colonial administrators.

Allied to this is the tendency of church and ecumenical statements to paint the plight of the world in ever more luridly apocalyptic colours, inducing a state of utter helplessness and despair unrelieved save for the hope of the gospel, of which the church is privileged bearer. This is apt to be not so much an exercise in responsible realism about the state of the world as a ploy by the church to secure for itself a superior vantage point over against the world. It is an assault on the world born (as aggression often is) out of insecurity, a prime example of what Bonhoeffer calls an attack on the adulthood of the world.[32] It is a simplistic view of the world that ignores the genuine ability of individuals and communities to make a positive difference – in other words under certain conditions to be justifiably optimistic. Writing in the winter of 1942–3, shortly before his arrest, Bonhoeffer defends optimism (all optimism, not just Christian) as a power of life, a power of hope when others resign, never to be despised however often it is mistaken:

> It is the health of life that the ill dare not infect. There are people who think it frivolous and Christians who think it impious to hope for a better future on earth and to prepare for it. They believe in chaos, disorder, and catastrophe, perceiving

---

30. Ibid., 36.
31. See D. L. Edwards, 'Signs of Radicalism in the Ecumenical Movement', in H. E. Fey (ed.), *The Ecumenical Advance: A History of the Ecumenical Movement Volume 2. 1948–1968* (Geneva: WCC, 1970), 373–409, especially 406–9.
32. DBWE 8, 427.

it in what is happening now. They withdraw in resignation or pious flight from the world, from the responsibility for ongoing life, for building anew, for the coming generations. It may be that the day of judgment will dawn tomorrow; only then, and no earlier, will we readily lay down our work for a better future.[33]

Bonhoeffer's question, about how followers of Christ can see themselves not only as called out but belonging wholly to the world, is not really answered simply by constant reiteration of calls for Christians and churches to witness prophetically for justice and peace, to respond compassionately to human need and the plight of the creation. These are right and just so far as they go but left to themselves they do not reach to that point of 'belonging wholly' to the world which Bonhoeffer is searching for. They do not reach to that point of profound identification with the world in its strengths as well as weaknesses, its hopes as well as its fears, which Bonhoeffer sees as the logic demanded by discipleship of the incarnate one and which alone enables effective and sustained engagement of the world. On the pastoral level it ignores the need for the spiritual resources required to energize and guide such witness and engagement, and to deal with the consequences for those who undertake them, and so they tend to lapse into cheap statements and fruitless gestures. The result of all authentic witness and engagement is not – one hopes – just the transformation of the world but the transformation of the church and believers too. At the end of *Discipleship*[34] and again in *Ethics*[35] Bonhoeffer teaches that it is not as though Christians and the church somehow bear the image of God and *then* take it into the world and bring it to bear on the lives of others. In Christ, God and world are united and neither God nor the world can be met without the other. It is in that engagement of faith with the world that the image of God in Christ is created in us. It is in sharing the sufferings of God in the world that one *becomes* 'a human being, a Christian'.[36] This is an invitation to be transformed, as much as to transform.

'Belonging wholly to the world' requires a much deeper identification than is usually sought with the human world of which one is a part yet which often one wishes one were not so. It is an identification with the world before God, in all its light and darkness, heights and depths. This is as much a spiritual exercise as one of political and social analysis (which is certainly required). It means that deep, daring and patient solidarity which makes its own the sighs of hope and fear, faith and doubt, of that part of the *oikoumene* whose life it shares. It means allowing people of faith to see *themselves* as part of the world in need of transformation, rather than trying to make people pretend that they are the ones who can put the world right – a way that leads either to fantasy or disappointment – it is first of all a truly *intercessory* identification of the kind Bonhoeffer himself had exemplified

33. DBWE 8, 51.
34. DBWE 4, 284–5.
35. DBWE 6, 82–7.
36. DBWE 8, 486.

in his prison poem 'Night Voices'[37] out of which true witness and engagement is born. Prayer and righteous action, together, are the form of faith in the world come of age. For such spiritual and moral formation we need to be truly ecumenical and to look for resources if necessary well beyond our own traditions. We need to learn from strangers (who may be angels in disguise!) more of what it means to live in Christ, to be a community of the new humanity. How interesting, that it was precisely in the period 1931–5 when he was so very Barthian, so heavily Christocentric in his theology, that Bonhoeffer was so anxious to travel to the East, to India, to visit Gandhi, in order to learn about non-violent resistance. In May 1934, on the eve of the Barmen Synod which effectively founded the Confessing Church, he writes to his grandmother,

> I'm thinking again of going to India. I've given a great deal of thought lately to the issues there and believe that there could be important things to be learned. In any case it sometimes seems to me that there's more Christianity in their 'heathenism' than in the whole of the Reich Church. Christianity did in fact come from the East originally, but it has become so westernized and so permeated with civilized thought that, as we can now see, it is almost lost to us. Unfortunately I have little confidence in the church opposition.[38]

Being ecumenical means being willing to travel, in every sense. It means, if I may quote the subtitle of my book *Ecumenical Dynamic*, 'living in more than one

---

37. DBWE 8, 462–70. Extract.

> Wide open my ear:
> 'We, the old, we the young,
> we the sons of every tongue, we the strong, we the weak,
> we the watchful, we who sleep,
> we the rich and we the poor,
> all alike in calamity's hour,
> we the bad, we the good,
> wheresoever we have stood,
> we whose blood was often shed,
> we witnesses of the dead;
> we the defiant and we the resigned,
> we the innocent and we the maligned,
> tormented by long loneliness in heart and mind.
> Brother, searching and calling are we!
> Brother, can you hear me?'

The poem 'The Death of Moses' (DBWE 8, 531–41) likewise powerfully exemplifies this intercessory identification with his country's fate before God.

38. DBWE 13, 152.

place at once'.³⁹ But we also need to travel in time as well as in space, looking for the surprising insights which reach far beyond the times in which they were first voiced. As explained in Chapter 4, I have, for example, become more and more impressed by the resonances between Bonhoeffer's worldly theology and the writings of the seventeenth-century English priest and poet Thomas Traherne, who could write,

> You never enjoy the world aright, till the sea itself floweth in your veins, till you are clothed with the heavens, and crowned with the stars; and perceive yourself to be the sole heir of the whole world; and more than so, because men are in it who are every one sole heirs, as well as you.⁴⁰
>
> Never was anything in this world loved too much, but many things have been loved in a false way: and all in too short a measure.⁴¹

Here is a kindred spirit to Bonhoeffer, who can help us extend Bonhoeffer's concern for a proper worldliness into a worldliness that sees itself as belonging not just to the human world but to the earth itself and all creatures with which we share a common home, a common *oikos*. I am sure that in your South African context you will know of avenues of exploration into African traditional religion and its understandings of belonging wholly to the created order.

The ultimate logic of ecumenism

In summary Bonhoeffer, we have seen, repeatedly challenged the ecumenical movement to act as the church. When in international session he called it to recognize itself *as* the universal church of the nations obeying the word of God. From the standpoint of his prison theology we may imagine him now calling for the churches, as before, under the word of Christ to act vicariously towards each other but also, now, to identify with their world in the deepest possible way; to confess that they do not have special privileges but themselves belong to the world in its longing for justice, forgiveness, reconciliation and peace and that they are simply the first hearers of the gospel. That means a fundamental reorientation away from themselves to belong to the world, the *oikoumene*, and through vicarious representative action in the *oikoumene* finding themselves more truly the body of Christ, and thereby finding their unity. This is truly worldly Christianity, and the ultimate logic of ecumenism.

---

39. Geneva: WCC, 2013.
40. Version taken from Thomas Traherne, *Poems, Centuries and Three Thanksgivings*, edited by Anne Ridler (London: Oxford University Press, 1966), 29. [Spelling and orthography modernized by KC.] On Traherne, see also Chapter 4.
41. Ibid., 244.

Chapter 11

'THE BURNING FIRE OF LOVE, THE NUCLEUS OF RECONCILIATION': RELEARNING WHAT LOVE MEANS

It should be no surprise that in the year of the seventy-fifth anniversary of his death the name of Dietrich Bonhoeffer should be called to mind in reflecting on the theme for the 11th World Council of Churches Assembly, 'Christ's love moves the world to reconciliation and unity.' Preaching in 1934 to one of the two German congregations he was pastoring in London he was typically forthright:

> It does nobody any good to protest that he or she is a believer in Christ, without first going and being reconciled with his or her brother or sister – even if this is someone who is a nonbeliever, of another race, marginalized, or outcast. And the church that calls a people [Volk] to belief in Christ must itself be, in the midst of that people, the burning fire of love, the nucleus of reconciliation, the source of the fire in which all hate is smothered and proud, hateful people are transformed into loving people.[1]

Bonhoeffer was deeply involved in the developing ecumenical movement during his short lifetime, and ever since his death at the hands of the Nazi regime in 1945 he has proved to be a major inspiration in ecumenical life and thought. Moreover, the themes of the love of Christ, the world, reconciliation and unity were central to him. Meeting at Karlsruhe – in Bonhoeffer's homeland – with a theme whose language so evidently resonates with his central concerns might suggest that the 11th Assembly will as a matter of course continue the ecumenical indebtedness to Bonhoeffer. But a word of caution should be voiced. Bonhoeffer, while deeply committed to the ecumenical movement as it was emerging in his own lifetime (up until 1936 he was in the category of youth participant), was never entirely at ease

---

Paper prepared in 2020 as a contribution to preparations for the World Council of Churches 11th Assembly scheduled for Karlsruhe, Germany, in 2021 but postponed to 2022 due to the Covid-19 pandemic. Published as '"The burning fire of love, the nucleus of reconciliation": Bonhoeffer and the WCC 11th Assembly theme' in *Ecumenical Review* 73, 2 (April 2021).

1. DBWE 13, 392.

with it, and indeed at times was sharply critical.[2] He sat restlessly at the ecumenical table, not because of any lack of commitment but precisely the opposite. He felt he was taking it more seriously than it took itself, and he was often wanting more from it than the official bodies felt able to give. At what points, we might well ask, might he be shifting uneasily in his seat at Karlsruhe? At the very least, we can imagine some of the comments he might make on the theme, not in order to seek direct advice from him but to gain some basic perspectives as we consider how he wrestled with the theological issues in his tragically short-lived career.

Christ's love: A very particular love

The Assembly theme echoes Paul: 'For the love of Christ urges us on' (2 Corinthians 5:14). Bonhoeffer, however, would surely ask that the rest of that verse be read as well: 'because we are convinced that one has died for all; therefore all have died'. It is here that the specific nature of Christ's love is seen, and right at the start of his theological career Bonhoeffer placed Christ's vicarious ministry and death at the centre of his understanding of God's self-revelation in Christ, and of the church as the community in which that revelation is earthed. This was expounded in his doctoral thesis *Sanctorum Communio* (The Communion of Saints) which he completed in 1927 at the early age of twenty-one.[3] Here, alongside his definition of the church as 'Christ existing as church-community', we meet a concept which, more than any other, runs like a thread through his theology from beginning to end. It is the German term *Stellvertretung*, 'vicarious representative action', that is, action which bears the needs of another and stands in for that person before God and before others.[4] For Bonhoeffer, *Stellvertretung* is most fully embodied by Jesus Christ himself, who as the incarnate Son of God took the place of sinners on the cross, bearing the wrath of God on their behalf and who always exists as the love shown in that relationship. It is specifically *this vicarious representative action* which is 'the love of Christ'.

Today, certainly in Western societies, love is typically conceived as an emotion, whether romantic, affectionate or aspirational, and thereby as a 'sentiment' confined to the inward, private life of individuals and to intimate relationships, having no place in the hard, competitive public world of social groupings, business and politics, and the collective interactions of nations (while nevertheless being susceptible to exploitation and manipulation by certain of those very same entities, the world of advertising being an obvious example).

Love conceived this way lives within, but does not challenge, the status quo of social relationships and structures. Moreover, even when Christians speak of the distinctive nature of *agape*, the Greek New Testament term for the love that Christ

---

2. See above, 116. On Bonhoeffer's whole ecumenical engagement and thought, see Keith Clements, *Dietrich Bonhoeffer's Ecumenical Quest* (Geneva: WCC, 2015).

3. DBWE 1.

4. See Chapter 1, 7–8, for a fuller exposition of the term.

has brought into the world, love for the other person's sake, it is still apt to be confined to the feeling of benevolence, or indeed compassion, rather than to what actually *happens* in this love. (We may note that the Good Samaritan, according to Luke's Gospel, *having been moved with pity, went to* the stricken victim and made his needs his own (Luke 10:33–34).) For Bonhoeffer, moreover, vicarious representative action is not confined to the private or intimate interpersonal sphere; by its very nature it manifests itself as justice, for collectivities too are called to responsibility for others. Lecturing on 'The Right to Self-Assertion', to technical college students in Berlin in 1932, he states,

> We are not only individuals, but we are also placed within life-communities... Our marriage, our church, Germany are called before the forum of responsibility... Every community, even the great community of the people, lives not only for itself but for the others, lives in responsibility for the brother, for the people to whom one is bound in brotherhood. There is absolutely no isolated life for the people. It is bound through its birth onward to the community and through its life to the peoples [*sic*] in brotherhood.[5]

A love strange and incomprehensible

In the ominous years just before Hitler came to power in 1933, the young Bonhoeffer as pastor and teacher was seeking not just to extend but to radically change people's understanding of love. Certainly as far as God's love is concerned, they have to begin all over again and be rid of the formulae and pious phrases that bedevil talk of God's love and doing God's will. During 1931-2 he preached some of his most striking sermons on the love of God, and its utter *strangeness* to comfortable, conventional Christianity. 'Your steadfast love is better than life'[6] (on Psalm 63:3) was preached in Berlin on Thanksgiving Sunday in October 1931, a time of growing unemployment and poverty for millions in Germany and elsewhere in Europe, not to mention the starving in India and China. What can such words about God's 'steadfast love' mean in such a time? The psalmist himself was praying in desperation 'far from home, consumed by suffering in body and soul, surrounded by mocking doubters and enemies of his God'. The thought of God's steadfast love comes not as a calm benediction upon an assuredly pleasant life but as a wrenching conflict within a person, the realization that knowing and faithfully obeying God matters more even than being alive. Surrounded by the hungry and powerless, if we regard ourselves simply as God's beneficiaries then we are worshipping our own selfishness: 'If we want to understand God's loving-kindness in God's gifts to us, we must see them as responsibilities for our brother ... The blessing and the loving-kindness of God are not possessions but

---

5. DBWE 11, 254.
6. Ibid., 401–8.

responsibility.'[7] Equally disturbing is the sermon he preached in a Berlin church in May 1932 on 2 Chronicles 20:12, 'We do not know what to do, but our eyes are on you.'[8] The text runs like a refrain through the sermon (and also through the address he gave at the ecumenical youth conference in Czechoslovakia two months later[9]). Preached just when Hitler was campaigning for power, when his speeches and his party rallies were exciting the nation with glib promises of answers to the country's predicament, the sermon includes a scarifying attack on the popularity of 'programmes' in public life, especially those which invoke the name of God and call him into their service. In contrast, in humility before God, faith confesses, 'We do not know what to do, but our eyes are on you.' But surely we know God's commandment to love our neighbour? No, says Bonhoeffer, we do *not* really know what *this* means amid the complexities of life, for the politician wrestling with decisions on war and peace; or what it means in marriage, or education. 'We recognize with trembling that God concealed his commandment from us – because we have violated, broken and blasphemed his commandment, out of which the world and we should have lived and now it comes towards us in thousands of human laws but it is not God's commandment.' The command to love our neighbour has in itself no clear meaning, except to make us cast ourselves on the judgment and grace of God and seek his wisdom when faced with our actual neighbour.

A radical relearning is required. Faithful obedience has to be reborn out of silent prayer which pauses with its eyes on the wholly other God, the God of the cross, whose mercy flashes out from his wrath. Nothing can be taken for granted. Even to claim that we understand those most familiar words 'God is love' as found in 2 John 4:16, is in Bonhoeffer's eyes dangerously presumptive, because it assumes that the love of God can be predicted and managed as if it was governed by the laws of this world. Whereas, asks Bonhoeffer, what can 'abiding in love', and God abiding in us, mean other than being called to break through the laws of the world as God breaks through them?

> To take the very special path that love takes, a path that is foreign and incomprehensible to the world? A path that can never lead one astray, that is completely self-sufficient, has its own laws, that is always right, even if it seems so strange? A path that is interrupted a thousand times. Because it is the path not of the priest who blindly passes by the man who had fallen into the hands of the robbers, but of the one who has eyes to see and sees everywhere. To abide in love means to have open eyes, to be able to see something that only a few see, namely, the outstretched, begging hands of the others who are along the way, and now not to be able to do anything else but to act, to help, to do one's duty, using

---

7. Ibid., 405.
8. Ibid., 434–40.
9. See below, 133.

everything one has. That may be here or there. Most important is that, wherever it is, one can always allow oneself to be interrupted by God.[10]

Stellvertretung leads to unknown destinations of responsibility. For God's Son it led to the ultimate in vicarious representative action, on the cross, the cross which faces human beings with the uncomfortable truth of their *untruthfulness* before God – and their only hope of knowing the truth which will set them free.

There are disturbing implications for both the believers and the world in which they live:

> The human being who loves because [he] has been made free by God's truth is the most revolutionary human being in earth. He is the overturning of all values; he is the explosive material in human society; he is the most dangerous human being … The path that God's truth took in the world leads to the cross. From then on, we know that all truth that wants to stand up before God must go to the cross. The congregation that follows Christ must go to the cross. For the sake of its truth and freedom, it will be hated by the world.[11]

Beware the ideal

'Reconciliation' and 'unity' are abstract nouns. Bonhoeffer knew the danger of great words, particularly religious words, and especially if they are used to denote an ideal state of affairs beyond the present-day world's experience of confusion, rootlessness, social conflict and upheaval. Ideals and utopian dreams are dangerously seductive. In June 1932, preaching on Colossians 3:1–4 ('If you have been raised with Christ, seek the things that are above'), he asks,

> What if one could finally find the key to wisdom for all areas of life? The ideal form of the state? The smoothest exchange of goods between all nations of the earth, the crisis-proof monetary system from which all instability would have been removed? The best possible educational method, the most sophisticated hygiene and diet, the infallible cure? The deepest analysis of the mind and maybe also the best philosophy, the finest art, and certainly the best of all forms of religiosity? Isn't it true that for a large segment of our people, salvation is expected from nothing else than from these things?[12]

But this dream-led search for an ideal world is never-ending and futile. It is in fact a flight from God, who faces us not with an ideal world but with the cross of Christ. 'Our future looks at us with hollow eyes.' Pious talk simply hides the truth

---

10. Pentecost Sunday sermon on 1 John 4:16, DBWE 11, 442.
11. Sermon on John 8:32, DBWE 11, 471–2.
12. Ibid., 453.

of our condition before God. It is those who dare to face the truth and drink the cup of nothingness, the cup of the wrath of God, the living and eternal God, who will find salvation. And with a word pertinent not least to ecumenical gatherings he declares,

> If we come together with some 'In the name of God, Amen,'[13] then we still come in our unbroken pride; then we never really find one another, then we never really meet each other, then we will always talk past each other, at the conferences and in our families. For it is simply impossible for us to give up our demands that seem so justifiable. But if we come together as the crucified and risen ones of Jesus Christ, as those who have lost their prideful human life in order to win it anew in Christ, as those who were sentenced to death but pardoned–then we will find one another, then we would look into one another's eyes and would recognize one another completely anew, as we are recognized by God. Then and only then could we love one another.[14]

How and for what do we pray, then? 'We are other-worldly or we are secularists' – so Bonhoeffer opens his address 'Thy Kingdom Come!' to the Protestant Continuing Education Institute for Women, in late 1932.[15] But the prayer for the kingdom is neither the prayer of the secularist who dreams of utopias on earth, nor of the pious soul who wishes to flee the earth. Rather, it is the prayer of the earthly church-community, of those 'who do not set themselves apart, who have no special proposals for reforming the world to offer, who are no better than the world, but who persevere together in the midst of the world, in its depths, in the daily life and subjugation of the world'. It is those who remain true to the earth in all its suffering and sinfulness under the curse of God, who will see and come to believe in the resurrection of Jesus Christ, the creation of a new world in the midst of the old. Loving God means loving God as Lord of the earth as it is, and loving God's kingdom as God's kingdom come on earth. We are unable to extricate ourselves from the cursed Earth, our death, loneliness and desire for utopias. 'But in fact we are not supposed to get beyond them at all. Rather, the kingdom comes *to us* in our death, in our loneliness, in our desire. It comes where the church perseveres with the world and expects the kingdom from God alone.'

The ecumenical context in the early 1930s was one in which ideals were certainly tempting. The wounds of 1914–18, in Europe especially, were still awaiting full healing, and new sores were festering. But the young Bonhoeffer was rigorously set against applying false cures in the form of ideals. He had joined the World Alliance for International Friendship Through the Churches in 1931, on his return from a year's study in the United States, and had been appointed one of its honorary youth secretaries. He threw himself uninhibitedly into the ecumenical

---

13. A phrase used by some politicians of the time when opening political gatherings.
14. DBWE 11, 456–7.
15. DBWE 12, 285–97.

peace witness – his position as youth secretary made him an ex officio member of the joint Youth Commission of the World Alliance and the Council of the Life and Work movement. Typically, however, he was also critical of some of the basic assumptions currently at work in these bodies. In particular, while he fully shared the opposition to war (he had lost one of his brothers in 1918) he equally called for a dethroning of peace regarded as an ideal state to be preserved above all other considerations and values. At the ecumenical Youth Conference in Ciernohorské Kúpele, Czechoslovakia, in July 1932, Bonhoeffer – no doubt to great surprise to many in his peace-campaigning audience – argued that such idealization was as serious an error as the nationalist desire, especially among the Nazi-sympathizing so-called German Christian movement, to exalt nationhood to the status of a divinely instituted 'order of creation'. Peace, Bonhoeffer argued, cannot be a good in itself but only for a purpose beyond itself, namely the reception of the gospel of Christ. Peace is not itself the gospel (though the gospel is indeed a gospel of peace) but is the command of God. The peace commanded by God respects two limits: truth and justice, for which there will at times need to be *struggle*. 'Wherever a community of peace endangers or suffocates truth and justice, the community of peace must be broken and the battle must be declared.'[16] By struggle, however, Bonhoeffer does not mean *war* which in the contemporary world means total annihilation of soul and body and therefore cannot be an order of preservation, 'and because war needs to be idealized and idolatrized in order to live, today's war, the next war, must be *condemned* by the church'.

Bonhoeffer carried his attack on ideals right into the heart of ecumenical life. The conference of the Council of Life and Work and the Ecumenical Youth Commission on the Danish island of Fanø in late August 1934 is famous in ecumenical history for several reasons. There, Life and Work declared its (almost) unequivocal support for the Confessing Church, much to the joy of Bonhoeffer. It was also the occasion where at a devotional session Bonhoeffer delivered his famous address 'The Church and the Peoples of the World', with its ringing call to act as 'the one Holy Ecumenical Council of the Church over all the world' and, in obedience to the command of God, to forbid war.[17] But the preparations for Fanø had also provoked one of Bonhoeffer's sharpest contretemps with the ecumenical leadership, and particularly with Hans Schönfeld, able theologian and economist who was in charge of the Ecumenical Research Office in Geneva. Schönfeld had invited Bonhoeffer to prepare some theses for discussion, expecting him to set out some basic principles about whether and in what way the church can speak and act on international problems. Bonhoeffer however was in no mood for such

---

16. 'On the Theological Foundations of the Work of the World Alliance', DBWE 11, 365. Bonhoeffer's refusal to endorse 'peace' if this meant evading unresolved issues of truth and justice was strongly echoed in the 1985 South African *Kairos Document* which rejected 'Church Theology' as based on reconciliation at the expense of facing up to the still-divisive injustices and inequalities of power under apartheid.

17. DBWE 13, 304–6.

generalities. Instead, in the spirit of his devotional address, and to Schönfeld's dismay, he presented a paper brusquely declaring God's command 'Thou shalt not kill', dismissing the basis both of this-worldly politics which justifies war, and 'secular pacifism' which looks for possibilities of holding back the outbreak of war and suppressing war 'so as to reveal the world as a good world'. The abolition of war would only be the suppression of a horrible symptom, 'but would not cut the root of the evil itself'. Then,

> The powers of evil will not be broken by means of organisations, but by prayer and fasting (Mark 9:29). Any other attitude under-estimates these powers and regards them as naturalistic or materialistic. The spirits of hell will be banished only by Christ Himself. Neither fatalism, nor organisation, but prayer! ... Prayer is stronger than organisation. It is easy to hide the burden of evil and struggle by organisation (not against enemies of blood and flesh. Eph. 6:12).[18]

The Fanø conference did not take up Bonhoeffer's challenge to speak as the great Ecumenical Council, and this led him to pursue his searching question: is the ecumenical movement *church*, that is, under the word of God, capable of taking an authoritative and concrete decision for truth, justice and peace? That would mean the ecumenical fellowship itself manifesting among the peoples that 'burning fire of love, the nucleus of reconciliation' which a few weeks later in his Reformation Sunday sermon he so passionately set before his London congregation. He was now investing the ecumenical movement with ever-greater theological significance, even as his frustrations with it were growing too. That became clear soon after his return from London to Germany in April 1935 to take charge of the Confessing Church seminary soon to be located in Finkenwalde in Further Pomerania.

No, not perfect – but under the promise of God

The ecumenical movement and its witness for peace were under pressure from all sides. In Germany they were under continual threat from the Nazis and other nationalists. In some ecumenical circles abroad, Faith and Order in particular, there was indifference to the Confessing Church's claim that the Church Struggle was a struggle about truth and heresy and therefore faced the ecumenical movement too with a decision. At the same time some within the Confessing Church evidently felt that their bold stand for the truth conferred a righteous self-sufficiency which discounted the need for ecumenical relations. In short, the ecumenical scene was in some disarray and hardly itself a credible witness to peace, reconciliation and unity. Bonhoeffer set out his response to these issues in his essay written in August 1935, 'The Confessing Church and the Ecumenical

18. Ibid., 306.

Movement', now widely regarded as his most significant statement on ecumenism, and one of the most important ecumenical documents of the twentieth century.[19] As expected, he deals with the German nationalists, and with the too-liberal-minded ecumenicals abroad who were indifferent to the truth question. He repeats his question of how the ecumenical fellowship can advance beyond its admirable range of joint studies and cooperative actions to find a basis for an authoritative decision; that is, to speak and act as a church. But equally, in the face of the Confessing Church sceptics he defends what has been happening in the movement, despite its imperfections and provisionality. Not least there has been common worship and preaching, all in the name of Jesus Christ and with prayer for the support of the Holy Spirit. 'Does one really have the right to summon the anathema over all such activity from the very outset? Is not this witness of all Christian churches at the very least something that must prompt a moment's pause and reflection?' The existence of the ecumenical movement does not of itself prove its truth and legitimacy but 'cannot it be at least an indication of the promise that God wishes to bestow on this activity?'.

By invoking the *promise* of God, as distinct from either claiming successful achievements or lamenting abject failures, at one stroke Bonhoeffer sets the ecumenical cause in a new perspective of hope from the side of God. That was timely, as further disappointments were in store for him. In 1937 he resigned from the Ecumenical Youth Commission, angered by the stubborn refusal of the Geneva office to acknowledge the right of the German members of the Commission (who were strong supporters of the Confessing Church) to appoint delegates to the Oxford Life and Work Conference and thereby in his eyes betraying the Confessing cause. While he now had no official position within the ecumenical bodies, he continued in friendship and cooperation with key ecumenical figures such as J. H. Oldham (Great Britain), Henry Smith Leiper (United States) and above all George Bell, Anglican bishop of Chichester. Then in 1938 Willem A. Visser't Hooft was appointed general secretary of the 'WCC in formation', which greatly improved the standing of Geneva in Bonhoeffer's eyes. As Europe, and eventually the whole world, slid into the deadliest war of all time in 1939, as Bonhoeffer's own situation in police-state Germany became ever more precarious and as he entered into uncharted ethical waters with his decision to join the political conspiracy against Hitler – how could the love of Christ now be expressed in a world at odds with itself and falling apart at every level, and by churches still caught in their own fragmentation? It is at just this apparently hopeless point that Bonhoeffer makes a new theological advance. From now on, he will be speaking less of human endeavour and more of God's action as the basis of ecumenical witness – and indeed of all Christian activity – and bound up with this comes a new emphasis on reconciliation as both the content and means of this witness, and on *the world* as where this reconciliation takes place.

---

19. The full text is found in DBWE 14, 393–412. An earlier, abridged translation is included in M. Kinnamon (ed.), *The Ecumenical Movement: An Anthology of Key Texts and Voices*, 2nd edn (Geneva: WCC, 2016), 7–12.

Reconciliation: Ground of all action and witness

The subject of reconciliation had of course been present in Bonhoeffer's thinking from his earliest theology onwards: 'In Christ humanity really is drawn into community with God, just as in Adam humanity fell.'[20] When God restores community between human beings and God's own self, community among us is also restored again. But he uses the actual term *reconciliation* surprisingly rarely – his 1934 Reformation Sunday sermon being an exception proving the rule – until starting to write his *Ethics* in the first year of the war and as he was entering into the political resistance. It now explicitly becomes the framework for understanding the totality of God's interaction with the world, and of human interrelationships. 'The central message of the New Testament is that God has loved the world and reconciled it with himself. This message presupposes that the world needs reconciliation with God but cannot achieve it by itself. Acceptance of the world is a miracle of divine mercy.'[21] 'There is no part of the world, no matter how lost, no matter how godless, that has not been accepted by God and reconciled to God.'[22] Reconciliation itself is not a goal to be reached by human efforts, but is the act of God; and in the incarnation, death and resurrection of Jesus Christ it has already been enacted. God's reconciling act embraces all creation: for Bonhoeffer the great cosmic Pauline scriptural texts are foundational: 'For in him all the fulness of God was pleased to dwell, and through him God was pleased to reconcile to himself all things, whether on earth or in heaven, by making peace through the blood of his cross' (Colossians 1:19–20; see also Ephesians 1:10, 22). This, declares Bonhoeffer, demands a radical rethink of such categories as 'sacred' and 'secular'. We cannot apprehend God apart from the world, nor the world without God. In Jesus Christ, God and world are united, confronting us with one reality, the world as reconciled to God. That is the situation in which humans are now placed. This equally demands a revolution in how we understand ethics itself. The common assumption is that ethics is about how one may be good and do good, and help to make the world a better place. But this is to make oneself and one's own idea of being good the ultimate reality. Such ideas (and ideals!) are abstractions, ignoring the fact that 'these realities, myself and the world, are themselves embedded in a wholly other ultimate reality, namely, the reality of God the Creator, Reconciler, and Redeemer' in the light of which the ethical problem takes on a whole new aspect.[23] The ethical now becomes not a matter of the abstract good or ideal but of allowing the reality of God whom we meet in Jesus Christ, whose way is that of *Stellvertretung*, vicarious representative action in and for this world, to take shape in our situation here and now. It is by Christ's vicarious representative action to the point of the cross that we and the world are reconciled to God, and it is in

---

20. DBWE 1, 146.
21. DBWE 6, 86.
22. Ibid., 67.
23. Ibid., 48.

such action, in each situation, that we ourselves are conformed to the will of God and find our true humanity as willed by the Creator. In Christ we are invited to participate in the reality of God and the reality of the world at the same time. We are not therefore called to identify a 'principle' which we have to apply to the world regardless of circumstances, nor some programme that we devise and seek to impose on the wayward, complex and confusing world. It is not our task to make ourselves the reconcilers of the world, for the decisive, fundamental reconciliation has already been accomplished by God's own self – that is our confidence and joy – in Jesus Christ. In summary, Bonhoeffer states, 'Rather, the question is how the reality in Christ – which has long embraced us and our world within itself – works here and now or, in other words, how life is to be lived in it.'[24] Christian action means action which within the exigencies of this world witnesses to and accords with this ultimate reality of God's reconciliation in Jesus Christ.

Bonhoeffer knew what this meant for those who, like himself in the most extreme situation of Nazi Germany, were seeking to be responsible before God, when all the conventional principles and norms for ethical action seemed vacuous and irrelevant faced with evil on such a massive scale. The question of what was responsible action could no longer appeal to established principles; rather it had now humbly to seek participation in vicarious action on behalf of others, action which could represent, in that dire extremity the reality of Christ who bore guilt for others' sake. But if the *ultimate* reality is God's reconciliation in Christ, can any human action, whether on a dramatic scale such as Bonhoeffer's own participation in the resistance (at greatest cost to himself yet morally ambiguous in the eyes of many), or in the day-to-day contexts of life in the world, the *penultimate* world as Bonhoeffer called it, witness to the ultimate? But for Bonhoeffer, the penultimate realm of 'the things before the last' is also claimed by Christ. This realm is to be kept in being and faithfully served in love, as the means of preserving the world for the sake of the ultimate, so that the ultimate word of reconciliation might receive a hearing at the right time. The way has to be prepared for the coming of the Lord:

> The hungry person needs bread, the homeless person needs shelter, the one deprived of rights needs justice, the lonely person needs community, the undisciplined one needs order, and the slave needs freedom. It would be blasphemy against God and our neighbour to leave the hungry unfed while saying that God is closest to those in deepest need. We break bread with the hungry and share our home with them for the sake of Christ's love, which belongs to the hungry as much as it does to us. If the hungry do not come to faith, the guilt falls on those who denied them bread. To bring bread to the hungry is preparing the way for the coming of grace.[25]

---

24. Ibid., 55.
25. Ibid., 163.

The world will be overcome not by destruction but by reconciliation, not ideals or programmes, not conscience, duty, responsibility or virtue,[26] nor by a general idea of love but by the actual love of God really lived in Jesus Christ. Such love engages with the reality of the world, suffering it at its worst. 'The world exhausts its rage on the body of Jesus Christ. But the martyred one forgives the world its sins. Thus, reconciliation takes place.' God's way in the world is the way of costly reconciliation, to the point of the cross. For Bonhoeffer, therefore, to say that Christ's love 'moves' the world to reconciliation will not mean a promise of untroubled progression to either an earthly paradise or the heavenly banquet but an invitation to a journey that cannot bypass the cross where pride and self-justification are broken, sins confessed and forgiveness begged for and received. It is a way that leads through risk. 'There is no way to peace along the way of safety', he had declared at Fanø in 1935. 'For peace must be dared. It is the great venture. It can never be made safe … Battles are won, not with weapons, but with God. They are won where the way leads to the cross.'[27]

Movement to reconciliation and unity: Where is the church?

To speak of reconciliation and *unity* raises the question of the relation of the church as the body of Christ to the whole of humanity and the whole created order embraced by the reconciling love of God in Christ. The question has proved inescapable for the ecumenical movement and has generated important discussion.[28] Bonhoeffer already anticipated the problems that arise if sight is lost of the reconciling action of God embracing the whole world, and the church within that world. The danger lies in the church claiming either too much or too little significance for itself in the reconciling work of God. So in *Ethics* we read,

> When God in Jesus Christ claims space in the world – even space in a stable because 'there was no other place in the inn' – God embraces the whole reality of the world in this narrow space and reveals its ultimate foundation. So also, the church of Jesus Christ is the place … in the world where the reign of Jesus Christ is to be demonstrated and proclaimed. This space of the church does not, therefore exist for itself, but its existence is already always something that reaches far beyond it;[29]

and 'the first task given to those who belong to the church of God is not to be something for themselves, for example, by creating a religious organisation or

---

26. Ibid., 83.
27. DBWE 13, 308–9.
28. For example, the WCC 1982–91 Faith and Order programme 'The Unity of the Church and the Renewal of Human Community'.
29. DBWE 6, 63.

leading a pious life, but to be witnesses of Jesus Christ in the world'.[30] Bonhoeffer states this even more starkly in his prison writings: 'The church is church only when it is there for others.'[31] But 'being there for others' means more than just being a charitable organization. Being-there-for-others means participation in Christ's own way of vicarious representative action, the way of love that takes upon itself the needs, sufferings and sins of others. We can therefore imagine Bonhoeffer saying that the ecumenical community likewise cannot be a body which merely announces to the world what its needs are and directs it to the journey it must take to reconciliation and unity. Rather it is called to be the community which wholly identifies with the suffering and fragmenting world in order to articulate from within the prayer 'Thy kingdom come'. As in Bonhoeffer's 1934 Reformation Sunday sermon, it is the church which is 'a burning fire of love, the nucleus of reconciliation' in the midst of the people, that points the world to the source of that fire, the love of Christ himself, the source and goal of reconciliation and unity. Here there is no room for 'religion', which is the attempt to use God for one's own benefit, or as a privilege.

Bonhoeffer in his prison writings underscores what he had been saying all through his career, that as human creatures we are to go where God is, and to share God's own life; not to enlist God for our own personal, class or political interests and ambitions but to be drawn to where God is and into what God is doing, entering into Christ's vicarious representative action and suffering in the world. Confessing its own condition and in humble, hopeful service, the church itself is on that journey to reconciliation and unity, and witnesses to its goal.

Bonhoeffer made his personal discovery of what the movement to reconciliation and unity involved, and expressed it poignantly in the nearly last poem he wrote in prison, 'The Death of Moses'. Here he plays himself into the role of Israel's first and greatest prophet, who is allowed to see from afar the promised land.[32]

Not an ideal but a commandment and a promise

That is the way in which the love of Christ moves the world to reconciliation and unity, by the appeal and example of love and unity themselves. Let the last word be Bonhoeffer's own, as in his 1935 essay, having surveyed all the reasons for doubting the effectiveness of the ecumenical movement of his time, he nevertheless writes of it in hope, knowing from where that hope comes:

> Whether the hope for the Ecumenical Council … will be fulfilled, whether such a council will not only witness for the truth and unity of the church of Christ authoritatively but also be able to bear witness against the enemies of Christianity

---

30. Ibid., 64.
31. DBWE 8, 503.
32. Ibid., 340. See Chapter 1, 10.

throughout the world, whether it will pronounce judgment on war, racial hatred and social exploitation, whether through such true ecumenical unity among all … churches in all nations war itself might one day become impossible, whether the witness of such a council will fall on receptive ears – that depends on our own obedience to the question now posed to us and on how God chooses to use our obedience. It is not an ideal which is set up but a commandment and a promise – it is not high-handed implementation of one's own goals that is required but obedience.[33]

Not an ideal but a commandment and a promise: might these words serve as a guide to prayer, reflection and action at Karlsruhe?

33. DBWE 14, 412.

Part IV

Taking Responsibility

Chapter 12

ULTIMATE AND PENULTIMATE: SOME BONHOEFFERIAN INSIGHTS FOR FAITH AND DEMOCRACY IN A TIME OF EXTREMISMS

The title, I hope, is not too misleading – it's certainly not meant to suggest that we can or should look for simple prescriptions from Dietrich Bonhoeffer for all the particular issues in our societies today. Further, regarding 'fresh insights' I hope you're not expecting to hear of newly discovered writings from Bonhoeffer or previously unnoticed ideas of his. All I offer is a rereading of some of the main themes in his theology in relation to what has recently been exercising our minds in what I call an age of extremisms. In particular I wish to explore his insights into what he called the relation between ultimate and penultimate things; between 'the last things' and 'the things before the last'.

Ultimate and penultimate

One of the most memorable events I've ever witnessed was in South Africa in April 1993. I was taking part in a World Council of Churches study group in Johannesburg. The day before we arrived a leading figure on the Black political scene, Chris Hani, was assassinated outside his Johannesburg home by a white supremacist. There was instant and widespread anger, and for a time it seemed that the whole political process towards the first elections for a democratic South Africa might be derailed and the country engulfed in violence. In fact that didn't happen. Political leaders like Nelson Mandela and church leaders like Frank Chikane and Desmond Tutu spoke and preached against violence and revenge: a racist murder must not be allowed to provoke a racist war. Chris Hani's funeral took place on the following Sunday evening, in the huge FNB stadium in Soweto, and our group attended it. It lasted several hours and was an amazing spectacle: some 80,000 people, nearly all Black, mostly young, chanting and singing songs of both grief and celebration, and at intervals listening to wise words from the podium. President F. W. de Klerk and other members of the white government were there,

Paper given as a public lecture hosted by the Religion and Social Policy Network (RASP) in Melbourne, Australia, 10 August 2017.

but the crowd erupted in excitement as the effective president-in-waiting, Nelson Mandela, stepped out of his car onto the floodlit turf. South Africans were saying that they were determined to go on holding the political process together for the sake of the democratic elections planned for a year hence, and thus dismantle peacefully the apartheid state. So it proved.

Next morning I was on my way out of Johannesburg and as arranged had a brief meeting at the airport with Gisela Nicholson, a leading member of the Baptist anti-apartheid group, the Fellowship of Concerned Baptists.[1] We talked about the funeral service in Soweto. She told me that the previous day at morning worship in her mainly white congregation someone had prayed that 'all the people in that stadium would be converted to Christ'. Apparently to such a person nothing mattered, not even the holding together of the tenuous fabric of society as whole, in comparison with the preaching of the gospel for personal decision. In principle of course that is right – the gospel is our ultimate concern. But if there is ultimate concern, does that entirely vitiate what is of not quite ultimate concern, the *penultimate*? This is a perennial issue in Christianity, which no-one saw more clearly than Dietrich Bonhoeffer when he was writing his major work *Ethics* during the Second World War. As a good Lutheran he believed and preached God's justifying grace for sinners as the last, the ultimate word of God, to be received by faith: and in his sermons he often did so very decisively. Such a word is in every sense the last thing. But as well as the last things, Bonhoeffer states, there are the things before the last, the penultimate sphere of life in the world where obedience to God is to be sought, where the way for the coming of the Lord is to be prepared. One can so radically insist on the ultimate word alone, that ongoing life in this world effectively vanishes in significance. Bonhoeffer sums up this radically negative attitude:

> Christ is the sign that the world is ripe to be consigned to the fire. Here there are no distinctions; all must come to judgment. In the judgment there is only one decision: to be for or against Christ Everything penultimate in human behavior is sin and denial. Faced with the coming end there is for Christians only the ultimate word and ultimate behavior. What will happen to the world as a result is no longer important: the Christian has no responsibility for that. The world must burn in any case. Let the whole order of the world break down under the word of Christ; here it is a matter of all or nothing.[2]

By contrast, in a nutshell, Bonhoeffer argues that for the ultimate word of grace to have any significance the penultimate sphere of everyday life needs to be

---

1. Gisela Nicholson died on 27 January 2021, aged eighty-four, in Pretoria. Born in Germany, she became a missionary in South Africa as a young woman together with her husband Ken. One of her close friends writes, 'During the apartheid years she boldly and passionately engaged in the struggle against apartheid and for reconciliation especially in her beloved Baptist denomination, always on the side of the oppressed.'

2. DBWE 6, 153.

preserved, otherwise there would be no-one left to hear that word; the preacher, however inspired, will be faced with an empty stadium. I expect a number of us can recall times when we've been involved in such arguments. I recall a meeting in England when an industrial chaplain, whose ministry was mainly in a large steel works, was confronted by an ardent evangelical demanding to know why he wasn't 'preaching the gospel' on the shop floor; the answer he got was that if God wanted us to make steel, on which so much of our life depends, then God would prefer us to make it in some ways rather than others, and it behoves us to find that out. Or, one of the best ways I knew of getting students to talk and think at the start of a course on Christian mission was to cite the theological college which one day in the 1960s announced that this week's project in mission would be a collection for the restoration of art treasures damaged during the recent floods in Florence.[3] The holding together of a society threatened by violence, the making of steel or other basic commodities, the creation and preserving of beautiful art are all penultimate things. In Bonhoefferian terms, they are not ends in themselves, nor are they substitutes for the ultimate, but in the light of the ultimate and for its sake they merit preservation.

It's not just absolutist preaching of the ultimate that discounts the penultimate. Events evidently announce that the End is upon us. Bonhoeffer was writing during the Second World War when it seemed that his country and all Europe was being consigned to the flames. What use was it to be concerned about lesser things when it was surely a matter of fleeing to the mountains, of not going down from the housetop or entering the house to take anything away (Mark 13:14–15)? So today it's not just extremist preachers but the threat of extreme events which call into question the value of simply trying to make the world a better place. We are beset by radical extremisms on every side, all marked by a hatred of this world: the most extreme being the world view espoused by so-called Islamic State, that everything and everyone not in accord with its own merciless theocratic ideal can literally be blown to pieces by suicidal martyrs who instantly receive the reward of heavenly bliss. No less, on the Christian fundamentalist wing, especially in the United States, are those who would gladly provoke a nuclear Armageddon in the Middle East, thereby to usher in the End. New fears are awaking. The kind of democracies many of us have grown up in suddenly feel very insecure, the dams threatening to burst under the pressures from populist movements and authoritarian leaders, often highly nationalist, racist, destructive. We have a world in which a megalomaniac dictator in North Korea suddenly becomes a nuclear threat on the international stage; and in which the United States elects a president whose declared overriding aim is to 'make his country great again' through whatever it takes and moreover claims quasi-divine powers to pardon anyone, including himself, as it suits his personal interests. We live on a planet where scientists warn of environmental catastrophe threatening the existence of life itself. Well, may we say that we live

---

3. The instance is cited in John V. Taylor, *The Go-Between God The Holy Spirit and the Christian Mission* (London: SCM Press, 1972), 38.

in apocalyptic times with the foundations of the world being shaken at every level. This is affecting our culture too. The cover story in last weekend's *The Age*, you may have seen, was a piece by Jake Wilson on the contemporary appeal of dystopian disaster movies, described by one commentator as 'fetish material for the progressive masochist'.

So it's not, apparently, a good time to go on talking about theology in the public square when the very survival of the public square itself is in doubt. We are tempted, either in fear or resignation, to give up and wait for the End, whatever form that End will take. The New Testament, however, while speaking of the end of all things, warns against presuming that disasters, wars and rumours of wars herald the immediate day of the Lord. 'The end is not yet' (Matthew 24:6), says Jesus, supplying therewith the title for a very timely forthcoming book by the South African theologian John de Gruchy, who addresses in an inspiring and yet realistic way the question of how we may go on living responsibly at such a time.[4] It was indeed in such a time that Bonhoeffer was writing his *Ethics*, a work unfinished when he was arrested in 1943. Yet his writing does not only reflect the extreme context of the ultimacy of evil that he faced in the Nazi regime. It does not only echo even the extreme ethical dilemmas posed by his involvement in resistance and conspiracy, which led to his death on the gallows in 1945. Nor is he too distracted by the strong possibility of his own premature end. At Christmas 1942, four months before his arrest, he wrote to his friends and family in the resistance that he and they had become very familiar with death: 'Deep down we seem to feel that we are his already and that each new day is a miracle.'[5] He is deeply aware of the ultimate judgment and promise of God but refuses to be either distracted or paralysed by the prospect. He has already in faith met God's last word in Christ, and in his light attends to the things before the last, the ongoing, day-by-day responsibilities of faith in the penultimate world. Christ's way needs to be prepared in the penultimate realm and its preservation: 'The hungry person needs bread, the homeless person needs shelter, the one deprived of rights needs justice, the lonely person needs community, the undisciplined one needs order, and the slave needs freedom.'[6]

With this thinking of Bonhoeffer in mind, let us look at four areas in the penultimate realm with which a public theology needs to engage today, in resistance to premature, abject or despairing submission to the End. Let me say right away: I take it as given that churches here in Australia will continue to have high on their agenda refugees, asylum seekers, Indigenous peoples, the environment and climate change – to name but some! What I have in mind may seem rather commonplace, well-worn, unexciting, even dull areas as compared with headline-hitting matters. But we are talking here about public theology, not *publicity* theology. They are very penultimate concerns, but as such are vital for that necessary preservation of life

---

4. John de Gruchy, *The End Is Not Yet* (Minneapolis, MN: Fortress Press, 2017).
5. DBWE 8, 51.
6. DBWE 6, 163.

for the advent of the gospel. They are: democracy; human rights; institutions; and 'the natural'.

A theology of democracy

Bonhoeffer himself, to the surprise of many, cannot be readily and unequivocally cited in support of the type of liberal democracy that we take for granted in the Western world. In his own time as a young adult the Weimar Republic had been born. It staggered fitfully through successive social and economic crises, and failed to withstand the mutual antagonism of the left- and right-wing parties. Not that he was anti-democratic: in 1933 he cast his vote in the last election following Hitler's accession – interestingly, and very unusually for a Protestant, for the Catholic Centre Party as the only one that now offered stability and independence thanks not least to its international ties. Ten years later in the midst of the Second World War, in commenting upon the views of his British ecumenical friends on prospects for post-Nazi Germany, he expressed severe doubts as to whether a defeated Germany would be ready for democracy on the 'Anglo-Saxon' model. A period of strongly authoritarian rule would be necessary to re-establish order on a scene where *all* order had been destroyed by dictatorship.[7] But these contextual perspectives apart, what powerfully motivates Bonhoeffer's political vision overall is the establishment of *justice* in society. 'By establishing justice, and by the power of the sword, government preserves the world for the coming of Jesus Christ.'[8] The question to put to democracies is therefore whether they promote justice, securing human rights and freedoms, protecting the vulnerable and encouraging the greatest possible participation of all citizens in both the benefits and responsibilities of a common life.

When people speak of the threats to democracies today they usually mean the activities of extremists like Islamic State. But the core dangers lie within the democracies themselves, with those who are bored with democracy and who do not see that the form of democracy is never fixed or final: it really is penultimate, always in need of extension and further development. Everyone quotes the saying attributed to Winston Churchill that 'democracy is the worst form of government, except for all the others'. But that can lead to complacency instead of real commitment to making one's democracy better, a willingness to ask the hard questions: Is our system really serving the cause of justice for all? Whose voices are not being heard? How vulnerable is it to being manipulated in the interests of powerful but minority groups endowed with wealth and control of the media? These should be on the agenda of a public theology, not in order to introduce

---

7. See Bonhoeffer's two papers 'Thoughts on William Paton's Book *The Church and the New Order*, Geneva, September, 1941', DBWE 16, 528–33, and (written with W. A. Visser't Hooft), DBWE 16, 533–9.

8. Ibid., 72–3.

religion into the debate but for the sake of preserving the moral element in that debate which is otherwise liable to become un-moralized by purely immediate and economic self-interests. Theologically democracy is vital because it reminds us all that none of us is God, we are all under God with an equally shared responsibility. Therefore much more is involved in democracy than just a voting system, more even than the vital checks and balances provided by a constitution with separation of legislative, executive and judicial powers which are the sine qua non of our Western democracies. John de Gruchy puts it very well:

> If we reduce democracy to a system only, then we fail to appreciate its character as an open-ended process shaped by a vision of a more just society. Democracy can then be frozen and co-opted to serve the interests of some, but not all citizens. The development of democracy is, for that reason, a constant struggle to extend and entrench civil rights, and promote human rights more generally. That is why it is sometimes said that democracy is a perpetual argument, something which is obvious if you watch proceedings in the British or South African parliaments as compared with a session of the Chinese People's Congress.[9]

Or, we might say with Bonhoeffer, it is in essence penultimate, very much a part of the penultimate realm which has to be kept open for the ultimate, and as such is a necessary sphere of faith's engagement.

A theology of human rights

We have already mentioned the upholding of human rights as a vital feature of democracy. We are immersed in the issues and debates all the time. These few weeks I have been here in Melbourne, they have been headline news: the possibility of new legislation on assisted dying; the dispute about what was agreed between the Australian government and the UN (and the United States) on refugees from Manus Island and Nauru; the case of the Sikh boy not allowed to wear a turban to a (Christian) school here in Melbourne. And so on. Particular individual cases provoke disagreement. But it is also the questions of fundamental principles about human rights, as to what they really are and to whom they apply, that make the whole area very penultimate: no clear and final answers. Indeed today the very concept of human rights is extremely vulnerable. Human rights seem to come low down on the priorities of even so-called liberal governments. That is all the more reason for a public theology to address them at this critical point. The penultimate sphere, including that of human rights, must be preserved for the ultimate judgment and grace of the Lord, and theology must surely be in on that debate because the central issue is not what we mean by rights but what we mean by *human*.

9. de Gruchy, *The End Is Not Yet*, 95.

Bonhoeffer has a great deal to say on human rights. 'Open your mouth for the dumb', he stated as the Nazi persecutions of Jews and dissidents began and the programmes to eliminate so-called physical and mental defectives were drawn up.[10] The one time I met the founder of Amnesty International, the late Peter Benenson, he told me that the single greatest inspiration for his work was Dietrich Bonhoeffer. In his *Ethics*, in his section on natural life and especially on 'The Right to Bodily Life', Bonhoeffer emphasizes the theological basis of human rights. 'Since by God's will human life on earth exists only as bodily life, the body has a right to be preserved for the sake of the whole person.'[11] It is remarkable how he underscores what is happening to people's bodies as the core issue in human rights. His discussion ranges widely and sensitively over issues including reproduction, abortion, suicide, war, torture and slavery. But it is all grounded in a belief in God as origin and safeguarder of natural bodily life. A special requirement is laid, he says, on those who defend their own or others' rights: 'Under all circumstances they must defend a right in such a way as to make it credible that God, not the individual, is standing up for the right.'[12] Such a blatant reference to God in the matter of human rights will irritate or embarrass many people today, including perhaps some Christians, since it is assumed that the whole concept of human rights is a creation of the Western Enlightenment, not religion, and is a secular matter to be determined on secular principles alone (despite, incidentally, the great landmark 1948 Universal Declaration of Human Rights having had significant church and Christian input into its formulation and early promotion[13]). God, it is argued, has no place in the public square. The contemporary human rights scene, however, is in some disarray on whether there can be a genuinely universal understanding of human rights in a multicultural world so complex and varied in its different contexts. Indeed, what is the basis of any 'human right' beyond what a bureaucratic government decrees, or what purely utilitarian motives dictate, which might simply be the greatest happiness of the greatest number or whatever suits that slippery concept of 'national security'? On such flimsy grounds there is no final protection against the most grisly utilitarian forms of violation of bodily life, like subjecting suspects to torture in the attempt to elicit information from them. Secularists are hard put to it, to identify a ground, transcendent of all other

---

10. In London, writing to George Bell on 19 January 1934, in English, Bonhoeffer cites Proverbs 31:8 in the King James Version: 'open [thy] mouth for the dumb in the cause of all such which are appointed to destruction' (DBWE 13, 89). Later that year, writing to his Swiss friend Erwin Sutz he cites the first part of the same verse in the German of the Luther Bible. 'Tu den Mund auf für die Stummen' (DBWE 13, 217). In the Luther Bible, it may be noted, the latter part of the sentence reads 'und für die Sache aller, die verlassen sind' – 'and for the cause of all those who are *abandoned*'.

11. DBWE 6, 185.

12. Ibid.

13. See John Nurser, *For All Peoples and All Nations: Christian Churches and Human Rights* (Geneva: WCC, 2005).

considerations, which invests human life with such unquestioned value as to make such violations unacceptable in any circumstances. What alternative is there to Bonhoeffer's belief that *God* is standing up for the right?

Rowan Williams has argued that while Christians in the human rights debate should not expect to be able to convert secularists to their theistic position, they should at least point out that what is really at issue is not just what 'rights' are but what *human beings* are. Human beings are not just atomized individuals but embodied persons who live by communicating with each other through their bodies. Defending the rights of the other is the according to him or her of a dignity, but more than that,

> the recognition that what they have to say (welcome or unwelcome …) could in certain circumstances be the gift of God … The recognition of a dignity that grounds the right to be heard is the recognition of my own need to receive as fully as I can what is being communicated to me by another being made by God.[14]

If the secularist can't stand this God-talk, let him or her at least recognize that such mutuality is the very stuff of which human society, at root, is constituted and which must be upheld for the healthy continuance of humankind on this planet. We all, refugees on Manus Island and Nauru included, are relational beings, which the powers that be, disregarding the refugees' close relations here in Australia, do not seem to recognize. If we are unable to bring God into the secular public sphere, let us at least talk about human beings and relationships in a way that only makes sense if God is real. So it is not just a matter of what will happen to people whose rights are violated or disregarded (though it is); it is a matter of what will happen to *us* as individuals and as a community if we do not uphold their humanity and dignity. This penultimate realm where the upkeep of human community, our own included, is at stake is one which both in practice and in understanding a public theology must engage.

A theology of institutions

I can almost see the yawns, and can well imagine the sighs of boredom as eyes turn upwards towards the ceiling, when institutions are mentioned. We live, we are often told, in an anti-institutional age. People are fed up with organizations which seem to exist only for the benefit of the people; the 'faceless bureaucrats' who run them; their overweening powers over people's lives; their inefficiency at delivering what they are supposed to do; their unaccountability; their toleration, and cover-up, of abuses of people supposedly in their care; not to mention, at times, their colossal expense. Which of us has never added our own grumbles to the chorus? Yet at the end of the day, is it possible to imagine a life without some

---

14. Rowan Williams, *Faith in the Public Square* (London: Bloomsbury, 2012), 156–7.

means of ordering our lives on the larger and even international scale? We have in fact a love–hate relationship with many of them. We both depend on them a lot and look to them for much that is vital whether in education or health care, finance or law enforcement or government itself, which is precisely why they generate such anger when they do not perform as well as we think they should. We might wish to compare the psychology of this with that of the child–parent relationship. They pose the question which runs throughout the penultimate realm: how to live creatively with what is provisional and imperfect?

In June 2016 the people of the UK voted in a referendum to leave the European Union (EU), of which the UK had been a member for over thirty years during which time it had grown to a membership of twenty-eight most notably since the end of the Cold War which allowed former Eastern Bloc countries to join. I won't spent time discussing in detail the reasons for that vote and its consequences, beyond saying that I think it was a serious mistake both politically and morally. Within the anti-EU vote there were many elements: a felt threat to national identity, a resistance to continuing substantial immigration, objections to what were seen as restrictions on business practices and consumer choices, and the supposed costs of British contributions to the EU budget. I believe that certain criticisms of the EU and its governance were justified but could have been addressed had we stayed in membership. But the leave vote was also aided and abetted by a long-running and often poisonous campaign of untruths by the right-wing press, not to mention a nostalgia, served up from the same quarters, for a supposed past of British independence, greatness and glory to which we could return, and that we would once again be better on our own. That the referendum campaign coincided with the centenary of the 1914–18 war was probably a significant factor in the outcome.

But I suspect also that the EU fell victim to anti-institutionalist feeling as a whole, and became the target of that widespread sense of what Kierkegaard and others saw as a feature of nineteenth-century Europe, namely *ressentiment*, 'a continuously grumbling exasperation' at whatever is seen as the source of one's frustrations:[15] in this case against government and governmental institutions as a whole. Such *ressentiment* left to itself is dangerous, and it manifests an inability to think both realistically and responsibly about our corporate social life. In the British EU referendum, along with this attitude went a refusal to look at the way the EU has been vital in developing a post–Second World War Europe of greater justice, peace, human rights and cooperation in so many cultural and educational as well as commercial fields. This populist anti-institutionalism came to a head after the vote, in November 2016. A panel of three judges had ruled in favour of a case brought by a private citizen claiming that, following the referendum vote to leave, it was the British Parliament, not the government solely, that had the power to enact 'Article 50' and so trigger the actual leave process. The entire right-wing press launched a tirade of vilification against the judges, the *Daily Mail*'s banner headline even calling them 'Enemies of the People' (a favourite term of abuse by

---

15. John de Gruchy explores this phenomenon in *The End Is Not Yet*.

both fascist and communist totalitarian regimes). How ironic that the judiciary – itself a vital institution for safeguarding rights and liberties as well as duties under the law – was being attacked in the name of patriotism for defending the most British of institutions, namely Parliament.

Most serious of all was the near-total failure by the British churches corporately to address the issues raised by the referendum, in the light of Christian beliefs about the nature of life together in community, both nationally and internationally. I read a statement by one pastor a few weeks before the referendum, that the vote one way or another had nothing to do with faith; that it was just a matter of deciding about political machinery. This view was probably typical of many, while the church leadership was effectively silent. This was a total abdication of theological responsibility in the public sphere. The omission by the churches was all the more troubling since in earlier phases of the EU's history the British churches, in cooperation with their European partners, had followed the development of the EU and other European institutions so closely. Indeed in Europe, both the Protestant and Roman Catholic churches, joined more recently by the Orthodox, have invested much input into study and dialogue with the European integration process as a whole. It was my privilege while working for the Conference of European Churches to know at first hand the constructive engagement that was established between the churches and many aspects of the EU's work.[16]

I doubt if this kind of scenario is unique to Britain, and we need to develop a faith-based, critical and constructive theological engagement with the institutions that order our societies at every level and in which vital decisions are made for human welfare. Bonhoeffer himself was suspicious about 'organizations' at large. But for most of his life he wrestled with how justice in society required both order and freedom under the law, and it could not just be left to individual action. In all their imperfections, in all their all-too-evident penultimacy, our institutions, both of government and in civil society, are to be taken seriously, neither simply accepted as they are nor demonized. The same is true no less of international bodies like the United Nations. But you will have in mind bodies within Australia too. They are part of the reality of the penultimate world, and it is in our responsible engagement with them, no less than with individuals, that we shall meet with Christ in whom God and reality are united, in service to the world. We cannot have God without the world, nor the world without God, is Bonhoeffer's constant refrain. 'The penultimate will be swallowed up by the ultimate, yet it retains its necessity and its right as long as the earth endures.'[17]

---

16. In some mitigation for the churches' inattention to Europe during the referendum debate was the publication (three years after the Brexit vote), by the Church of England and the Evangelische Kirche in Deutschland, edited by Matthias Grebe and Jeremy Worthen, *After Brexit? European Unity and the Unity of European Churches* (Leipzig: Evangelische Verlagsanstalt GmbH, 2019).

17. DBWE 6, 167-8.

A theology of the natural

Closely connected with his understanding of the penultimate is Bonhoeffer's highlighting of 'natural life', that is, human life as created by God, now fallen and marred by sin but nevertheless still under God's loving preservation, still accorded God-given rights, and thus preserved for the coming of Christ. The natural includes that whole area of relative freedom in which, even in its fallenness, life is sustained and enriched. It includes work and friendship, culture and play, for example. (Bonhoeffer himself, be it noted, was both a gifted pianist and a formidable tennis player.) The significance of the natural, he believed, had long been overlooked in Protestant ethics as compared with Catholic doctrine. Some strands in Protestant theology saw the natural as so sunk in sin as to be fit only for burning, or the material and fleshly world as of no real interest to God who is spirit. I'm not sure how he regarded the traditional Catholic view that 'grace perfects nature'. Perhaps he would have preferred to say 'grace *protects* nature' – certainly as an ethical guide. Writing against the background of wanton violence and destruction of life wrought by war, the Nazi-enforced euthanasia programmes and, of course, the final solution of the holocaust, the reasons for his concern for the natural are obvious. But he also warns against the threats to natural life from 'organization'. The natural itself, he says, cannot be organized, though it can certainly be disorganized. 'For example, one can organize the undermining of respect for parents, whereas respect for parents is simply practiced and in its essence cannot be organized.'[18] This was a source of optimism for Bonhoeffer. In *Ethics* he speaks of the resilience of natural life which has a kind of inbuilt protective will, countering attempts by the unnatural to violate, repress or over-organize it:

> The natural guards life against the unnatural. In the end, it is life itself that tends towards the natural and ever again turns against the unnatural and breaks it down. Here lies the ultimate basis of health and healing, both of body and soul. Life, whether of the individual or of the community, is its own doctor. It fends off the unnatural as life-destroying. Only when life itself is no longer capable of this necessary defense are the destructive powers of the unnatural victorious.[19]

One can cite, for example, the responses of the local communities in Britain to recent events like the terrorist attacks in Manchester and London, together with the Grenfell Tower fire in Kensington, London, in which over eighty people are thought to have died. The refusal by Manchester people to be intimidated by an inhuman attack on Ariana Grande's concert-goers produced simply another pop concert by the singer attended by thousands expressing both their defiance and compassion. The Grenfell Tower tragedy released an extraordinary, spontaneous

---

18. DBWE 6, 177. Bonhoeffer has in mind some of the activities of the Hitler Youth movement, which encouraged children to spy on their parents ideologically.
19. Ibid., 176.

outpouring of relief and mutual help by the local community, including churches and mosques in the shadow of that tower-block, which put to shame the paralysis and ineptitude of both local and central government (the Prime Minister's office had to telephone the bishop of Kensington with the request that he convene a meeting to coordinate the local relief effort, the voluntary part of which was already underway happening on the streets).

Bonhoeffer writes that 'the natural persists and prevails by its own strength, since life itself is on the side of the natural'.[20] There is an evident need for humility by the churches and public theology here. We do not have to take charge of natural life; rather, it is enough to be alongside it. Some versions of public theology, including high-level ecumenical ones, seem to assume that the world is everywhere in direst need and darkness unless and until we come in with our ideas, insights and solutions (and maybe our money too).[21] A vital part of our role should be simply to recognize, affirm, uphold, cherish and celebrate the good that is already happening in the public realm. Jesus sat down and enjoyed communal meals and wedding feasts; he let little children be little children, for of such is the kingdom of God. He wasn't always lecturing them. He was prepared to let birds and lilies do the talking, which is a good cue for drawing to a conclusion.

Conclusion

The extremists object to – or disregard – democracy, human rights, institutions and much of natural life because these obstruct their obsessions with complete control and final solutions – and a final solution was a threat about which Bonhoeffer himself knew all too well in his context. The penultimate must be maintained, as in a mass funeral rally in Soweto, a steel works or an art gallery or a pop concert, and not prematurely cast aside either politically or religiously. It is best preserved by living out what the extremists hate, what religious fanatics fear and what the power-hungry political bullies grab for their own ends. I hope it's not too much of a trivialization to cite the advice issued by Her Majesty's Government on posters in wartime Britain, and today reproduced on postcards for our amusement if not encouragement, 'Keep Calm and Carry On' – as did Bonhoeffer himself from April 1943 even in his prison cell. He remained an optimist even under Hitler and even after the failure of the conspiracy against him. His optimism stemmed both from his faith in the faithfulness of God in Christ in the midst of a faithless world, and his sense of the long-term resilience of natural life. Therein lies his legacy for our responsibility.

20. DBWE 6, 177.
21. See 123–5 in Chapter 10.

Chapter 13

THE 'WHO AM I?' QUESTION WRIT LARGE: BRITAIN, EUROPE AND THE CHURCHES

Statements by church figures on public occasions can be very predictable. I know, because in the course of my ecumenical work I often had to draft them myself. The predictability was apparent in the kind of things we heard from church leaders in the UK following the 23 June 2016 referendum vote to leave the European Union, and certainly when the divorce between Britain and the European Union was formally declared on 31 January 2020. The presidents of the Conference of European Churches (CEC) stated, 'This does not change the mutual ecumenical commitment if European churches that grew in the last century under different political contexts. On the contrary, there is a call for us to intensify the commitment of churches towards reconciliation, cooperation and solidarity in Europe.' I have to admit that it would probably have made very little difference to the statement if I had still been general secretary of CEC then. But I would also have felt uneasy if that was all that could be said. For beneath all the noble statements about reconciliation, cooperation and solidarity there swirl, in the UK and in Europe as a whole, turbid currents of emotions generated by words such as nationhood, sovereignty and identity, which this sort of statement barely touches. It is with these dangerous currents that we must engage if we are to have anything meaningful to say to the crisis of our time and place.

As we well know, much of the Brexit debate centred on economic issues, on whether the UK would be materially better or worse off outside the EU. But there were voices saying, 'It's not really about economics, or even issues like security; or at any rate not these alone. It's about our *identity* as a nation, about *who we are*.' Closely bound up with the issue of identity is that of sovereignty, as conveyed by phrases such as 'taking back control' of our affairs from Brussels. But sovereignty and identity are not quite the same issue. Sovereignty refers to an entitlement which is claimed by virtue of our presupposed identity as a nation. So while I was and am a Remainer, I have a certain innate sympathy with those leavers who feel that the identity issue has been underplayed, and heartily endorse what the vicar of St Martin-in-the-Fields, Sam Wells, wrote in the *Church Times*: 'The referendum,

Chapter based upon a lecture given to the Severn Forum, Cheltenham, 2 April 2019, revised for presentation to the Peterborough Theological Society in March 2020, but not given due to the Covid-19 pandemic.

and almost all the foregoing and subsequent debate, have concentrated on economics and politics but the real issue is one of identity.'[1] Precisely because identity is such a highly charged issue, it is a theological issue: it has to do with what really matters; it raises what the theologian Paul Tillich called our 'ultimate concern'. So, we must dare to talk about these things and reflect on them in a theological light. Put another way, theology has to become controversial. It has to get under the skin of sensitive issues of our time and raise basic questions about society's assumptions, especially when it comes to nationhood, national identity and relating to other nations. It is good to see that in the wake of Brexit there has appeared the symposium *After Brexit? European Unity and the Unity of European Churches* published by the Church of England and the Evangelical Church of Germany,[2] which I hope will prompt much more searching discussion than has so far emerged from the churches, certainly in the UK.

So, to some basic observations.

Nations are facts

This may sound obvious but always has to be restated. When just over thirty-five years ago I was writing a book called *A Patriotism for Today: Dialogue with Dietrich Bonhoeffer*, it was Reinhold Niebuhr, the great American theologian and social ethicist of the 1930s, who rubbed my idealistic nose in the inescapable realities of collective life:

> The modern nation is the human group of strongest social cohesion, of most undisputed social authority and of most clearly defined membership. The church may have challenged is pre-eminence in the Middle Ages, and the economic class may compete with it for the loyalty of man in our own day; yet it remains, as it has been the since the seventeenth century, the most absolute of all human associations.[3]

This did not stop Niebuhr from describing the state as 'human egoism in its great proportion'; but just as our abhorrence at the egotist personality cannot make us pretend that the personality as such is unreal, no more can we shy away from the fact of nationhood and the undoubted benefits that stem from it. It is a powerful means of socialization which a common life requires. Much of what we take for granted is possible because it is organized on a national basis and draws upon a sense of shared responsibility and communal values and cooperation at the national level: education, health care, provision of infrastructure and so forth. The

---

1. 'A Manifesto for a post-Brexit United Kingdom', *Church Times*, 28 February 2020.
2. Matthias Grebe and Jeremy Worthen (eds) (Leipzig: Evangelische Verlagsanstalt, 2019).
3. Reinhold Niebuhr, *Moral Man and Immoral Society* (London: SCM Press, 1963), 83 (originally published 1932).

answer to the prayer 'Give us this day our daily bread' comes in large (though not of course total) measure through national provision and organization.

More recently the late Professor Anthony Smith of the London School of Economics concluded his influential study *National Identity* (1991), in much the same vein as Niebuhr: 'A growing cosmopolitanism does not itself entail the decline of nationalism: the rise of regional culture areas does not diminish the hold of national identities';[4] and 'National identity does in fact today exert a more potent and durable influence than other collective cultural identities; and ... this type of collective identity is likely to continue to command humanity's allegiances for a long time to come, even when other larger-scale but looser forms of collective identity emerge alongside national ones'.[5]

If nations are real, so too are national sentiments

We might reckon sentiments and emotions of national loyalty and identity to be naïve and attaching to fiction, to fantasy even, rather than fact, but they are real factors in what we mean by national identity. We can describe what a particular nation is in very prosaic, factual terms of geography and population. The UK, for example, is an island country situated off the north-west coast of northern Europe, with a land area of approximately 242,000 square kilometres and a population of approximately 66,436,000 people. That however does not convey what people feel they belong to. For that, geography has to give way to sentiment and poetry, to this sceptred isle, this precious stone set in the silver sea, this teeming womb of royal kings, this home of football and Strictly Come Dancing. In Scott Fitzgerald's novel *Tender Is the Night*, set in the 1920s there is a scene in which the character Dick Diver is showing a group of mostly American tourists around one of the still-scarred French battlefields of the recent world war. In response to their bafflement at what could have engendered such conflict and carnage, he says,

> You have to have a whole-souled sentimental equipment going back further than you could remember. You had to remember Christmas, and portraits of the Crown Prince and his fiancée, and little cafés in Valence and beer gardens in Unter den Linden and weddings at the mairie, and going to the Derby, and your grandfather's whiskers. ... This kind of battle was invented by Lewis Carroll and Jules Verne and whoever wrote *Undine*. ... Why, this was a love battle.[6]

It took some time for political scientists and historians to admit that this psychological, emotional phenomenon is a real part of what national identity, indeed nationhood itself, is. Long gone is the time when nationhood and conflicts

---

4. Anthony D. Smith, *National Identity* (Reno: University of Nevada Press, 1991), 175.
5. Ibid.
6. F. Scott Fitzgerald, *Tender Is the Night* (London: Penguin Books, 1955).

between nations could be explained wholly by material and economic factors. I well remember going to Chatham House in London (home of the Royal Institute of International Affairs) in 1991 to hear a lecture by Eduard Shevardnaze, minister of state for foreign affairs in the last years of the Soviet Union, and Mikhail Gorbachev's right-hand man in bringing about the eventual changes there. It was in the early stages of the conflicts in former Yugoslavia and in the course of his lecture Shevardnaze remarked that if life in society was all about economics, Serbs and Croats would not now be fighting each other. That, from one who no doubt knew his Marxist theory as well as anybody else!

National identity is at least in part a *choice* made by a people as to who they think they are. It is partly a given, but it is also a choice, a social act', and most often it centres upon a story which people believe is their history and which can sustain them as a collective self.[7] It involves powerful myths, by which is not necessarily meant fictions or fantasies, but stories and figures to which people look for the meaning of the collective narrative and which supply inspiration for the present and guidance for the future. Within the UK of course there are several narratives and a variety of myths depending on the particular nation we are talking about: Scotland, Wales, Northern Ireland and England will have their particular takes to tell and icons to display, and it is getting harder to talk about an overall British narrative and a sense of national identity. As well as the growth of a parliamentary democracy and an independent judicial system, a typically English collective historical memory and its 'whole-souled sentimental equipment' is likely to include all sorts of events, artefacts and images, like Magna Carta, the Spanish Armada, the Glorious Revolution of 1688, Florence Nightingale, Isambard Kingdom Brunel and Spitfire pilots running to their aeroplanes. The historical memory is a selective mixture of fact and interpretation, depending on what the people particularly wish to claim are their distinctive features, that which makes them recognizably different from other peoples. That is not always a convincing claim to sustain.

When successive British prime ministers try to set out a list of what makes Britain distinctively British, the typical list – democracy, freedom of speech and a free press, the rule of law, toleration and so on – tends to look remarkably like those of most of our European neighbours, which leaves us having to play up our tourist attractions as distinctives. Sigmund Freud identified a trait in some of his patients, which he called 'the narcissism of minor differences', that is, the felt need to exaggerate even the smallest features of oneself in order to lend an air of distinction and importance one might otherwise not possess. Churches can behave this way too, which probably accounts for why ecumenical discussions seem to make so little progress. (This happens at every level. When my wife and I moved to Portishead on our retirement some years ago, about twice a month we started to attend the Anglican church close to our home. Portishead is an unusual

---

7. Bill McSweeney, *Security, Identity and Interests* (Oxford: Oxford University Press, 1999), 165.

parish in that there are two Anglican churches in it, St Nicholas, the one we attend, and the larger congregation of St Peter's. After we'd been attending St Nicholas for some time, we were puzzled as to why, although the church has a choir and organ, we never actually sang the Gloria at Sunday morning communion but just recited it. When we asked someone about this the answer we got, not entirely tongue in cheek, was 'because at St Peter's they do'. Thankfully, we do now sing the Gloria.) The collective identity we choose can be a way of keeping our distance from others.

British identity and Europe

All along, British attitudes to the European project and British decisions on how to relate to it have reflected the British sense of identity at the time. In the immediate aftermath of the Second World War, Britain still saw itself as only marginally European, choosing to emphasize its transatlantic and Commonwealth links which had after all been so important in the defeat of Nazi Germany. When the European Trade area was first mooted in 1950, setting up the European Coal and Steel Federation of Belgium, France, Germany, Italy, Luxembourg and the Netherlands, followed by the 1957 Treaty of Rome establishing the Common Market, Britain positively decided not to join. This was in contrast to the new Federal Republic of Germany which from the start saw itself at the centre of a democratic European family. Bill McSweeney of the Irish School of Ecumenics observes that both Germany and Britain like many other countries faced the same problem 'which individuals and collectivities routinely address at critical junctures in their lives, but which now posed itself with unprecedented starkness: Who are we?'.[8] Britain's answer then, with all the emotional undertow of the wartime and Commonwealth alliances, engendered a deep-seated Euroscepticism which continues today as the default position for many people. McSweeney deserves quoting more fully here:

> Britain chose to distance itself from the [European Community] because its post-war governments saw the possibility of reconstructing its pre-war identity in line with economic and strategic interests alien to the [European] integration project. While ... one cannot separate out the material self-interest from the moral choice in respect of identity, the British case sharpens the focus on identity. The idea that Britain was in Europe, but not of it, and must disentangle itself from the legacy of wartime involvement with the European allies in order to reassert its role as a major world power, proved a powerful motive for rejecting the Schuman plan for European integration ... This appeared to entail the surrender of a centuries-old tradition of imperialism and independence to the uncertain benefits of integration with the 'lesser' states of Europe.[9]

---

8. Ibid., 185.
9. Ibid.

The tradition of imperialism may not carry so much weight today (except as a form of nostalgia) but the desire for independence certainly does, as was manifest in the leave vote. This is not to minimize the other factors in what was a complex scenario – such as fears about migration, and the resentment of large sections of the population especially in areas of the north of England, who felt that their economic deprivation was being ignored by the political classes and that any change would be better than none. But the national picture was varied. As one observer noted, 'Different communities are rooted in different values and different versions of the past, in different interpretations of Brexit, and in different hopes and fears for the future'[10] – to say nothing of the Northern Ireland border issue. Scotland is especially distinctive here. It was no surprise that Scotland strongly voted Remain, and the Church of Scotland moreover was the only British church representative body which formally (and firmly) resolved firmly for Remain. (Sixty percent of Anglicans, reportedly, voted Leave, the overall stance of their bishops notwithstanding.[11]) The Scottish stance was no surprise; when I used to visit the Church of Scotland offices at 121 George Street in Edinburgh, one was met by the St Andrews flag and the European flag hanging side by side over the entrance. The message, 'We are Scottish – in Europe!', was clear. The identity issue is real: indeed, who are we? Put crudely, are we nationalists or internationalists? British independents or British Europeans? Identities are certainly competitive at the moment. Which identity should triumph?

One of the realities to be faced is that notwithstanding all the formal aspects of ending membership of the EU, still to be negotiated over the coming months, 'getting Brexit done', or 'taking back control', or 'leaving Europe', is in practice going to be far more limited than the rhetoric implies. The reality is nicely symbolized by the fact that our post-Brexit passports, reverting to the traditional British blue, are in fact having to be printed in Poland, an EU country. The Channel is no wider than it was before. The EU member states are still our closest neighbours. We will have to trade with them, and to do so effectively whether we like it or not we will still have to meet many EU standards. Or what will we do if we lose our membership, for example, of the European Centre for Disease Prevention and Control,[12] which plays an invaluable role in providing early warning and reporting on outbreaks such as the Coronavirus epidemic? Do we really want to be without the highly effective and valued Erasmus programme of youth and student exchanges and international courses in education? Leaving the EU does not by itself mean taking no more notice of the European Court of Human Rights which is a quite separate institution, while our relation to the European Court of Justice, which is the judicial branch of the EU, is a matter for difficult negotiation. Quite

10. Tina Beattie, 'The Human Factor', *Tablet*, 23 February 2019, 4.

11. It should also be noted that the Quaker Council of European Affairs also 'discerned' in favour of Remain. On further referendum voting figures by denomination see *After Brexit?*

12. Based in Stockholm.

apart from all this, the UK will still be a member of the Council of Europe (which in fact predates the EU) and the Organization for Security and Cooperation in Europe. 'Leaving Europe' is more fiction than reality, not because the tentacles of the evil monster of Brussels are still determined to embrace and strangle us but simply because of the way the world is today. It is a world of interrelationships and interdependence at every level, of which we in the UK are a part and through which we have to navigate according to the rules of that wider world. That being so, we need a motivating vision of ourselves which, our non-membership of the EU notwithstanding, helps us to engage creatively with Europe, the Europe from which we cannot escape, and of course the wider world. Otherwise we shall be left to foster self-indulgent fantasies about independence and entitlement which merely stoke up fruitless antagonisms with our neighbours. Freedom comes not by detachment and isolation but by engaging with others in the common good, and it is only in that engagement, not apart from it, that we find out who we really are.[13] The cat that habitually chases its own tail may as an individual cat be independent but it is not free, being merely in thrall to itself. In this quest for identity the churches of Britain and Europe have a crucial role to play.

Faced with this situation, let us move towards some theological reflection.

How important is nationhood?

A very basic question: if nationhood is a fact, just *how* important a fact is it in the grand scheme of things, such as theology envisages? In the early 1930s in some circles in Germany the significance of nationhood, thanks to the Nazi ideology of blood, race and soil, was being so exalted as to become demonic. That exaltation owed something to those German Protestants, the so-called German Christian Movement (*Deutsche Christen*) who viewed nationality as an 'order of creation'. On this understanding, each nation with its particular racial basis and inherited culture was ordained as of God and had to be preserved in all its racial, cultural and religious purity. In Germany, above all, it meant that any admixture of so-called 'non-Aryan' (in practice, Jewish) blood to the truly Germanic physical inheritance was a violation of the Creator's will. Bonhoeffer saw in this order of creation theology a heretical misreading of Scripture, because it presupposed that the world as it is, is wholly as God wants it to be. It ignored the reality of sin, and bypassed Christ as the true revelation of the Creator's intent for human life. It provided, he said, the justification of war, and was 'a dangerous and treacherous foundation'.[14] But he did not thereby throw overboard all theological significance of nationhood. As an alternative to orders of creation, he argued for the notion of *orders of preservation*; that is, features of human life such as marriage, family and nation are allowed by God to arise in history as providential means of sustaining

---

13. On Bonhoeffer and freedom, see Chapters 2 and 8.
14. DBWE 11, 365.

and enhancing life but are not in themselves 'very good'. They have a positive, but relative, provisional, importance in the light of God's ultimate purpose. They remain justifiable so long as they remain open to the word of God for judgment and renewal. If they do not so remain open, or directly countermand God's will as known in Christ, they are to be dissolved. Bonhoeffer himself felt that point had certainly been reached by the time of the outbreak of war in 1939, as he prayed for the defeat of his country and began to work in the conspiracy to overthrow its leadership.

The theological concept of nation as an order of preservation is useful, I believe, because it offers the possibility of acknowledging what is good in national community and identity, without making it fixed, final and absolute. What is good in it can be affirmed and cherished, and at the same time critical flexibility can be allowed. Like all human phenomena, even the best and most to be cherished are subject to historical development and revision. They are not fixed and final. They have recognizable continuity with their past but there is more to come. That means that the sense of identity, of who we are as a community, has yet to hear the last word and can develop too, as it does in our personal lives. I like the Anglican theologian Paul Avis's description of identity as 'not so much a given but a quest',[15] never settled once for all, and 'belonging within an unfolding narrative quest for meaning'.[16] It is work-in-progress.

Relativizing identity

Now if 'Who are we?' is the dominant question of the hour, what may come from a theological perspective, that is, through speaking out of the Christian tradition, the thrust of the biblical witness and the experience of faith-based life and thought that we have inherited? I wish to draw some insights from the Bible, and from some of the struggles in modern times where nationhood has become a crucial issue for ethics and theology, in particular from Western Europe's darkest hour in the 1930s and the witness of people like Dietrich Bonhoeffer; and in more recent times to the traumas of the conflicts in the Balkans in the 1990s.

What follows here may well sound heretical in an age and culture consumed by assertions of and quests for identity, at every level from the most personal to the communal and national. It is that while very important the question of identity, the 'Who am I?' or 'Who are we?' question is not *the* most important question facing humanity. Now, having heard mention of Bonhoeffer, some of you who are familiar with his writings will be quick to point out that one of the most striking poems he wrote while in prison was titled 'Who Am I?' In it he expresses puzzlement that he seems to have two selves: the one that other people see and admire, the calm, cheerful, self-assured prisoner who comes out of his cell like a

---

15. Paul Avis, *The Identity of Anglicanism* (London: T&T Clark, 2007), 31.
16. Paul Avis, *Reshaping Ecumenical Theology* (London: T&T Clark, 2010), 200.

squire taking his morning walk, ready for whatever the day may bring; the other, the person he knows himself to be inwardly, often trembling, fearful, lonely and longing to be either free or to say farewell to it all. 'Who am I? This one or the other?', he asks. And what conclusion does he come to? He can't answer the question, and in the end it doesn't matter:

> Who am I? They mock me, these lonely questions of mine.
> Whoever I am, thou knowest me; O God, I am thine![17]

He can only come to an answer by going beyond the 'who?' question to the 'whose?' question. Beyond his identity question of what he is as a self, a person with certain characteristics and experiences and outlooks is the question of his ownership by a reality quite other than himself and to whom he is accountable, namely God. The 'whose?' question doesn't deny the importance of the 'who?' questions but transcends them and keeps them in their place. What Bonhoeffer is saying is more than a matter of personal piety. It is opening up a wholly different dimension to human life at every level. To be human is not to be a self-enclosed individual but it is to be relational through and through. We only truly live as humans in relationship to what is other than ourselves, to other people and ultimately in our relation to God, our origin and our goal. Therefore, the question is not who are we but *whose* we are. This qualification applies to every aspect of our created life, which in the light of Christ we see is created in and for relationships with others and with God, the supremely Other who is unfathomably relational in the freedom of his love. In 1932, as the Nazi movement was gaining strength and would come to power the following year, Bonhoeffer was lecturing in Berlin on the creation story in the book of Genesis. Pointedly, as narrated in Chapter 1,[18] he dealt with the highly topical issue of 'freedom', which is always an aspect of our identity when we think of ourselves as sovereign individuals. But, says Bonhoeffer,

> in the language of the Bible freedom is not something that people have for themselves but something they have for others. No one is free 'in herself' or 'in himself' – free as it were in a vacuum or free in the same way that a person may be musical, intelligent, or blind in herself or in himself ... Freedom is not a possession, something to hand on ... an object ... To be precise, freedom is a relation between two persons. Being free means 'being-free-for-the-other', because I am bound to the other. Only by being in relation with the other am I free.[19]

In a lecture given at about the same time, on 'The Right to Self-Assertion' he spoke even more pertinently on how this applies to the *nation*, at just the time the Nazis

---

17. DBWE 8, 460.
18. See below, 8.
19. DBWE 3, 62–3.

and their religious accomplices were demanding Germany's right to assert its own way and vaunt the advance of its power in the world:

> Every community, even the great community of the people, lives not only for itself but for the others, lives in responsibility for the brother, for the people to whom one is bound in brotherhood [*Brudervolk*]. There is absolutely no isolated life for the people [*das Volk*]. It is bound through its birth onward to the community and through its life to the peoples in brotherhood.[20]

In our own time the Croatian theologian Miroslav Volk, who in his native context has known more than enough of national or ethnic self-assertion, has similarly critiqued the assumed foundation of freedom and identity in the isolated individual, whether the individual person or the individual community or nation. In his seminal work *Exclusion and Embrace* he writes of how *dialogue* is not just one among other possible human activities but is at the very heart of what it is to be human:

> The self is dialogically constructed. The other [person] is already from the outset part of the self. I am who I am in relation to the other; to be Croat is, among other things, to have Serbs as neighbours; to be white in the U.S. is to enter a whole history of relation to African Americans (even if you are a recent immigrant). Hence the will to be oneself, if it is to be healthy, must entail the will to let the other inhabit the self; the other must be part of who I am as I will to be myself. As a result, a tension between the self and the other is built into the very desire for identity.[21]

On this view, we cannot decide what it means to be British without owning the common history we have with other peoples, not least those in Europe. 'Breaking free of Europe' would mean breaking free of a lot of our own historical identity, like the man trapped in a glacier with his arm frozen into the ice, who could only free himself by cutting off his arm. We cannot get out of our vocation to what Karl Barth called co-humanity.

Beyond identity: Whose are we?

This brings us to the still outstanding question, of how to move beyond competing identities. If the most important question is not who but whose we are, this also means that the really important question is 'What are we to *do*?' Earlier I quoted Bill McSweeney to the effect that the choice of identity is partly a moral act. I would wish to state that from a Christian perspective any question of identity

---

20. DBWE 11, 254. Also see Chapter 1, 8–9.
21. Volf Miroslav, *Exclusion and Embrace* (Nashville, TN: Abingdon Press, 1996), 91.

is actually transcended by the ethical question. The question of what is right, or, if you prefer the will of God, cannot be determined wholly by the understanding of who you are unless the 'who' includes the 'whose', and so indicates the ultimate source of moral authority for you. Ethics trumps identity. In the Bible we see several occasions where the claim of identity is used in an attempt to *evade* the imperative of God's command or the warnings of God's prophets. John the Baptist forestalls any attempt by the Pharisees and Sadducees to avoid the demands of repentance when they say 'We have Abraham as our ancestor.' The axe is laid at the root even of that genealogical, ethnic claim (Matthew 3:10) Most striking of all is how the prophet Jeremiah responds to the grave crisis which threatens Judah's very survival during the reign of King Zedekiah, as the armies of King Nebuchadnezzar of Babylon finally close in on Jerusalem. Zedekiah appeals to Jeremiah for a word from the Lord, Yahweh (Jeremiah 21:1-12, 22:1-5), the national God whose job it is to safeguard Judah and turn back her enemies, as he had done so many times in the past. But the message that comes from Jeremiah is rather unexpected. Yahweh is going to turn around Zedekiah's tanks lined up against Nebuchadnezzar and train them instead on ramparts of Jerusalem. 'I myself will fight against you with outstretched hand and mighty arm, in anger, and fury, and great wrath.' What sort of national god is this? Hardly a refuge and strength, a very present help in times of trouble (Psalm 46), one who can always be depended upon to save the nation from defeat and boost its advancement in the world. The people are so far gone in corruption and idolatry that they can't escape Yahweh's judgment. Only those who surrender will be spared.

But Jeremiah is also calling for something else: 'Execute justice in the morning, and deliver from the hand of the oppressor, or else my wrath will go forth like fire, and burn with no one to quench it, because of your evil doings.' And soon after: 'Act with justice and righteousness, and deliver from the hand of the oppressor anyone who has been robbed. And do no wrong or violence to the alien, the orphan, and the widow, or shed innocent blood in this place.' Note: execute justice *in the morning*. There is to be no delay. The first item on your agenda is not your survival as an independent nation, or what you think is important for your identity, but justice and compassion. These are paramount: they are the imperatives of the One *whose* you are. The rest can follow. When the nations will be gathered before the Son of Man, it will not be a matter of 'Who are you?' but 'What have you *done*?' to the Son of Man in the form of his brothers and sisters who are strangers, hungry, naked, sick or in prison (Matthew 25:31-46). With what shall I come before the Lord, asks the prophet Micah: 'He has shown you, O mortal, what is good; and what does the Lord require of you but to do justice, and to love kindness, and to walk humbly with your God' (Micah 6:8). It is a matter of living out our *co-humanity* as reflective of God the one whose we are, creator, reconciler and sanctifier of all life, and to be expressed in all our relationships; seeking partnership and cooperation, rather than partisanship and competition, reconciliation rather than rivalry. We are to seek that identity which serves our need to live together, not an identity which simply sets us apart and provides an excuse for not relating to one another.

Europe: The ethical question

A properly ethical dimension was almost completely lacking in the Brexit debate, on the Remain side as much as the leave side. By properly ethical I mean not just considerations other than ones of economic or material advantage or disadvantage, or political ones too – though I acknowledge that in many people's eyes these will have some moral connotations (e.g. where the matter of sovereignty is concerned). By properly ethical I mean the consequences of our actions for the wider good of our country and of Europe. Here the question has to be not just 'Is the EU a good or a bad thing?' but the more concrete one of 'What are the consequences of leaving the EU now, not just for us but for the EU and its member countries?' We heard almost nothing about this amid all the campaigning, shouting, mutual abuse and confusion. There is a myopia that renders people oblivious to what our European neighbours might be thinking and what may happen to them as a consequence.

Who, for example, gave a thought to why, on the other side of the EU geographical reach, the small Baltic states of Latvia, Lithuania and Estonia were so eager to join the EU, Western-oriented but perched on the doorstep of an increasingly unstable and unpredictable Russia? They may be forgiven for thinking that we are deserting them. Or take the Balkans. During the conflicts in the former Yugoslavia in the 1990s, one almost despaired at times at the entrenched nationalist emotion, fuelled it has to be said by religious loyalties that generated brutal wars and ethnic cleansing. Those of us who during those conflicts were involved in ecumenical and interfaith efforts at peacemaking, frankly, had little to show for our efforts. But following the Dayton Accords which brought some sort of peace to Bosnia, and later the abatement of violence in Kosovo, by 2004/5 one noticed a growing change of atmosphere. It was in part a generational change. In Belgrade one met young adults who were sick of the old nationalism, determined not to keep fighting all over again the ethnic and religious battles of the fourteenth century. And where were their hopes now centred? On the EU, which was offering a very different way of living together, and a much more creative future for their aspirations. Even at that time I did not dream that in a very few years the CEC human rights desk in Brussels would be occupied by a young Serbian woman, but so it proved. Will our actions encourage or discourage such people and their hopes?

The outstanding question, certainly from a Christian point of view, and of all the other world faiths, is what will help to foster stability and cooperation in Europe and the influence of these values in the wider world? What, in short, will encourage 'the things that make for peace' (Luke 19:41)? One cannot rehearse too often that the EU from its origins in the 1950s has been a moral and not just an economic project: how the vision of the founding figures Robert Schuman and Jean Monnet was to rebuild a post-war Europe which would make war impossible and would make the desire for war impossible by placing the values of cooperation and mutual solidarity central to its life, at every level; how this vision has owed so much to Christian influence, not just Catholic social teaching, though that has been very significant to it, but also from the mainline Protestant churches and increasingly the Orthodox too. In 2004 I was with a small group of international church representatives who met with the then UN Secretary-General Kofi Annan in New York. At that time, he was under immense pressure, especially from the White House, and we had gone to offer him support in his role in the Middle East following the invasion of Iraq the year before and also in his standing at the world level. During the course of our discussion he turned to the two of us from Europe, and choosing his words carefully said that in Europe we had a remarkable and unique model of cooperation of which the whole world should take note. Whatever criticisms are to be levelled at the EU – and there are many that can rightly be made – they have to be set against both its intent and its actual story and its likely future significance. It does not need to be praised to the heavens as if it were the kingdom of God on earth. But neither does it warrant demonizing as if it were the dragon of the apocalypse. It should be respected, indeed cherished, for what it is: indeed, as another order of preservation, not replacing the nation-states but enabling them to act as closely together as possible in the direction of justice, peace and the preservation of creation.[22] It is a matter of fostering a culture as much as strengthening intergovernmental structures of Anthony Smith, whom I cited earlier, who nearly thirty years ago said that a further European integration process was unlikely to succeed without the growth of a common European culture, and I think events have proved him right.[23]

But, if the ethical trumps the claim of identity, where does this leave our sense of national identity? Are we bereft? Not necessarily at all. We are simply challenged to find a revised identity which serves the wider purpose.

Conclusion: A new identity?

Some might still say that to seek a non-EU-membership attachment to Europe is still asking too much, an admission that says 'So much for our national pride and sense of identity as a nation. It's a final farewell to all that we have been over the centuries, to all that has made Britain great.' To which, it can be said that a nation, being in Bonhoeffer's words an order of preservation, is a good but provisional manifestation in history serving the common good, and finds its true destiny under God in serving the wider good of its neighbours in justice and peace. With Miroslav Volf, we can say that in the relational world which God has created for us, we find out who we are not by excluding others from us but by examining how our life has interacted with theirs. Being aware of a new kind of ethical commitment, for co-humanity, sends us as a nation back to look at our store of

---

22. The question of a theological understanding of the EU as an institution is pertinently raised in *After Brexit?* 25. One would hope that Bonhoeffer's concept of an order of preservation might be drawn into the discussion, together with his notion of the 'mandates', among which is government, which he proposes in his *Ethics*.

23. Smith, *National Identity*, 175.

historical memories, some perhaps half or even completely forgotten, from which we can draw wisdom, strength and inspiration for this task. Not a wholly different identity but one which is work-in-progress, giving a new perspective on what we are and can be. Simply to react to an invitation or challenge by saying 'It's not me', without asking what relevant capacities and experiences might lie within us, can be the most self-denigrating and impoverishing stance, whether for a person or a people. So, let's go back to our identity and take a fresh look at the traditions it rests on. It won't always be a matter of giving up our stories, for it's the way we tell them that matters, as well as the content.

First, for example, if the memory of our imperial past still dogs us today and lies behind our persistent unique entitlement to sovereignty, why can't we at least equally cherish the way *we let go* of our empire, for the most part relatively peaceably? Isn't that a good element in our historical identity, relevant for the continuing project of pooling our sovereignty with that of our neighbours?

Second, in the religious area, our history has already taught us how much we owe to Europeanization. In the run-up to the 2016 referendum the Anglican priest and writer Giles Fraser wrote in the *Guardian* to the effect that the English Reformation was a sort of proto-Brexit, the doughty English led by Henry VIII throwing off the yoke of Rome, just as it was hoped the yoke of Brussels would be treated likewise.[24] One can bring in all sorts of historical precedents for Brexit, but the Reformation is hardly one of them. The Reformation might have been anti-Rome but it was hardly anti-Europe for it was itself a European movement that came our way (yes, John Wycliffe with his Lollards ran a proto-Reforming project a century earlier, but he closely related to his European counterpart in Prague, Jan Hus). William Tyndale's printed English New Testament was indeed the cornerstone of the early reform movement here. But such was the opposition to it by King and Church that Tyndale had to find hospitality on the continent to finish translating it, among other things visiting Martin Luther at Wittenberg, and it had to be printed in Worms and then smuggled into London. Meanwhile, Cambridge and Oxford teamed up with Basel, Strasbourg, Zurich and Geneva to form in effect a rolling transnational seminar in Reformed theology.

Third on the list for revision must be the memory of *war*, which is often cited as the great reason for cherishing our separateness from Europe. There's a paradox here. On the one hand some argue that while the EU was indeed born out of the tragedy of continental and world wars, that founding motivation no longer carries much weight with today's generation for whom even 1939–45 is effectively pre-history and is not relevant to their concerns.[25] But if that is so, why was it that the image of 'Britain standing alone' in war was so often cited in Brexit talk – 'What did all those men die for?' The experiences of two world wars in the twentieth

---

24. 'Brexit recycles the defiant spirit of the Reformation', *Guardian*, 5 May 2016. A similar argument was more recently been made by Ben Macintyre, 'History Tells Us This Is just the Beginning', *Times*, 31 February 2020.

25. See the discussion in *After Brexit?*, 13–15.

century do still shape much of the British consciousness (it is also the case that over much of the continent the memories are still in the process of healing). But it is extraordinary how parochial are the lenses through which those wars are seen in retrospect. Were they just about keeping the Union Jack flying above our green and pleasant land? If so, why are so many of our war graves on the continent? Were not those wars about and for *Europe*, about what rules Europe should be governed by and the values by which its peoples should live?

The story of war, and its significance, without losing any of its inspirational heroism, can be told in a way quite other than self-congratulatory nationalism, as part of our story in Europe.

This is not a matter of academic historians rewriting history but of listening to the voices of those who themselves fought and suffered in the conflicts and whose belief in what they were fighting for contradicts the simplistic nationalist version. Take, for example, RAF Group Captain Derek Rake, who died in December 2020 aged ninety-eight. He was a Spitfire pilot in the Second World War, decorated for bravery and with an adventurous tale to tell (worthy of *Boys' Own* Paper) of escape after being shot down in the Balkans, and also flew on highly secret reconnaissance missions during the Cold War. He recalled that of the seventy-seven pilots in his training unit in 1941–2, only two survived the war. In retirement, according to his obituary, he had two passions: golf and Europe. 'He was pro-EU and contemptuous of Brexiteer politicians. "Many of my friends died ... and all we wanted was peace and prosperity in Europe."'[26]

Let us also attend to the late Paddy Ashdown's eloquent plea to recall the resistance movements in occupied Europe in the Second World War, and, equally, the British support for them:

> Looking back today, it seems to me extraordinary that our besieged little country committed so many of its young men and women and so much of its resources to secret and extremely hazardous operations to free the countries of Europe, which we have now chosen to be no part of. It seems extraordinary that a nation which today does less than any other member of the European Union to help those fleeing the misery of war, was, so short a time ago, their only refuge. After the shock of the Referendum result, I still cannot believe that our country, which has now turned its back on solidarity with our European neighbours, was then so much their last hope that, from the alpine pastures of Norway to the mountaintops of Greece, those desperate for freedom from every nation in Europe gathered on moonlit nights to listen for the tiny reverberation in the air which would tell them that the dark shadow of an RAF Halifax from London would shortly pass over them, with a largesse of weapons and its message that they were not alone.[27]

---

26. 'Group Captain Derek Drake', *Times*, 2 February 2021.

27. Paddy Ashdown, in collaboration with Sylvie Young. *Game of Spies: The Secret Agent, the Traitor and the Nazi* (London: William Collins, 2016), xii. Ashdown (1941–2018) was a British politician and diplomat, and leader of the Liberal Democrat Party 1988–99.

Fourth, we have a lot to share with Europe from our own experience of *diversity in society*, not least in religion. In an increasingly secularized society there is not much public interest in our religious history, while at the same time both here and on the continent anxieties are rising about cultural differences and religious extremism, and the threat these pose to a democratic society. Let's just remember that until relatively recently Roman Catholics in England were seen as the Fifth Column of a tyrannical Rome, while the English Free Churches and the Church of England were at loggerheads, often bitterly, over continuing Anglican privileges and discriminations against non-Anglicans, not least in the field of education. That we are now in a very different scene is not just because the churches have declined in strength; still less is it because they have kept themselves to themselves and out of the public sphere (which they haven't though the secularists believe they should), but because all three traditions have found that they can contribute positively to the common life from out of their respective inherited beliefs and practices.[28] There is a lesson there not just for Christian ecumenical relations but for wider interfaith relations in society, both here and in Europe as a whole. Our identity has been about more than tolerance; it has learnt positive inclusivity for the common good.

Fifth, as for *race*, like most nations we have never been as homogenous in ethnicity and national origin as we imagine. Now known to us, for example, are the studies on the DNA of some of the crew of Henry VIII's flagship, *Mary Rose*, which sank in 1545, indicating that as well as many from England, other crewmen were likely to have been from Italy or northern Spain, from the North African coast and possibly including some Moors. We have a multi-ethnic history. We have much of which to repent, from the slave trade and slavery right down to the recent scandal over the *Windrush* generation. But the fact that we have for centuries had a multi-ethnic population right here in Britain itself should be seen as one of the strengths in our actual national identity.

Sixth, there is what many will feel is the most distinctive and precious commodity in our identity, our language.

> We must be free or die, who speak the tongue That Shakespeare spake.

So wrote William Wordsworth, and who could disagree with him? But 'English' is itself an extraordinary synthesis of previously existing European tongues: Celtic, Anglo-Saxon, Viking Scandinavian, Norman French, with the odd Latin surviving here and there, and it is precisely this diverse inheritance that gives English its subtlety and power, which Shakespeare knew. A vital part of our identity, it can encourage us to think of ourselves as the great synthesizers of Europe, both indebted to Europe for who we are and what we have, and with much to continue to give in return.

---

28. This is not of course the whole picture in Britain. Religious-political sectarianism is still a factor, for example, in Northern Ireland.

What else would they be saying?

Many British people admit to having family relatives on the continent. But as well as ties of blood and kinship there is another familial bind to be claimed, by those belonging to the Christian Church:

> There shall be peace because of the Church of Christ, for the sake of which the world exists. And this Church of Christ lives at one and the same time in all peoples, yet beyond all boundaries, whether national, political, social, or racial. And the brothers who make up this Church are bound together, through the commandment of the one Lord Jesus Christ, *more inseparably than men are bound by all the ties of common history, of blood, of class, and of language.* All these ties, which are part of our world, are valid ties, not indifferent; but in the presence of Christ they are not ultimate bonds.[29] (Italics mine)

So declared Bonhoeffer in 1934, in the face of the deadly nationalism of the time, at an ecumenical conference in Denmark. It's the kind of forthright statement which makes one ask, 'If we don't believe this, when what *do* we think belonging to the Church of Jesus Christ means?' If for Christians this is our most fundamental community of belonging, then how does it relate to our various human identities? The churches in this country and across Europe are faced with a question very similar to that of the countries and churches of Europe ninety years ago as they seek to find their identities in a fast-changing and fragile world. The very conditions of life facing the entire human family and the natural order are pressurizing us towards a planetary consciousness and the demands for solidarity and cooperation. Yet at the same time these pressures are perceived as threats towards the distinctive identities of communities and the individuals who comprise them. This is both the ecumenical challenge for churches and faith communities, and for nations, whether in the EU or not. For an almost final word I turn to someone who has long served the ecumenical movement as a leader both in this country and at the world level. Echoing the Apostle Paul's teaching on belonging to one another as members of the body of Christ, Mary Tanner has written of the ecumenical calling of the churches, which is at the same time a sign to the nations in a fragmenting world: 'It is about how we are all held in communion – when we agree and when we disagree – so that we refuse to say "I have no need of you".'[30]

The challenge for both churches and nations is to find a form of identity which enables, motivates and inspires us for a life, not of self-sufficient isolation or oppositional separation from others but of growing interdependence. That means a radical kind of conversion from 'Who am I?' or 'Who are we?' to 'Who are we for one another?'; and going beyond all these 'who?' questions, asking the 'whose?'

---

29. DBWE 13, 308.

30. Mary Tanner, 'Celebrating Edinburgh 1910: Reflections on Visible Unity', *Theology*, November–December 2010, 403–10.

questions about our ultimate accountability for justice, truth and humanity which are the footstool of God. 'What else would they be saying?' Let us hope that the churches collectively could dare to say to another, and encourage the countries of Europe, to say, 'Identity is important – but it isn't everything.' That would be transformative for the churches, and could help to ignite a transformative vision for Europe.

Chapter 14

'ARE WE STILL OF ANY USE?' WORDS FOR FAILING PUBLIC SERVANTS AND FRIGHTENED CITIZENS

And he said to me, 'You are my servant, Israel, in whom I will be glorified.' But I said, 'I have laboured in vain. I have spent my strength for nothing and vanity; yet surely my cause is with the Lord, and my reward with my God.' And now the Lord says ... 'It is too light a thing that you should be my servant to raise up the tribes of Jacob and to restore the survivors of Israel: I will give you as a light to the nations, that my salvation may reach to the end of the earth.'

(Isaiah 49:3–6)

So Jesus called them and said to them, 'You know that among the Gentiles those whom they recognize as their rulers lord it over them, and their great ones are tyrants over them. But it is not so among you; but whoever wishes to become great among you must be your servant, and whoever wishes to be first among you must be slave of all. For the Son of Man came not to be served but to serve, and to give his life a ransom for many.'

(Mark 10:42–45)

Dear friends, it is an honour to be invited to address this Civic Service, and for that I am truly grateful. It is also something of a challenge. You gather here as citizens of Bath and North-East Somerset, and among you are those elected and appointed to serve the public good of this area. You gather today to give thanks for all the blessings you enjoy in civic society here, and to uphold in thought and prayer all those who serve as councillors and those who work as servants of the local authority for the community and its welfare.

But no-one needs telling – I certainly don't – that at the present time in our country anyone addressing such a public gathering is engaging in a high-risk operation. And it might well be asked what a minister of the church can offer at this present time

---

Sermon preached at the Bath and North-East Somerset Civic Service, at Radstock Methodist Church, 21 July 2019, on the seventy-fifth anniversary of the attempt by the German resistance to overthrow Hitler.

of division, anxiety and frustration.[1] Well, the answer is straightforward: nothing, if it is a matter purely of his or her own mind and insight. But a preacher of the Christian gospel is not called to speak for him- or herself. He or she invites people to give an ear to what we find in Holy Scripture, and to the testimony of those saints and servants of the faith who have gone before us, and in their own times and turmoils have wrought guidance and encouragement for responsibility in their world and ours. I wonder, for example, whether as you heard our first reading this afternoon, from the book of Isaiah, you felt an affinity with what the prophet was saying, evidently in a moment of frustration and exhaustion: 'I have laboured in vain, I have spent my strength for nothing and vanity.'

But we don't have to go back twenty-six centuries or more to hear words that may resonate similarly. Listen to this:

> Are we still of any use? We have been silent witnesses of evil deeds. We have become cunning and learned the arts of obfuscation and equivocal speech. Experience has rendered us suspicious of human beings, and often we have failed to speak to them a true and open word. Unbearable conflicts have worn us down or even made us cynical. Are we still of any use? We will not need geniuses, cynics, people who have contempt for others, or cunning tacticians, but simple, uncomplicated, and honest human beings. Will our inner strength to resist what has been forced on us have remained strong enough, and our honesty with ourselves blunt enough, to find our way back to simplicity and honesty?[2]

'Are we still of any use?' You might be wondering which of our leading political figures in the thick of our national debates and controversies was baring his or her soul here. Or maybe, even, some of you may feel, 'I could say this, too', having tried so long to serve the public good, and at times finding it a wearying and depressing business of 'unbearable conflicts', in which honesty does not always come out on top, ending in a sense of failure, and cynicism. If so, you are in good company. In fact, these words were written at Christmas 1942, by Pastor Dietrich Bonhoeffer. They are part of an essay he wrote as a present for members of his close family and friends who like him were members of the German resistance network plotting to overthrow Hitler and put in place a non-Nazi government. In it, he is expressing the pressures and questions and doubts that involvement in the resistance had brought them. Quite apart from the continual fear of being discovered and all that that would bring, there was the burden of being decent people yet having to keep low, to camouflage themselves, to pretend to be friends of the regime in order to be close enough to the serpent's head and strike when the right moment came. It is a piece of searing honesty, which asks: having learned to be conspirators in a

---

1. The latter half of 2019 in the UK was marked by increasingly fractious debate, in Parliament and in the country, on the terms of the treaty to be negotiated by the UK government and the EU for Britain's departure from the EU.

2. 'After Ten Years', DBWE 8, 52.

Germany of lies, and where in order to stay alive you had to lie and deceive, will we be any good as leaders of a new, post-Hitler Germany where public honesty and straight talking will be required?'

When Dr Eleanor Jackson invited me to give the sermon at this service, she pointed out that this weekend sees the seventy-fifth anniversary of the tragic culmination of that conspiracy in the attempted overthrow of Hitler, on 20 July 1944. Commemorations have been taking place in Germany, here in Britain and elsewhere in the world. All these years later, the courage of the men and women who took part in the conspiracy, and the sacrifice of the more than two-hundred who were brutally executed following its failure, still stands as a challenging and inspiring instance of civil courage and responsibility. Extreme cases, it's said, make bad law. But they can also give us precious insights, just as the extreme pressures of volcanic eruptions and seismic shifts in the earth's crust can produce gemstones of everlasting beauty. At the ceremony in Germany yesterday, Chancellor Angela Merkel highlighted its message for today in a world where extreme racist and nationalist movements are astir again.

Dietrich Bonhoeffer was just one of the resisters, though by now one of the most well-known, partly because he was a surprising figure to be involved in such a plot. A Lutheran pastor, a brilliant academic theologian, he had been a leading figure in the Confessing Church, that section of German Protestantism which resisted the church being taken over as an arm of the Nazi state. In 1939 he returned to Germany from the safety of temporary sojourn in the United States, saying that after the war that was now inevitable, he would have no right to take part in the rebuilding of Christian life in Germany if he had not shared the trials of his people during that war; Christians in Germany, he said, were faced with the terrible alternative, either of praying for the defeat of their country so that Christian civilization might survive, or of willing its victory which would mean the end of that civilization. Back in wartime Germany, he went much further in resistance than most pastors did, joining the actual political conspiracy to overthrow the regime, acting as a courier between the resisters in Germany, and churches and governments abroad, using his important ecumenical contacts. Already under suspicion by the Gestapo, he was arrested in 1943 and placed in a military prison in Berlin. After the failure of 20 July 1944, he was under even greater suspicion. He was transferred to the Gestapo cellars in Berlin, then to Buchenwald concentration camp; and finally, with other last surviving members of the conspiracy, was done to death at Flossenbürg execution camp on 9 April, barely a month before the war in Europe ended.

The German resisters were, to say the least, a mixed bunch. There were military types like Colonel Claus von Stauffenberg who on 20 July placed the ill-fated bomb in Hitler's headquarters; and high-ranking civil servants like Hans von Dohnanyi, Bonhoeffer's brother-in-law. There were Protestants and Catholics, and people of no particular religious faith.

There were men and women. There were landowning aristocrats like Count Peter York von Wartenburg and James von Moltke and their wives Freya and Marion. There were idealistic diplomats like Adam von Trott. There were many lawyers (more lawyers than clergy in fact!); some social workers like Gertrud Staewen. There were academics and office workers. Some were socialists, some were conservatives and traditionalists – some even wanted to restore the monarchy and have a Kaiser again. In a Monty-Pythonesque-moment, can you imagine, if they had succeeded and survived, and they had television, what *their* televised debates would have been like? But many were motivated by a vision of a truly non-Nazi Germany and a Europe free from the nationalisms that had wrought such havoc in the past. It's moving to go to Flossenbürg, and stand in the execution yard where on that April morning in 1945 Dietrich Bonhoeffer and six other conspirators were hanged including Admiral Wilhelm Canaris, who had been in charge of German Military Intelligence where much of the conspiracy had been secretly located. A rather touching story has gone the rounds that Bonhoeffer's death was very dignified, and that after kneeling in prayer at the gallows his end ensued very quickly. It's now known it was quite otherwise. The SS guards at Flossenbürg were the most sadistic of Hitler's minions; no pieties would have been allowed and the deaths of these seven were horribly prolonged. But more importantly for us, the simple memorial tablet in that yard states that these people gave their lives 'for justice, freedom and human dignity': the very things which had been banished from Germany and which especially the resisters were denied in their manner of dying.

To stand before that spot at Flossenbürg, and read those words – justice, freedom and human dignity – is moving and humbling. They are familiar words to us, and we might feel that still living as we do in a free and democratic society under the rule of law, they don't convey anything new to us. But standing there makes you realize that these were the values which united this diverse company of people, and remaining true to these values cost them everything, even life itself. No mere lip-service but literally a matter of life and death. So at Flossenbürg you feel you are standing on holy ground. Some of us would say that in recognizing the ultimacy of these values we are face to face with God; or if you don't like the word 'God', you can say we are up against what it means to be truly human, and what has to be the foundation of genuine human community at every level, from our most intimate and local spheres to the national and global level. It is a searching experience to stand there, because you can't help asking, 'What is it that *I* really believe in, what would *I* be prepared to risk everything for?' That's the significance of 20 July 1944.

There's something more on that memorial stone: the chapter and verse number of a biblical text: 2 Timothy 1:7. I have to confess that although I'm a minister (a Baptist one at that), and therefore expected to know every verse of the Bible by heart, I had to wait till I got back to my car where I had my Bible and look up 2 Timothy 1:7. It's where St Paul says, 'God did not give us a spirit of cowardice, but rather a spirit of power and of love and of self-discipline.' How apt, for all those who resisted, and those who died following 20 July 1944. Apt, because they did not give in to fear, to resignation at the terror of the totalitarian state, its rank militarism, its racism, its false patriotism which was in fact idolatry of the nation. Indeed, they were prepared to be found guilty of what the state called treason but which in truth was the real love of their country, a country which had been so shamed.

To live by a spirit not of cowardice but of power, the power of love, and of self-discipline: how do we respond to this in our time and place? And how far do those stark words, 'for justice, freedom and human dignity', express our core values in Britain today? Or are we resigned to the inexorable slide away from community, towards a society run purely by economic self-interest: a society of isolated, self-centred individuals and a world of increasingly self-centred nationalisms? That is a way that leads to death, death either by loneliness or by conflict. There are many calls today for our country to become more united, to move beyond the divisive and polarizing polemics of the past three years. Who could disagree with that? But what is to be the basis of any real unity? 'No new leader can unite the country now', ran the headline above one newspaper article this last week. Perhaps it is because we no longer really *believe in unity* any more, that we no longer appreciate what it costs; that we're making our particular group- and community-loyalties, our own boxes, the be-all and end-all of our morality. Perhaps we should take up that term that St Paul uses in 2 Timothy, 'self-discipline'. We know what that must have meant for the conspirators, having to work determinedly, but always covertly, waiting patiently for the right moment. But it is a good word for us too. Doesn't true democracy always require self-discipline? How about the discipline of political leaders only making promises they fully intend to keep? And how about all of us honestly trying to understand the actual consequences, for others no less than ourselves, of what we wish for and vote for? That way, we might begin to understand more of what 'unity' requires.

Religion, it must be confessed, has often been a dark force here. Religious loyalty is prone to blinkering us, investing our particular cause, our class, our race, our nation, our ideology – our own 'box' in current jargon – with a kind of special divine significance, to be preserved at all costs, a sacred temple on its own, so entrenching division: instead of enabling us to think outside our particular box. Dietrich Bonhoeffer challenged this tendency in the first weeks of the Nazi regime, in 1933, when he was asked by senior people in his church to prepare a position paper on the persecution of the Jews, which was just really beginning. In his paper he said three plain things. First, the church has an unconditional obligation to care for the victims of state-sponsored violence, whoever they are, Jews or whoever. Second, the church in the name of justice has a responsibility to question the state on its actions. Third, if all else fails, then it must be asked if the time has come, not just to bandage up the victims crushed beneath the wheel but to put a spoke in the wheel of the state itself – the thought which eventually led him and others into conspiracy. That was quite remarkable given the intense nationalist, racial and religious group loyalties in Germany at the time. I believe that what Bonhoeffer wrote may well have been what inspired his older colleague, Pastor Martin Niemöller, who was himself to endure eight years in concentration camp, to say in his famous statement after the war:

First they came for the socialists, and I did not speak out – because I was not a socialist. Then they came for the trade unionists, and I did not speak out – because I was not a trade unionist. Then they came for the Jews, and I did not speak out – because I was not a Jew. Then they came for me – and there was no one left to speak for me.

The great heresy of our time is that it is our separateness, our apartness, from other human beings, from other communities, from other nations, which ensures our identity and security. This is not to advocate a sameness, or uniformity of belief, or nationality, or culture. It is rather to assert that it is only by positively relating to one another as those who share a common humanity that we shall survive and thrive on this one planet to which we all belong. We are relational beings, who can only thrive in a relationship with others. One of Bonhoeffer's great mentors, the Swiss theologian Karl Barth, spoke of truly human existence as 'co-humanity'. Or as the poet W. H. Auden said, 'We must love one another, or die.'[3] That sounds a lofty, starry-eyed thing to say. And it is true that the challenge facing all the major faiths is how we can dig into our traditions to find resources not for competitive impulses seeking domination and generating violence but for living together in the one world we share. What is remarkable about Dietrich Bonhoeffer is that while he was deeply and passionately loyal to his Lutheran Christian faith centred on Jesus Christ as Saviour of the world, he did not use this to preach a Christian superiority, still less a nationalist Christian superiority. Instead, he saw following Christ as leading us to a new kind of love and solidarity embracing all humankind. Towards the end of his great book *Discipleship* he says, 'In Christ's incarnation all of humanity regains the dignity of bearing the image of God. Whoever from now on attacks the least of people attacks God. … Since we know ourselves to be accepted within the humanity of Jesus, our new humanity now also consists of bearing the troubles and sins of all others.'[4]

We shall soon be singing William Blake's stirring words 'Jerusalem', words committing us to build Jerusalem in our green and pleasant land. A lot of arguments are going on as to whether this should now be our National Anthem – for the English nation at any rate. When you sing it, you don't have to imagine you are a member of the Women's Institute (WI), like my dear mother-in-law who was a voluntary county organizer of the WI in Derbyshire who could play 'Jerusalem' from memory on the piano, and probably did so in just about every village hall in the county. Nor do you have to pretend you're bursting your lungs at the Albert Hall on the Last Night of the Proms in a sea of Union Jacks. But you could bring to mind what the city of Jerusalem represents in the Bible. Jerusalem in the Hebrew Bible was the place where God's glory dwelt, where the countenance divine really does shine on the people. And *therefore* for the Hebrew prophets it was a city that was called to be marked by the true godliness of justice and peace within its borders,

3. From 'September 1939'.
4. DBWE 4, 285.

and to be open to all the world which God loved. We've heard from the book of Isaiah already. Dietrich Bonhoeffer's favourite prophet was in fact Jeremiah. 'Oh no,' I reckon some of you will be thinking, 'not that old pessimist, the Eeyore of the Old Testament!' Jeremiah in fact was a prophet of hope. What earned him his negative reputation was his determination to destroy false and illusory hopes for the sake of *real* hope. Indeed he held out hope just when Jerusalem was falling into a hopeless situation, besieged by the forces of King Nebuchadnezzar of Babylon, and about to fall. When the leaders of the people in despair went to Jeremiah and asked for a word from the Lord, his message was clear: if you want hope, if you want a future, you must practise justice, for God is a God of justice; 'Act with justice and righteousness and deliver from the hand of the oppressor anyone who has been robbed. And do no wrong or violence to the alien [the stranger, the foreigner], the orphan, and the widow, and shed no innocent blood in this place. … Judge the cause of the poor and needy.' Moreover, he says, 'Execute justice *in the morning*.' That is, the first item on your agenda each day, not your prosperity or your prestige over other peoples, must be justice. A city indeed, where justice, freedom and human dignity are upheld and celebrated. A city, moreover, which witnesses to that openness and universality of God's salvation and peace for all peoples, a light to the nations, a salvation reaching to the end of the earth. The prophet who in our Isaiah reading complained about the futility of his labours, was answered by God not with a more comfortable task but a wider commission embracing the whole earth.

That is Jerusalem, set in the world as an embodiment of peace and justice and a witness to peace in all the earth. There can be no escape from that, no exit from that, if you want hope for your future, that is what you must be. Whatever the outcome of the momentous deliberations of the next few months, there can be no exit from the divine calling for us as for all nations for justice and peace. There can be no exit from this world as it is, no exit from its tangled relationships and complexities. No exit from compassion for refugees and asylum seekers. No exit from the ongoing joint search for peace in the flashpoints of the world. No exit from sharing with our country's neighbours searching for how to preserve life on our planet for ourselves and future generations. Like Jerusalem, we are inextricably part of that world. There is no freedom apart from that world. Real freedom, as Bonhoeffer knew and constantly taught, does not come by detaching ourselves from all relationships and obligations, and living in a kind of vacuum, but in meeting them in the freedom of the power of love. He himself was never so free as when in 1939 he made that decision to go back to Germany, with all its risks and dangers and the eventual suffering it entailed. Just as Jesus showed that true greatness is not the freedom to lord it over others but the willingness to become the servants of others, 'for the Son of Man came not to be served, but to serve, and to give his life as a ransom for many'. We are called to both a wider vision and a greater humility.

'Are we still of any use?' On the personal level that question may well trouble each one of us, as we try to assess how successful or unsuccessful we have been in our public service. Was it all worth it? The people we commemorate this weekend certainly knew that question. While yesterday, 20 July, was the actual anniversary date of the attempted coup, today, 21 July, is also an especially significant date in the story of Dietrich Bonhoeffer. For it was on this day that, in Tegel prison, he wrote what many of us would say was the most remarkable of all the many letters he secretly wrote in that prison cell, and smuggled out to his close friend Eberhard Bethge. He had heard the news that the coup attempt had been made, that it had failed and that Hitler's revenge on the ringleaders was already being wreaked. As he contemplated the bitter fact of failure, and knowing what his own fate was very likely now to be, he writes this very personal letter, reflecting on where his life has led him and what he has learnt from it. He regrets nothing, he says.

> I discovered, and am still discovering to this day, that one only learns to have faith by living in the full this worldliness of life. If one has completely renounced making something of oneself ... then one throws oneself completely into the arms of God, and this is what I call this-worldliness, living fully in the midst of life's tasks, questions, successes and failures, experiences and perplexities – then one takes seriously no longer one's own sufferings but rather the suffering of God in the world. ... How should one become arrogant over successes or shaken by one's failures when one shares in God's suffering in the life of this world?[5]

A wider vision and a deeper humility. Those humble enough to be the willing servants of others rather than of their own ambitions, forever worrying about themselves, will always be of use, perhaps in ways they cannot yet imagine; just as those whom we commemorate today serve us seventy-five years on, still serve us by the example of their living by the spirit of power, of love and self-discipline, in the service of justice, freedom and human dignity. May you who serve in leadership in this community, and of all you who live here, be inspired, strengthened and guided, by that same spirit, which thanks to the divine generosity is still alive and available to us all, and thereby know that you are indeed still 'of use'.
Amen.

---

5. DBWE 8, 486.

Chapter 15

A NEW ETHIC – OR THE END OF ETHICS?
LOVE AGAINST THE PLAGUE

To add to all the issues over the past ten years which have supplied the contexts for the chapters of this book, at the time of writing (April 2021) the Covid-19 pandemic is still upon us. It has wrought personal loss and grief, social disruption and economic hardship, throughout the world, on a scale unprecedented in the lives of many of our generation It has challenged assumptions about unhindered economic progress and the capacity of our political structures to respond adequately to such crises. Biologists had for some years been warning of the potential dangers to world health posed by organisms and viruses as yet unknown or only partly understood, but nothing of this nature was really imagined until early 2020. We were taken by surprise. Would Bonhoeffer have been taken by surprise? That, we cannot know. But he is one of the figures about whom people have been asking, 'What would he say about the pandemic?' In February 2021 that question was put to me by a church in Bristol as the subject for a Zoom discussion evening, to which I was invited to speak. I began by saying what has been said more than once in these chapters, that we should not go too quickly to Bonhoeffer (or anyone else for that matter) hoping to find instant answers to specific problems. His role is not that of an instant oracle. Rather, he takes us onto a certain fundamental plane for our thinking about faith, God and engagement with the world, with his basic insights into what it means to be human as created by the God who is revealed in Jesus Christ. He sets a framework within which we ourselves can think creatively, perhaps in new ways, about the challenges meeting us in our contemporary situation.

In the later stages of the pandemic, one could read press columnists waxing eloquent on how the experience of isolation during lockdown had shown how important relationships are in our lives. Yes indeed, but to call relationships important is surely a massive understatement if, as we have seen Bonhoeffer asserting, as humans we are created in, by and for relationships, and that only in relationships are we truly free.

Throughout these chapters, integral with this relational emphasis, is woven Bonhoeffer's concept of *Stellvertretung*, vicarious representative action, which is the most authentic form of human relationship because it reflects God's own act and being in the incarnate, crucified and risen Jesus Christ, the supreme embodiment of vicarious representative action: life with, for and on behalf of others. *Stellvertretung* is the resonance between the life of the transcendent God and the immanent, social life of human beings. It is also, in particular, embodied in the community of faith, the body of Christ, Christ existing as community offering itself to the world in further vicarious action. Sadly, I would note, the past ten years have seen further decline in the ecumenical interest of the churches, which for a renewal will need the kind of basic theology of the communion of saints, and the church for others, which Bonhoeffer has bequeathed us.

Why be moral?

Morality and ethics have for long had a hard time in seeking to be taken seriously in any area other than the purely personal, but the issue has become even more serious in these past years, which have seen a progressive de-moralization of large areas of our public life in favour of purely economic interests or the claims of unexamined community identities. Just what is the status of morality or ethics in decision-making, where the main players are huge financial institutions with little public accountability though often, it seems, with plenty of covert political clout thanks to dubious relationships with individuals in power, or seeking power? Where are the restraints on venality and corruption, and blatant untruth-telling? Not that there are no persons in the public arena with a strong ethical awareness, but they are the ones who sense that the overall tide is against them.[1] In the 1990s the president of one major venture capital bank in London, with a strong Christian commitment and active church affiliation, told me that in his view it was in the mid-1980s that personal greed had begun to make real inroads. Now it seems to be widely accepted as the norm. It may have been a tongue-in-cheek remark by the British prime minister Boris Johnson, but his comment in March 2021 that the relative success of the British Covid-19 vaccine programme was 'because of capitalism, because of greed my friends'[2] seems to presuppose a culture of acceptance, and hardly signals a wish for probity, or any awareness of the gross inequalities within and between nations accentuated by the pandemic. We might well wish to echo Bonhoeffer's remark in his Christmas 1942 essay that his generation, ethically, 'had so little ground under their feet'.[3]

Traditionally, morality has been regarded as a gift (or imposition) from the gods or one god in particular; or if not from heaven then embedded in the immutable order of things. But what if there is now no god, or gods, or if the order of things is seen to be in an endless state of flux? It was Friedrich Nietzsche (1844–1900) who pronounced the death of God (with the churches as his sepulchres). Yet

---

1. See, e.g. the book by former governor of the Bank of England Mark Carney, *Values: Building a Better World for All* (London: HarperCollins, 2021).
2. As reported in the *Guardian*, 24 March 2021.
3. DBWE 8, 38.

Nietzsche was no less concerned to shake even the most determined atheists into a realization of just what a drastic deed had been done in 'murdering' God, creating an unprecedented situation for humankind:

> But how have we done this? How were we able to drink up the sea? Who gave us the sponge to wipe away the whole horizon? What did we do, when we unchained this earth from its sun? Whither is it moving to now? Whither are we moving now? Away from all suns? |Are we not perpetually falling? Backward, sideward, forward, in all directions? Is there any up or down left? Are we not straying through an infinite nothing?[4]

In this 'infinite nothing', with nothing outside or above humankind to hold humans and their history to account, humans were now free for the exhilaratingly daunting task of a 'transvaluation of all values'.

Where no kind of transcendence is acknowledged, the nature and authority of any accepted morality is in doubt. In Chapter 13 I argued that decisions of ethical commitment cannot be determined simply by asking 'who we are' without also asking '*whose* we are', that is, acknowledging a claim upon us transcending even that precious commodity, identity. That obviously invites the secularist retort that there is no 'whose' beyond the communities and shared lived experiences that make up our life on earth, and the sum total of knowledge that we have acquired. Central to that knowledge today is that which has and is being gained through science. Can science supply the answer to the ethical question – or if not, demonstrate that it is a question that need not trouble us further? Recent years have seen major advances which merge evolutionary biology, anthropology and neuroscience, to give an account of how 'morality' emerged and developed in *Homo sapiens*. On this kind of approach, as presented in the recent readable and insightful study by Chris Paley,[5] morality emerged during the hunter-gatherer stage of early human history, when survival depended on living in relatively small communities needing defence against intruders and enemies, and requiring bonds of shared mores relating to punishment of transgressors against those communal mores. 'It is coalitional punishment that guided the evolution of morality.'[6] This was genetically determined. It was those genes which promoted such communal behaviour (and the individuals possessing such DNA of course) which natural selection favoured and so survived. One legacy of this makes for an uncomfortable aspect of morality (or what we think morality is), in the relation between personal behaviour and the dominant expectations of one's community: 'One of the functions of our distinctive moral beliefs is to signal which group we're in. They are less about

---

4. From Nietzsche's *The Gay Science* (1882), in R. J. Hollingdale (ed. and trans.), *A Nietzsche Reader* (London: Penguin, 1977), 202–3.

5. Chris Paley, *Beyond Bad: How Obsolete Morals Are Holding Us Back* (London: Coronet/Hodder & Stoughton, 2012).

6. Ibid., 180.

making people's lives better, and more about choosing sides.'[7] Thus, it is more important to *seem* to be moral in line with the group mentality, than actually to *be* moral. These are highly interesting and pertinent insights which touch the nerves of any of us with an ounce of honesty about how we behave much of the time. But it leaves unanswered the question of what it actually *means* to be moral, as distinct from appearing to be moral – a matter familiar to us in reading the Gospels. Can we find the answer to *that* in evolutionary science? At this point I find myself in parallel with the American writer Marilynne Robinson: 'It is a triumph of science to have, in some degree, described the electron, and preposterous to suggest it has been explained.'[8] Something similar might be said of evolutionary accounts of moral values. In particular, what do we make of moral actions which, far from conforming to group mores, or seeking group approval, actually run counter to them and can even represent, to borrow Nietzsche's words, a transvaluation of values?

In a secularist age the 'whose?' question can certainly be dismissed, ignored or laughed out of court. That is the right of free enquiry. But the dismissal comes at considerable cost to our view of what is essential to our humanity. Khaled al-Asaad, a Syrian archaeologist and head of antiquities in the ancient city of Palmyra, a UNESCO World Heritage site, was beheaded by the 'Islamic State of Iraq and Syria' (ISIS) on 18 August 2015, aged eighty-three. His murder followed several weeks of interrogation and torture, during which he refused to reveal to his captors the location of the ancient artefacts which ISIS wished to seize and destroy as 'idolatrous'. There is a report that when ordered to kneel down before his captors he said, 'I bow down to no one except God.' It is hard to see how such commitment fits wholly into a narrative of ethics as conformity to group mores, or even as wishing to give the appearance of such conformity, though some forms of martyrdom, notably for example as displayed by ISIS followers themselves, where self-immolation for the cause is part of the cult, undoubtedly would do so. Or, as T. S. Eliot's Thomas Becket puts it,

> The last temptation is the greatest treason:
> To do the right deed for the wrong reason.[9]

But it is not only the extremity of martyrdom that tears open the immanent moral consciousness to the claim of what is other and transcendent. It can happen with any serious venture in responsibility, any attempt to depict the universal significance of that responsibility. In Chapter 1 it was noted how in 1932 Bonhoeffer lectured to students at the Berlin Technical University on 'The Right to Self-Assertion' and argued that 'self-assertion, whether of an individual or a community, cannot be divorced from responsibility in the wider relational, communal context, the given

---

7. Ibid., 159.
8. Marilynne Robinson, *The Givenness of Things* (London: Virago Press, 2015), 222.
9. From 'Murder in the Cathedral'. *The Complete Poems and Plays of T. S. Eliot* (London: Faber and Faber, 1969), 258.

reality in which life is lived'.[10] Much later, in his *Ethics*, he refuses to dichotomize self-assertion and self-denial in opposition to one another.[11] This happens when, for example, discussion of the Sermon on the Mount becomes polarized between those who regard obedience to Jesus' command of non-violence as 'unrealistic' and utopian in the world as it is, and those who posit an abstract ethic of self-denial regardless of the actual circumstances, as the true form of Christianity. In fact, says Bonhoeffer, in calling for self-denying *love*, love of one's neighbour in his or her actual situation of need, the Sermon on the Mount calls us into historical responsibility, including political responsibility, and in that respect a degree of self-assertion. 'It addresses a person with the necessity of responsible historical action. It addresses the individual, not to give status to individuals as such, but so they may be what they already are before God, namely, persons faced with historical responsibility.'[12] To regard 'self-affirmation as the only law of political action and self-denial as the only law of Christian action, and to consider them as mutually exclusive opposites, as a dual morality'[13] is to ignore the reality of God's becoming human in love for the world, which includes political action, 'and that the worldly form of Christian love is therefore able to take the form of a person fighting for self-assertion, power, success, and security'.[14]

To dismiss all political life and public responsibility as inherently antithetical to Christian love is therefore misguided. The self-denial required in discipleship of Christ is the placing of others' needs above one's own in fulfilment of responsibility, not in abrogation of that responsibility. One wonders what part Bonhoeffer's encounter with Black communities and writings during his year in the United States during 1930–1 played in his reflections here. For Bonhoeffer and his fellow conspirators responsibility meant the ultimate sacrifice, not the ultimate excuse for inaction. In the present context of Western society, however, the question being repeatedly raised is whether there can be any ethical imperative outside the call to assert the identity and rights of one's particular group or community, be it ethnic, religious, gender-based or national, and particularly where the reality of that human group and identity is being denied by the majority or those with most power. Are we condemned in our social futures to endless wars of identities and mutual cancellations? Or can the right to self-assertion somehow be harmonized with belief in a wider, even universal, common identity and loyalty, as Bonhoeffer argued in his 1932 lecture? Can we hold together the here-and-now commitment with the transcendent and universal?

Here, the limitations of abstract concepts become all too apparent. It is imagination rather than theorizing that is required: the work of the novelist, the poet, the artist, the musician, who at their most creative enable us to glimpse or

---

10. See above, 8–9.
11. DBWE 6, 241–5.
12. Ibid., 242.
13. Ibid., 244.
14. Ibid., 245.

hear a universal resonance in a particular event, story, scene or sound. I take as an example the American Ralph Waldo Ellison (1913–1994) whose 1952 novel *Invisible Man*[15] quickly became a classic of Black American writing in highlighting, through the story of one individual, the situation of being Black in urban society. In one sense, it is an essay in self-assertion on behalf of those who, while physically seen on account of their Blackness, are invisible in their humanity, their inner feelings, thinking and aspirations, and are either patronized, manipulated or simply ignored by the wealthy and powerful (who might on occasion include other Blacks). But the book is not just a piece of self-assertion on behalf of the community to which Ellison belongs. It is revelatory of features of American society as a whole, and opens up questions of what it means to be human in America, and thereby of what can be hoped for by Americans as a whole. Ellison comments that one of his aims was that of 'endowing his inarticulate characters, scenes and social processes with eloquence. For it by such attempts that he fulfils his social responsibility as an American artist.'[16] The aims of art and democracy converge. He continues,

> By way of imposing meaning upon our disparate American experience the novelist seeks to create forms in which acts, scenes and characters speak for more than their immediate selves, and in this enterprise the very nature of language is on his side. For by a trick of fate (and our racial problems notwithstanding) the human imagination is integrative – and the same is true of the centrifugal force that inspirits the democratic process. And while fiction is but a form of symbolic action, a mere game 'as if', therein lies its true function and its potential for effecting change. For at its most serious, just as is true of politics at its best, it is a thrust towards a human ideal.[17]

The particular stories of diverse individuals, highly placed and lowly, southerner and northerner, native-born and immigrant, 'are combined to tell us of transcendent truths and possibilities such as those discovered when Mark Twain set Huck and Jim afloat on the raft'.[18] In effect what we have here in literary form is a kind of *Stellvertretung*, vicarious representative action, on the part of the narrator and his characters, pointing to the *possibility* of such action in society for real. This is not to assume any specifically religious commitment on the part of either Ellison or Twain but a discernment of how things are and can be in social life. Bonhoeffer, we will shortly note, during his imprisonment turned to writing a novel, drama and poetry, much of it reflecting on the future of Germany. His closest English

---

15. Ralph Ellison, *Invisible Man* (London: Penguin, 2014). First published 1952 by Random House, United States.
16. 'Author's Introduction', *Invisible Man*, xix–xx.
17. Ibid., xx.
18. Ibid. The reference is to Mark Twain's characters in *Adventures of Tom Sawyer* (1876) and *Adventures of Huckleberry Finn* (1884).

friend George Bell, incidentally, was not only a prophetic figure but also a notable patron of the arts,[19] and memorably described the arts as 'auxiliaries' to the gospel.[20]

A village in France

High on the plateau of the Massif Central in France is the village of Le Chambon-sur-Lignon. Here and in the surrounding area hundreds of Jewish people, mostly children, were hidden and protected during the German occupation of 1940-4 and in many cases were enabled to travel to safety in Switzerland and elsewhere.[21] So outstanding is this epic that Le Chambon is one of only two *places* in the world to be honoured by inclusion among the 'Righteous among the Nations' at the Yad Vashem holocaust memorial in Jerusalem. High in the gallery of the heroes and heroines in the story of Le Chambon are André Trocmé, pacifist pastor of the Reformed Protestant Church there from 1934 to 1949, and his wife Magda. It was Trocmé's forthright character and powerful, biblical preaching that inspired much of the rescue effort, although, as often in cases of resistance, the narrative has become a contested one as regards the respective roles of the personalities and groups involved. Popular journalistic and hagiographical accounts have also led to some gross exaggerations of the number of Jews rescued, even running to claims of several thousands. Eight hundred is in fact the most likely approximate number, which of course is impressive enough by any standards.

In any case, nothing can detract from the main features of the story and its principal actors, especially those who were courageous and faithful even unto death. Trocmé himself remained steadfast under arrest and interrogation, and survived. It was a truly cooperative exercise in which Protestants, Catholics and Jews were all involved and put themselves under a common risk; and little could have been done without the willing help offered by those who came from elsewhere to teach in the school specially set up for the children who were 'hidden' among the local children, sometimes right under the noses of the occupying military. But no less impressive were the villagers themselves, not only Trocmé's mainstream Protestants but also members of the fundamentalist Darbyist wing of the Brethren movement. Unsophisticated in the niceties of ethics and political responsibility, they could nevertheless tell basic right from plain wrong. Mentally soaked in the Old Testament they were inoculated against the latent anti-Semitic culture of many of their more sophisticated and urbane fellow-citizens who stayed silent when the transports to the death camps started from France. It was a time of

---

19. See above, 82.
20. G. K. A. Bell, *Christianity and World Order* (London: Penguin, 1940), 146.
21. For an informative and balanced account of the Le Chambon story see Moorehead, Caroline, *Village of Secrets. Defying the Nazis in Vichy France* (London: Chatto & Windus, 2014).

incredible strain under which the villagers put themselves. Some years afterwards, when one of them was asked how she would sum up the experience, the reply was simply 'fear'. Two generations on, a reticence is still evident. When my wife and I visited Le Chambon in 2018 we stayed in an inn just outside the village itself. On a shelf by our table in the dining room were displayed photographs and newspaper cuttings about a film that had been made about the war years and the rescue operation, and featuring several of the people who had been involved. As the landlady served our dinner I asked her if any of these were her relatives. She shook her head, smiling, 'But I knew them.' Modesty, we suspected, was having the first and last word. Overt virtue signalling during the occupation would have proved fatal. Now, it was simply improper.

Le Chambon, though conveniently isolated (especially in winter) for such dangerous activity, was nevertheless part of a wider network of resistance both within and beyond France, and this enables us to make a connexion between the story and Bonhoeffer. Le Chambon was closely tied in with CIMADE (*Comité intermouvement auprès des évacués*) set up by French Protestant youth organizations in 1939 to work with refugees and evacuees in internment camps. From 1942, due to its increasing involvement with helping Jews to escape to Spain or Switzerland, it went underground. It had outstanding leadership in its secretary Madeleine Barot who worked closely with her Jewish counterpart Madeleine Dreyfus of OSE (*Organisation de Secours aux Enfants*), and the CIMADE president Marc Boegner who was also president of both the French Reformed Church and the French Federation of Protestant Churches. Both Barot and Boegner were seasoned ecumenical workers with active contacts in the World Council of Churches, and it was in the WCC office in Geneva that much of the reception of children smuggled over the border from Le Chambon and elsewhere was organized. But one figure in Le Chambon itself was especially important in the communication with Geneva: Charles Guillon. A staunch socialist, he preceded André Trocmé as pastor in Le Chambon, and was mayor of the commune during 1931–41. As secretary of the French YMCA, and being its reporting member to the YMCA international headquarters in Geneva, he was in a position to visit Geneva even in wartime – in effect he had dual residency in Le Chambon and Geneva – and regularly met with staff of the WCC and other organizations there.

Dietrich Bonhoeffer on his two 1941 visits to Geneva[22] met Charles Guillon, and we have records of the meetings at which both Guillon and Bonhoeffer were present with W. A. Visser't Hooft, Alfred Freudenburg (WCC secretary for refugee relief work), Nils Ehrenström (codirector of the Ecumenical Research department of the WCC) and others.[23] There were intensive discussions on work among Jewish refugees, the situation in France and Switzerland, the World Alliance, peace aims, the wider ecumenical scene and the whole German situation – 'Amazing news: the

---

22. See above, 12.

23. DBWE 16, 169, 223–8. Bonhoeffer also met with Ehrenström in Sweden in 1942, when both were visiting George Bell there. See above, Chapter 7, 81.

opposition plans to get rid. of Hitler and the Nazi regime are getting increasingly crystallised' Ehrenström recorded after these September 1941 meetings.[24] Guillon found these encounters with Bonhoeffer memorable. He told Marc Boegner soon after the March 1941 meetings that Bonhoeffer had said to him 'our churches are for the collaboration and have thus betrayed the cause.'[25] One imagines that by 'our churches' Bonhoeffer was not just meaning the |French churches. It was during the August–September 1941 visit that, Visser't Hooft recalls, Bonhoeffer was asked by someone in the group what he prayed for in the present situation. He replied, 'The defeat of my country, for I believe that this is the only way in which it can pay for the suffering which it has caused in the world.'[26] With his collaborators in France and Switzerland, as well as in Germany, Bonhoeffer was at the apex of an enterprise which was pushing through the bounds of conventional moral behaviour. Far from reflecting the moral norms of group-induced virtue and virtue-signalling, he and other resisters and conspirators were defying those conventions. His prayer for the defeat of his country was treasonable. Whereas ethics may scientifically be described as a child of evolution, ethics in this case was impelling a new stage and direction of evolution. It was an answer to '*Whose are we?*' a call to a transcendent responsibility beyond the norms that mere identity would impose. Here it was not a matter of action determined by the moral conventions necessary for the survival of a community; it was action creative of a *new* and emerging community, united in prayer and righteous action, come what may, and embodying *Stellvertretung*, vicarious representative action, to a rare degree.

Beyond prayer and blasphemy: Albert Camus

The mountain air of the plateau made Le Chambon and its vicinity a favoured treatment and convalescence centre for sufferers from tuberculosis and other diseases. In the summer of 1942, a French writer arrived from Algeria for that reason, staying in the Le Panelier Hotel. He was Albert Camus, busily at work on the novel that would after the war make him world-famous, *The Plague*.[27] Already involved in resistance activities himself, he could not have been unaware of much

---

24. Ibid., 215.
25. Ibid., 169 n.6.
26. W. A. Visser't Hooft, *Memoirs* (London: SCM Press, 1973), 153. Note the similarity in spirit with Bonhoeffer's reported letter to Reinhold Niebuhr while in New York in June 1939, concerning the 'terrible alternative' for Christians in Germany in the coming war: either 'willing the defeat of their nation in order that Christian civilization may survive, or willing the victory of their nation and thereby destroying our civilization.' E. Bethge, *Dietrich Bonhoeffer: A Biography* (Minneapolis, MN: Fortress Press, 2000), 665.
27. The French original *La Peste* was published in 1947. Citations here are from the English translation by Robin Buss, *The Plague* (London: Penguin Random House, 2020).

that was happening in the village. The context was in fact highly pertinent to the concern that underlies the novel. The story is set in the Algerian town Oran, beset and closed off to the outside world by an epidemic of bubonic plague which strikes the population progressively and mercilessly. Medicine seems helpless to arrest the spread and to save the already infected. It is known that Camus was using the plague as an allegory of the spread of nationalism, fascism and – under the occupation – Nazism, which led many of his countrymen to resignation if not collaboration but which called for a drastic willingness to resist. The question is posed, what is the point of resistance against such seemingly overwhelming odds? The central character in the story, Bernard Rieux, is a skilled and compassionate doctor, indefatigably dedicated to doing what he can but knowing that realistically he can do so little to change a terrifying situation, one in which his own survival is always at risk. Rieux's existential experience of his struggle is mirrored in several accounts of medical staff on the front line against Covid-19, and other grim scenarios.[28]

In *The Plague* Camus writes as a free-thinker, not overtly antireligious. Rieux is critical of Christians who talk about collective punishment for sin but 'who are better than they appear to be'.[29] He gives a respectful hearing to the sermons of the well-meaning priest Father Paneloux who was at least wrestling with how the hand of God might somehow be in the plague. One of Rieux's interlocutors asks, not if God exists or not but whether there can be saints without God,[30] for the situation in which Rieux and his close colleagues are working demands a kind of holy dedication to relieving suffering come what may, and *not* to engage in it, not to try *anything* for the dying child choking and shrieking in agony; or still worse, to slope off away from the plague city to safety until the epidemic has burnt itself out would be to become part of the plague itself. Rieux says, 'When you see the suffering and pain that it brings, you have to be mad, blind or a coward to resign yourself to the plague.'[31] He sees Father Paneloux as an ally in the fight, but not on the priest's theological terms of God's gracious love for the world – Rieux refuses to love a world in which children are tortured. He tells the priest, 'We are working together for something that unites us at a higher level than prayer or blasphemy, and that's all that counts.'[32]

---

28. For example, the celebrated trauma surgeon David Nott has movingly described working in situations of unimaginable suffering and danger in war zones including Syria and Yemen: *War Doctor: Surgery on the Front Line* (London: Picador, 2019). Yet, working in a London hospital during the current pandemic he describes Covid-19 as 'the most frightening enemy' he has faced. See https://www.thetimes.co.uk/article/david-nott-interview-fighting-the-coronavirus-is-worse-than-operating-in-syria-s2g9ptkq2. See also Rachel Clarke, *Breathtaking: Inside the NHS in a Time of Pandemic* (London: Little, Brown, 2021).

29. Buss, *The Plague*, 96.

30. Ibid., 196.

31. Ibid., 96.

32. Ibid., 169.

Might Bonhoeffer have recognized in Rieux's 'something' what he himself describes in his prison letters as 'the beyond in the midst of our lives?'[33] That 'something' appears indeed to be a transcendent, summoning source and core of humanity, and the response is not determined by 'who we are' but for who we are *called* to be. For the sake of suffering humanity the plague in Oran had simply to be fought, and likewise the plague of fascism and Nazism in occupied France, and all over Europe. Bonhoeffer too once likened Nazism to a disease that had to be fought in all its manifestations. In a novel which he started to write while in prison, some young friends are hiking through a forest on a hot day and, coming to a lake, take a dip. A uniformed employee of the estate comes upon them, and coarsely orders them out of the lake and off the land, threatening them with his whip. Two of the young men face up to him, one of them grabs the whip and gives him a lecture on proper behaviour. At which point the owner of the estate, a Major von Brake, arrives on the scene and reprimands the official (a cameo Nazi) for his bullying behaviour. The major proves to be the uncle of one of the young men and he invites the group to supper that evening. They reflect on the unpleasant incident of the afternoon, and the Major, effectively Bonhoeffer's mouthpiece, says,

> It is the petty tyrants who destroy a nation from the inside. They are like the invisible tuberculosis bacteria that secretly destroy a young life in full bloom ... They are like a contagious disease. As these petty tyrants suck the life force out of their victims, they infect them their own spirit. Then, as soon as those who until now had only been victims of violent deeds get hold of the least bit of power, they take revenge for what they have suffered. But this revenge – and this is the terrible thing – is not directed against the guilty party, but against innocent, defenceless victims. And so it continues, endlessly, until at last everything has been infected and poisoned and dissolution can no longer be stopped.[34]

The fight against this disease of tyranny, says the Major, must go on wherever and in whatever form, however apparently trivial, it is found. It is a serious matter, not

---

33. DBWE 8, 367. Perhaps not surprisingly, some commentators have drawn parallels between Camus and Bonhoeffer who in his prison letters asks what it means to live faithfully *etsi deus non daretur*, 'as if God were not given'; see William Hamilton, *The New Essence of Christianity* (London: Darton, Longman & Todd, 1961). 52, and the discussion by Eleanor McLaughlin, 'Dietrich Bonhoeffer and the Death of God Theologians', in Matthew D. Kirkpatrick (ed.), *Engaging Bonhoeffer: The Impact and Influence of Bonhoeffer's Life and Thought* (Minneapolis, MN: Fortress Press, 2016), 25–43; and André Dumas, *Dietrich Bonhoeffer: Theologian of Reality* (London: SCM Press, 1971), 191–2, although it is Camus's later novel *The Rebel* (1951), not *The Plague*, to which Dumas refers. For a recent reference to *The Plague* in relation to Bonhoeffer see John de Gruchy, 'Playing God during the Pandemic: Bonhoeffer on Civil Courage, Responsibility & the Ethics of Necessity', *Ecumenical Review* 72, 4 (October 2020), 660–72.

34. DBWE 7, 120–1.

to be smiled at, for that would be 'as foolish and irresponsible as smiling about the tiny size of bacteria or about the doctor who saves a few lives during an epidemic and then falls victim to the disease himself'.[35]

A new ethic – or the end of ethics?

'Groupishness has become a problem rather than a benefit', states Chris Paley,[36] summarizing the evolutionary biologist's perspective on the legacy which the survival of the fittest of our genes has bequeathed us from the time when 'it was us versus the animals and tribes kept out of each other's way and the hard smack of intra-group punishment kept us in line'. Morality conceived in that way, he says, has been good to us. 'But we're grown-ups now. It's time we left home.' Bonhoeffer, who in his orison writings was exploring the significance of humankind's 'coming of age' would be extremely interested in that remark.[37] Both in his actions and thinking on vicarious representative action he was prophetically moulding from his Christian tradition a new kind of ethic of solidarity, of persons with each other; no longer determined by the distinctives of genetic inheritance, ethnicity, nationality and religion but of truly global dimensions; a solidarity, moreover, foreshadowing a new relation with the natural, extra-human order of the *oikoumene*. There is also however a feature in Bonhoeffer's thought which puts a radical question mark against too-easy ventures into our understanding of ethical responsibility.

> Those who even wish to focus on the problem of a Christian ethic are faced with an outrageous demand – from the outset they must give up, as inappropriate to this topic, the very two questions that led them to deal with the ethical problem: 'How can I be good?' and 'How can I do something good?' Instead they must ask the wholly other, completely different question: what is the will of God?[38]

So Bonhoeffer begins the section of his *Ethics* 'Christ, Reality and Good'. Later in the book, the same startling approach meets us head-on at the start of the chapter 'God's Love and the Disintegration of the World': 'The knowledge of good and evil appears to be the goal of all ethical reflection. The first task of Christian ethics is to supersede that knowledge.'[39] One of Bonhoeffer's most provocative pronouncements, at first it sounds wilfully contradictory to the most basic moral sensibility. How could anyone living in Hitler's Germany, and witnessing the murderous agenda being put into effect, not be aware of good and evil as the

---

35. Ibid.
36. Paley, *Beyond Bad*, 202.
37. DBWE 8, 426–8, 450, 451, 457, 461, 475, 476, 478, 500.
38. DBWE 6, 47.
39. Ibid., 299.

great divide in the world? Good was surely the obverse of the most blatant evil imaginable taking place. Bonhoeffer however was thinking not so much of good and evil as entities which humans can observe, identify and pronounce upon as lying outside of themselves but rather of their own actions which they seek to judge as good or evil. That involves a very problematic assumption. It ignores the biblical view that as humans who have fallen away from the divine origin of our life we are in any position to be judges of our own actions. As usual, Bonhoeffer takes us back to the pages of the Bible and the basic picture we are given of our human situation *before God*. The primal relation that humans enjoyed with God was of union with their Creator, of total harmony with God. But they have seized an equality with God, an equality which they imagine they can have apart from God, and this apparent equality includes their knowledge of good and evil. 'Out of the original has emerged a usurped equality with God. Human beings as the image of God live completely out of their origin with God; having become equal with God, they have misappropriated the origin and made themselves their own creator and judge.' Instead of accepting God's gracious choice of them to live with him, they 'want to choose on their own and thus be the origin of election.'[40] They are now cut off from life. 'Their life is now divided, estranged from God, material things, and themselves.'[41] From this follows the disunion of all things, the fragmentation of the world.

The usurped knowledge of good and evil becomes a possession, a righteousness of our own, which separates us from God. The question, 'What is the good thing to do?' subtly replaces 'What is the will of God?' A system, religiously based or quasi-legal, a checklist of 'goods' against which we can measure our behaviour or intentions, is substituted for our relationship with God. That relationship can now in any case only be restored through God's grace. By that grace, we are not back in Paradise, but in the new creation, plunged into the world with God. God is with us, and we with God, abiding in God's love for ourselves and for others, with consequences far surpassing 'morality'. As Marilyn Robinson puts it, 'Our sacred dignity and our supreme vulnerability are the basis of a profound obligation to weigh our actions in the scales of grace, not by our corrupted notions of justice and retribution.'[42] It means letting go of our limiting preconceptions about ourselves and other people, about what they deserve or don't deserve, or whether they belong or not. Bonhoeffer reminds us that Jesus, after all, did not teach a morality, a body of universally valid controlling principles and edicts.[43] Unlike, says Bonhoeffer, the great philosopher Immanuel Kant, 'Christ was not concerned about whether "the maxim of an action" could become "a principle of universal law", but whether my action now helps my neighbour to be a human being before God.' 'God became human. That means that the form of Christ, though it certainly

---

40. Ibid., 301.
41. Ibid., 303.
42. Robinson, *The Givenness of Things*, 272.
43. DBWE 6, 98–9.

is and remains one and the same, intends to take form in real human beings, and this in quite different ways.' Jesus proclaimed the reign of God, liberating people from religiously sanctioned control (often designed to ensure people's respectability, or prosperity, or the security and greatness of their country, or what is claimed to be its 'Christian' nature), yet inspiring in them a life of love far costlier and more demanding than the righteousness of the scribes and pharisees. Such a life cannot be programmed, circumscribed or predicted in its outcomes, as illustrated in the course of Bonhoeffer's own varied life, as cumulatively pastor, peace activist, teacher, conspirator and martyr, summed up in the line from his almost-final poem 'O God, this people this people I have truly loved'.[44] Such love is life out of normal control. It embraces the humblest duties and joys of everyday life, and is capable of enabling us, with others, to inspire our responsiveness to the most daunting and complex challenges of the public sphere. To repeat what Bonhoeffer preached in 1932,

> The human being who loves because [he] has been made free by God's truth is the most revolutionary human being in earth. He is the overturning of all values; he is the explosive material in human society; he is the most dangerous human being … The path that God's truth took in the world leads to the cross. From then on, we know that all truth that wants to stand up before God must go to the cross. The congregation that follows Christ must go to the cross. For the sake of its truth and freedom, it will be hated by the world.[45]

In a fragmenting world we are invited to become, however modestly, part of its healing and restoration, in hope of the end of all things in the reconciling grace of God.

---

44. Poem, 'The Death of Moses'. DBWE 8, 540.
45. DBWE 11, 472.

BIBLIOGRAPHY

Published works of Dietrich Bonhoeffer

The Dietrich Bonhoeffer Works in English series published in 16 volumes by Fortress Press, Minneapolis. These are referenced in the notes by 'DBWE' + the respective volume number.

Vol. 1, *Sanctorum Communio: A Theological Study of the Sociology of the Church*. Ed. Clifford J. Green. Trans. Reinhard Krauss and Nancy Lukens. 1998.

Vol. 2, *Act and Being: Transcendental Philosophy and Ontology in Systematic Theology*. Ed. Wayne Whitson Floyd and Hans-Richard Reuter. Trans. Martin Rumscheidt. 1996.

Vol. 3, *Creation and Fall: A Theological Exposition of Genesis 1–3*. Ed. John W. de Gruchy. Trans. Douglas S. Bax. 1997.

Vol. 4, *Discipleship*. Ed. Geffrey B. Kelly and John D. Godsey. Trans. Barbara Green and Reinhard Krauss. 2000.

Vol. 5, *Life Together* and *Prayerbook of the Bible: An Introduction to the Psalms*. Ed. Geffrey B. Kelly. Trans. Daniel W. Bloesch and James H. Burtness. 1996.

Vol. 6, *Ethics*. Ed. Clifford J. Green. Trans. Reinhard Krauss, Charles West and Douglas W. Stott. 2005.

Vol. 7, *Fiction from Tegel Prison*. Ed. Clifford J. Green. Trans. Nancy Lukens. 2000.

Vol. 8, *Letters and Papers from Prison*. Ed. John W. de Gruchy. Trans. Isabel Best, Lisa E. Dahill, Reinhard Krauss and Nancy Lukens. 2009.

Vol. 9, *The Young Bonhoeffer: 1918–1927*. Ed. Paul D. Matheney, Clifford J. Green and Michael D. Johnson. Trans. Mary Nebelsick and Douglas W. Stott. 2003.

Vol. 10, *Barcelona, Berlin, New York 1928–1931*. Ed. Clifford J. Green. Trans. Douglas W. Stott. 2008.

Vol. 11, *Ecumenical, Academic, and Pastoral Work: 1931–1932*. Ed. Victoria J. Barnett, Mark Brocker and Michael B. Lukens. Trans. Isabel Best, Nicholas S. Humphreys, Marion Pauck, Anne Schmidt-Lange and Douglas W. Stott. 2012.

Vol. 12, *Berlin: 1932–1933*. Ed. Larry L. Rasmussen. Trans. Douglas W. Stott, Isabel Best and David Higgins. 2009.

Vol. 13, *London: 1933–1935*. Ed. Keith Clements. Trans. Isabel Best. 2007.

Vol. 14, *Theological Education at Finkenwalde: 1935–1937*. Ed. H. Gaylon Barker and Mark S. Brocker. Trans. Douglas W. Stott. 2013.

Vol. 15, *Theological Education Underground: 1937–1940*. Ed. Victoria J. Barnett. Trans. Claudia D. Bergmann, Scott A. Moore and Peter Frick. 2011.

Vol. 16, *Conspiracy and Imprisonment: 1940–1945*. Ed. Mark Brocker. Trans. Lisa E. Dahill and Douglas W. Scott. 2006.

Select list of secondary material on Bonhoeffer

Bethge, Eberhard. *Dietrich Bonhoeffer: A Biography*. Revised and edited by Victoria Barnett. Minneapolis, MN: Fortress Press, 2000.
Burnell, Joel. *Poetry, Providence and Patriotism: Polish Messianism in Dialogue with Dietrich Bonhoeffer*. Eugene, OR: Pickwick, 2009.
Clements, Keith. *A Patriotism for Today: Love of Country in Dialogue with the Witness of Dietrich Bonhoeffer*. Eugene, OR: Wipf & Stock, 2011.
Clements, Keith. *Bonhoeffer and Britain*. London: Churches Together in Britain and Ireland, 2006.
Clements, Keith. *Dietrich Bonhoeffer's Ecumenical Quest*. Geneva: WCC, 2015.
Clements, Keith. *What Freedom? The Persistent Challenge of Dietrich Bonhoeffer*. Eugene, OR: Wipf & Stock, 2011.
Gardiner, Craig. *Melodies of a New Monasticism. Bonhoeffer's Vision, Iona's Witness*. Eugene, OR: Cascade Books, 2018.
Green, Clifford, J., and Carter, Guy C. (eds). *Interpreting Bonhoeffer: Historical Perspectives, Emerging Issues*. Minneapolis, MN: Fortress Press, 2013.
Matthews, J., *Anxious Souls Will Ask: The Christ-Centered Spirituality of Dietrich Bonhoeffer*. Grand Rapids, MI: Eerdmans, 2005.
Mawson, Michael, and Ziegler, Philip G. (eds). *The Oxford Handbook of Dietrich Bonhoeffer*. Oxford: Oxford University Press, 2019.
Metaxas, Eric. *Bonhoeffer. Pastor, Martyr, Prophet, Spy*. Nashville, TN: Thomas Nelson, 2010.
Nielsen, Kirsten Busch, Wüstenberg, Ralf K. and Zimmermann, Jens (eds). *Dem Rad in die Speichen fallen. Das politische in der Theologie Dietrich Bonhoeffers/A Spoke in the Wheel. The Political in the Theology of Dietrich Bonhoeffer*. Gütersloh: Gütersloher Verlagshaus, 2013.
Plant, Stephen. *Bonhoeffer*. London: Continuum, 2004.
Schlingensiepen, Ferdinand. *Dietrich Bonhoeffer 1906–1945: Martyr, Thinker, Man of Resistance*. Translated by Isabel Best. London: T&T Clark International, 2010.
Schmidt, Florian, and Tietz, Christiane (eds). *Dietrich Bonhoeffers Christentum: Festschrift für Christian Gremmels*. Gütersloh: Gütersloher Verlagshaus, 2011.
Tietz, Christiane. *Theologian of Resistance: The Life and Thought of Dietrich Bonhoeffer*. Translated by Victoria J. Barnett. Minneapolis, MN: Fortress Press, 2016.

Further secondary published literature

Ashdown, Paddy. In collaboration with Sylvie Young. *Game of Spies: The Secret Agent, the Traitor and the Nazi*. London: William Collins, 2016.
Avis, Paul. *The Identity of Anglicanism*. London: T&T Clark, 2007.
Avis, Paul. *Reshaping Ecumenical Theology*. London: T&T Clark, 2010.
Baillie, John. *Our Knowledge of God*. Oxford: Oxford University Press, 1939.
Barth, Karl. *The Epistle to the Romans*. Translated from 6th edition by E. C. Hoskyns. Oxford: Oxford University Press, 1933.
Beeson, Trevor. *Discretion and Valour: Religious Conditions in Russia and Eastern Europe*. London: Collins, 1974.
Bell, G. K. A. *Christianity and World Order*. Harmondsworth: Penguin, 1940.

Bell, G. K. A. *The Kingship of Christ*. Harmondsworth: Penguin, 1954.
Best, Thomas F., and Granberg-Michaelson, Wesley (eds). *Costly Unity*. Geneva: WCC, 1993.
Best, Thomas F., and Robra, Martin (eds). *Costly Commitment*. Geneva: WCC, 1995.
Best, Thomas F. and Robra, Martin (eds). *Ecclesiology and Ethics: Ecumenical Formation and the Nature of the Church*. Geneva: WCC, 1997.
Best, Thomas F. (ed.). *Faith and Renewal: Reports and Documents of the Commission on Faith and Order Stavanger 1985, Norway*. Geneva: WCC, 1986.
Camus, Albert. *The Plague*. Translated from *La Peste* (1947) by Robin Boss. London: Penguin Random House, 2020.
Carlile, Lord Alex. 'Bishop George Bell: The Independent Review' (October 2017). https://www.churchofengland.org/sites/default/files/2017-12/Bishop%20George%20Bell%20-%20The%20Independent%20Review.pdf
Chambers, P., and Franklin. P. *Baron von Hügel: Man of God. An Introductory Anthology Compiled with a Biographical Preface*. London: Geoffrey Bles; Centenary Press, 1945.
Chandler, Andrew. *George Bell, Bishop of Chichester: Church, State and Resistance in the Age of Dictatorship*. Grand Rapids, MI: Eerdmans, 2016.
Clements, Keith. *Ecumenical Dynamic: Living in More Than One Place at Once*. Geneva: WCC, 2013.
Clements, Keith. *Faith on the Frontier: A Life of J. H. Oldham*. Edinburgh: T&T Clark; Geneva: WCC, 1999.
Clements, Keith. *The Theology of Ronald Gregor Smith*. Leiden: Brill, 1986.
de Gruchy, John. *The End Is Not Yet*. Minneapolis, MN: Fortress Press, 2017.
de Gruchy, John. *This Monastic Moment*. Eugene, OR: Wipf & Stock, 2020.
de la Bedoyere, Michael. *The Life of Baron von Hügel*. London: J.M. Dent, 1908.
Ellison, Ralph. *Invisible Man*. London: Penguin, 2014. (First published 1952 by Random House, USA.)
Fey, Harold E. (ed.). *The Ecumenical Advance: A History of the Ecumenical Movement Vol. 2. 1948–1968*. Geneva: WCC, 1970.
Gooder, Paula. *Heaven*. London: SPCK, 2011.
Grebe, Matthias, and Worthen, Jeremy (eds). *After Brexit? European Unity and the Unity of European Churches*. Leipzig: Evangelische Verlagsanstalt, 2019.
Hastings, Adrian. *A Century of English Christianity 1920–1985*. London: Collins, 1986.
Hastings, Adrian. *Oliver Tomkins: The Ecumenical Enterprise*. London: SPCK, 2001.
Hollindale, R. J. (ed. and trans.). *A Nietzsche Reader*. London: Penguin, 1977.
Jasper, R. C. D. George Bell. *Bishop of Chichester*. London: Oxford University Press, 1967.
Jenkins, Daniel. *Beyond Religion: The Truth and Error in Religionless Christianity*. London: SCM Press, 1962.
Keller, Adolf. *Karl Barth and Christian Unity: The Influence of the Barthian Movement Upon the Churches of the World*. London: Lutterworth, 1933. (Translation of Der Weg der dialektischen Theologie durch die Kirchliche Welt (1931).)
Kinnamon, Michael, and Cope, Brian E. (eds). *The Ecumenical Movement: An Anthology of Key Texts and Voices*. Geneva: WCC; Grand Rapids: Eerdmans, 1977.
Limouris, Gennadios (ed.). *Church Kingdom World: The Church as Mystery and Prophetic Sign*. Faith and Order Paper No. 120. Geneva: WCC, 1986.
Malouf, Amin. *Disordered World: Setting a New Course for the Twenty-first Century*. Translated by George Miller. London: Bloomsbury, 2011.
Matthews, Melvyn. *Awake to God: Explorations in the Mystic Way*. London: SPCK, 2006.
McSweeney, Bill. *Security, Identity and Interests*. Oxford: Oxford University Press, 1999.

Moorehead, Caroline. *Village of Secrets: Defying the Nazis in Vichy France*. London: Chatto & Windus, 2014.
Morgan, D. Densil. *Barth's Reception in Britain*. London: T&T Clark International, 2010.
Newbigin, Lesslie. *The Open Secret: Sketches for a Missionary Theology*. Grand Rapids, MI: Eerdmans, 1978.
Niebuhr, Reinhold. *Moral Man and Immoral Society: A Study in Ethics and Politics*. London: SCM Press, 1963 (1st British edition).
Paley, Chris. *Beyond Bad: How Obsolete Morals Are Holding Us Back*. London: Coronet/Hodder & Stoughton, 2021.
Robinson, Marilynne. *The Givenness of Things*. London: Virago Press, 2015.
Smith, Anthony D. *National Identity*. Reno: University of Nevada Press, 1991.
Smith, Ronald Gregor (ed.). *World Come of Age: A Symposium on Dietrich Bonhoeffer*. London: Collins, 1967.
Taylor, Charles. *A Secular Age*. Cambridge, MA: Belknap, 2011.
Traherne, Thomas. *Poems, Centuries and Three Thanksgivings*. Edited by Anne Ridler. London: Oxford University Press, 1969.
Traherne, Thomas. *The Works of Thomas Traherne Vol. 1*. Edited by Jan Ross. Cambridge: D.S. Brewer, 2005.
Vidler. A. R. (ed.). *Soundings: Essays Concerning Christian Understanding*. Cambridge: Cambridge University Press, 1962.
Visser't Hooft, W. A. *Memoirs*. Geneva: WCC, 1987.
Volf, Miroslav. *Exclusion and Embrace*. Nashville, TN: Abingdon Press, 1996.
von Hügel, Friedrich. *The Mystical Element of Religion as Studied in Saint Catherine of Genoa and Her Friends Vol. I Interpretation and Biographical*. Vol. II Critical. London: J.M. Dent, 1908.
von Hügel, Friedrich. *Essays and Addresses on the Philosophy of Religion*. London: J.M. Dent, 1921.
von Hügel, Friedrich. *Letters from Baron Friedrich von Hügel to a Niece*. London: J.M. Dent, 1928.
von Hügel, Friedrich. *Selected Letters 1896–1924*. London: J.M. Dent, 1928.
von Hügel, Friedrich. *The Reality of God and Religion and Agnosticism*. London: J.M. Dent, 1931.
Warnock, Mary. *Dishonest to God*. London: Continuum, 2010.
WCC. *The Church Towards a Common Vision*. Faith and Order Paper No. 214. Geneva: WCC, 2013.
Williams, Rowan. *Christ the Heart of Creation*. London: Bloomsbury, 2018.
Williams, Rowan. *Faith in the Public Square*. London: Bloomsbury, 2012.
Zimmermann, Wolf-Dieter, and Smith, Ronald Gregor (eds). *I Knew Dietrich Bonhoeffer*. London: Collins, 1966.

INDEX

Abyssinian Baptist Church, Harlem 115
al-Assad, Khaled 184
Amnesty International 27, 149
Annan, Kofi 167
apartheid, struggle against 28, 108, 122, 133 n.16
arts as auxiliaries of gospel 187
Ashdown, Paddy 169
asylum seekers 110, 146, 179
atheists 121, 183, 190
Auden, W. H. 26 n.13, 178
Avis, Paul 162

Baillie, John 56, 59
Baptists 15, 16
Barmen Theological Declaration 65, 68, 71, 74–7, 99, 125
Barnett, Victoria 74–6
Barot, Madeleine 188
Barth, Karl 5, 51, 54, 58, 70, 106, 164, 178
 influence in Britain 59–65
Bell, George 11, 24–5, 55, 56–7, 69, 116, 135, 149, 187
 Bonhoeffer's final message to 110
 2015 allegation against Bell 81–9
 wartime meeting with Bonhoeffer 81
Benenson, Peter 26, 149
Bethge, Eberhard 25, 38, 55, 95, 105, 111, 117, 180
 biographer of Bonhoeffer 4
 recipient and editor of prison writings 12
Black communities in USA 115, 185–6
Black Lives Matter 31
Blackman, Cyril 72–3, 79
Blake, William 178
body, human 38–40, 43, 149
 created from earth 39
body of Christ 7, 44, 76, 79, 99, 100, 103, 114, 119, 126, 138, 171, 182
 church as body of Christ 40

as means of Christ's ministry 40
 seen in every soul 48
Boegner, Marc 188, 189
Bonhoeffer, Karl-Friedrich 46 n.29, 70
British churches and Europe
British Council of Churches 29
Bruay Conference 1934 71–80
Brunner, Emil 61, 76
Buber, Martin 25, 76

Camus, Albert 189–91
Canaris, Wilhelm 176
Carlile, Lord Alex, QC 85–6, 88
Catherine of Genoa 53
Catholic Modernist movement 51–2
Chambers, Franklin 59
Chandler, Andrew 83
Chikane, Frank 143
Christian Democratic Union (GDR), 13
Christian Peace Conference 17
church as Christ existing as community, 5
church and kingdom of God
church for others 5, 16, 107, 116–17, 119, 132, 139
Church of England and child abuse 82
Church of Scotland 29, 160
Church Struggle in Germany 44, 61, 71, 97, 99, 100, 114, 115, 134
Church of Sweden 97
church, as transnational/universal, 24, 71, 94, 116, 118, 119, 126
Churchill, Winston, 147
civil courage 14–15, 175
coming of age
 in Bonhoeffer 4, 13, 25, 46, 105, 117, 129, 192
 in spiritual nature 111
 in Traherne 46–7
communism, churches under 11–21
community, human 98–9, 101, 106, 119–21, 129, 136, 150, 152, 162, 164, 189

all people on earth 113
authentic humanity 8–10, 30
  in Christ, 78, 103–4, 115, 118–19, 125, 171, 176–7, 182
  Christian forms 67, 73, 74
  church as, 5, 53, 73, 74–5, 78–9, 101–2, 114–15, 117, 119, 128
Conference of European Churches 67, 152, 155
Confessing Church 4, 11–12, 13, 19, 41, 55, 65, 71–2, 77–80, 81, 97, 99, 109, 134–5, 175
  attitudes to Finkenwalde seminary 98
  and ecumenical movement 67–8, 114, 116, 133, 134–5
Council of Europe 160
Covid-19 pandemic 181–2, 190
creation 8, 9, 36, 38–41, 58, 123–4, 133, 136, 161
cross of Christ 7, 48, 66, 100, 101, 103, 109, 128, 130, 131, 136, 138, 194
Czechoslovakia 11, 16–18, 21

Davidson, Randall 61
de Gruchy, John 146, 148
De Klerk, F. W. 143
democracy 16, 18–29, 143–54, 158, 177, 186
dialogical life 88, 164
dialogue, inter-religious 119, 121–2
Dilthey, Wilhelm 46
Discipleship 4, 5, 6, 17, 24, 27, 44, 78, 100, 102, 103, 178
diversity in society and religion 119, 170
Dohnanyi, Hans von 105, 175

earth, love of 5, 25, 36–8, 39–42, 110, 113, 126, 132
Ecumenical Council, hopes for 71, 114, 115, 116, 133–4, 139
ecumenical fellowship as global 110, 113–26
ecumenical movement in development 24, 132, 182
  Bonhoeffer's relationship with 127–8
  as command and promise 135–40
  theological basis for 115–35
ecumenical social thought 24, 71–80

Ecumenical Youth Commission 71–3, 116, 133, 135
Ehrenström, Nils 188
Eidem, Erling 98
Eliot, T. S. 26, 184
Ellison, Ralph Waldo 186
ethical dimension in Europe debate 165–7
Ethics 4, 5, 6, 7, 12, 13–15, 19, 20, 27, 42, 78, 87, 102, 104, 114, 121, 136, 144, 146, 149, 185, 192–4
ethics, basis of Christian 136–8, 182
ethics, contextual 71–8
ethics and identity 165
ethics, public 23–31
European Court of Human Rights 160
European Court of Justice 160
European Union, Britain and 9, 151–2, 155–71
  British churches and 9, 155–71
extremism, 143–54, 170

Faith and Order movement 114
  and Confessing Church 67, 68, 134
  WCC Commission 114, 119, 122, 138
Falcke, Heino, 15
Falklands/Malvinas War 9, 28
Fanø Conference 1934 17, 71
Fellowship of Concerned Baptists in South Africa 144
Finkenwalde seminary 19, 41, 63, 97–102, 109–12, 134
First World War 93, 132, 157, 168–9
Fitzgerald, Scott 157
Flossenbürg 4, 81, 94, 97, 105, 175–6
Forrester, Duncan 29
Forsyth, P. T. 59
Fraser, Giles 168
freedom
  divine 5, 163
  human 45
  not individual possession 8, 9
  in love 131, 179
  in relationship 78, 161, 163, 164, 179
  of speech 158
Freudenberg, Alfred 188
Fuhrmann, Klaus 21

Gandhi 125
George Bell Group 83–5

German Christian Movement 13, 68, 115, 133, 161
German Democratic Republic (GDR) 12–16, 20–1
German resistance to Hitler 12, 104, 146, 174. *See also* 20 July 1944 plot
Gooder, Paula 47 n.34
grace, cheap and costly 48, 100
Grenfell Tower tragedy 153–4
Griesebach, Eberhard 76
Guillon, Charles 188–9

Haddad, Frieda 119–21
Hammarskjöld, Dag 47 n.35
Hani, Chris 143
Hastings, Adrian 54
Henkys, Jürgen 21
Hickman, Rebecca 30
Hodgson, Leonard 55, 68–9
Holocaust 104, 153, 187. *See also* Jewish persecution
Hoskyns, E. C. 60–3
Hromádka, Josef 16–17
Hügel, Friedrich von 51–70
human being as heir 37, 45, 46, 126
human rights 11, 19–20, 122, 147, 148, 148–50, 154
humanists 121
Hussite Church 16

identity
  British identity and Europe 159–62
  communal 109
  contemporary obsession 118
  ethnocentric 95
  national 19, 95, 151, 155–8
  as relative to ethical imperative 162–80
image of Christ 78, 103
image of God in humanity 6, 39, 44, 48, 58, 88, 103, 104, 124, 178, 183
incarnate God and human life 10, 18, 43–4, 58, 78, 103, 124, 128, 181
India 109, 125, 129
individuality and selfhood 8, 9, 76, 161, 163–4, 184
Inge, W. R. 52
institutions in public life 150–4
intercession 109–10

inter-religious relations 110 n.39, 119–21
Islamic State 145, 184

Jackson, Eleanor 175
Jenkins, Daniel 26
Jeremiah 165, 178–9
Jerusalem 165, 178–9
Jewish persecution 7, 103, 149, 177, 187
  efforts to save Jews 187–8
July 20 1944 plot 13, 48, 107, 111, 175–9. *See also* German resistance
justice 165, 167, 171, 175–80

Kairos Document 133 n.16
Kant, Immanuel 193
Kierkegaard, Søren 25, 57–8, 60, 65, 67, 70, 151
Kilborn, Trevor 72–3
King's College Chapel 93–5
kingdom of God 5, 37, 39, 41–7, 94, 106, 117, 119, 132, 139, 154
knowledge of good and evil 136, 192–3
Koopman, Nico 122
Krötke, Wolf 14
Kuron, Jacerk 20

language in Britain 170
Lasserre, Jean 72
Le Chambon-sur-Lignon 187–90
Lebanon 119–21
Leibholz, Sabine and Gerhard 55
Leiper, Henry Smith 135
liberation theology 4
Life and Work Movement 63, 67, 68, 69, 71, 73 n.5, 114–15, 116 n.12, 132–3, 135
Life Together 17, 100–2
Liguš, Jan 17–18
Lochmann, Jan M. 17–18
love of Christ 128–9, 178
love of God 41, 64, 127–40, 193, 209
  known in world 30–3, 38
love as mystery 66
love as true freedom 194
love not ethical ideal 131–4
Luther, Martin 7, 13, 21, 40, 43, 100, 168

Maechler, Winfried 72–3
Malouf, Amin 95

mandates, divine 14, 78, 80, 167 n.22
Mandela, Nelson 143
martyrdom 123, 184
Marxism 12–13, 17–18, 20, 158
materiality of human being 38–41
Matthews, John 111
Matthews, Melvyn 47
Maturity. *See* coming of age
McSweeney, Bill 159, 164
Metaxas, Eric 4
ministry, shared 102
monasticism, call for new 40, 99
Moravians 21
Morawska, Anna 19
Morgan, D. Densil 60
Morris, Jeremy 83
Müller, Hanfried 13–14
mystery 45–6, 60, 63–7

narcissism of minor differences 158
national identity 155–9
national sovereignty 9, 155, 166, 168
nationhood, status of 161–2
natural life 153–4
Newbigin, Lesslie 121
Nicholson, Gisela 144, 144 n.1
Niebuhr, Reinhold 156
Nietzsche, Friedrich 182–3
North Korea 145

Occupy City/Wall Street movement 28
oikoumene 113, 119, 121–2, 124, 192
Oldham, J. H. 23–4, 26, 51, 55 n.14, 56, 63, 75–6, 77, 108, 135
orders of creation 40, 133, 161
orders of preservation 133, 161, 167
Oxford Conference on Church, Community and State (1937) 23, 56, 77, 116 n.12

Paley, Chris 183, 192
Pardoe, Judge Alan 83
participation in Christ 18, 47–8, 107, 137, 139
Pascal, Blaise 57
peace, international 70, 71, 94, 95, 98, 110, 114, 133, 136, 138, 169, 178–9
peace and the church 171
peace not an ideal state 132
peace as command of God 133

personalist thought 8, 76
plague as metaphor for tyranny 189–91
Poland 18–20
polis, body politic 121
Pope John Paul II 19
Pope Pius X 52
populist movements viii, 9, 145, 151
post-Christian world 97–112
poverty 3, 29, 79, 80, 129
Prague Spring 16
prayer 37, 54, 63–5, 98, 102, 109, 122, 125, 130, 132, 134, 135, 139, 189
public discourse as chatter 87–9, 129
public ethics and theology 23–31, 43, 71–80, 146–50, 152–4

race 40, 94, 109, 127, 170
reconciliation
   as calling 9, 82, 94, 108, 118, 126, 127–40, 155, 165
   as God's act 135–7
Reformation, English 168
Reformation, Lutheran 13
refugees 81, 110, 146, 148, 150, 179, 188
relationality of life 5, 7–9, 88, 163, 167, 178, 181, 184
religion, 13, 17, 19, 26, 29
   Bonhoeffer's critique of 6, 105–7
   as negative social influence 29, 94, 107, 109
responsibility 7, 8, 15, 19, 250, 46, 70, 74, 75, 76–80, 121, 124, 129, 148, 164, 175, 184, 185–6, 189, 192, 166
Robertson, Edwin 27
Robinson, John A. T. 27
Robinson, Marilynne 184, 193
Roman Catholic Church 16, 18–20, 29, 51–2, 109, 115, 152
Russia 12, 166

Saint John of the Cross 57, 60
Sanctorum Communio 5, 7, 24 n.7, 99, 115, 128
Schönfeld, Hans 133
Schönherr, Albrecht 16
science and ethical question 183–4
sciences 35, 45, 53
Second World War 108, 135, 145, 159, 162, 168, 175

Shevardnaze, Eduard 158
Simpson, John 47 n.35, 108
Smith, Anthony 157
Smith, Ronald Gregor 25
spirituality 47–8, 52, 63, 67, 109, 122
Stauffenberg, Claus 175
Stellvertretung 7–8, 9, 78, 99–100, 101, 103–5, 107–10, 115, 117, 128–31, 136, 181–2, 186, 189

Tanner, Mary 171
Taylor, Charles 106
Temple, William 53, 61–2
terrorist attacks 153
Tomkins, Oliver 51–9
Toronto statement 118
Traherne, Thomas 35–49, 126
transcendence and ethics 183
transcendence, God's 54, 56, 58, 63, 64–5, 66, 183, 107
tribalism 7, 93–5
Trocmé, André 187–8
Trott, Adam von 175
Trump, Donald 4
truth-telling 81–9
Tutu, Desmond 108, 143
Twain, Mark 186
two realms thinking 42, 78–80
tyranny, nature of 5, 11, 191

ultimate and penultimate 10, 32, 137, 143–7, 148, 150, 151, 152
United Nations 152, 166
Universal Declaration of Human Rights 149

vicarious representative action. *See Stellvertretung*
Vidler, Alec 26
Visser't Hooft, W. A. 12, 55, 67, 70, 77, 135, 188, 189

Warnock, Mary 29–30
Weimar Republic 5, 147
Weizsäcker, Carl von 46
Welby, Justin, 85, 89
Wells, Sam 155
Williams, Rowan 7, 150
Wojtvla, Karol. *See* Pope John Paul II
World Council of Churches 11, 24, 55, 67, 68, 77, 82, 94, 117, 188
  Karlsruhe Assembly 2022 127
World Alliance for International Friendship through the Churches 63, 72, 93–4, 113–14, 115–16, 132–3, 188

Yugoslavia, Former 158, 166

www.ingramcontent.com/pod-product-compliance
Lightning Source LLC
Chambersburg PA
CBHW062228300426
44115CB00012BA/2260